SELFWATCHING

To Dee, Gay, Michael, Melanie and Rachel

SELFWATCHING
Addictions, Habits, Compulsions:
what to do about them

Ray Hodgson and Peter Miller

FACTS ON FILE, Inc.
460 Park Avenue South
New York, New York 10016

This book was devised and produced by
Multimedia Publications (UK) Ltd
1 Ballards Lane, London N3 1UZ

Editor: Christopher Fagg
Production Director: Arnon Orbach
Design and layout: Youé and Spooner Ltd
Picture Researchers: Angela Baker, Miranda Innes, Sarah Waters

First published in Great Britain in 1982 by
Century Publishing Co. Ltd, 76 Old Compton Street, London W1

This edition published by Facts On File Publications
460 Park Avenue South, New York, N.Y.10016

Library of Congress Cataloging in Publication Data

Hodgson, Ray
Selfwatching: addictions, habits, and compulsions and what to do about them

Includes index
1. Substance abuse — Psychological aspects.
2. Obsessive-compulsive neurosis.   3. Habit.   4. Behavior modification.
I. Miller, Peter Michael, 1942- II. Title.
RC564.H6 1982   616.85'227024   82-9188   AACR2
ISBN 0-87196-726-X

First American edition 1982
10 9 8 7 6 5 4 3 2 1

Printed in Great Britain by Fakenham Press

CONTENTS

INTRODUCTION

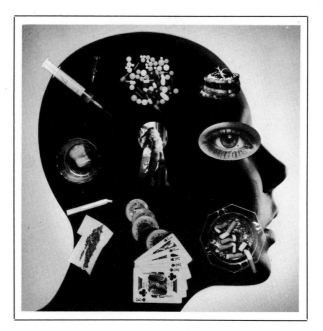

Selfwatching and Self-help

The shrine of the oracle at Delphi has the injunction 'Know thyself' inscribed on the walls, along with a further exaltation 'Nothing to Excess'. This book is a modest contribution to mankind's eternal striving for these two goals of self-knowledge and self-control.

If a scientist wants to understand the behaviour of frogs, elephants or human beings, then it is essential that at some stage he watches them. If we are to understand and then change our own behaviour we must observe ourselves in a systematic fashion. This activity is what we have called 'selfwatching'. One of the aims of our book is to offer practical ways of observing and understanding one's own addictive and compulsive behaviour, along with effective methods of bringing about a change and achieving self-control.

A second aim is to provide information about a wide variety of addictions and compulsions, including smoking, alcoholism and other forms of drug dependence, obsessional compulsions like checking and excessive washing, compulsive gambling, overeating, sexual compulsions and workaholism. This knowledge will help sufferers and their families to understand these types of complaints. It should also help those involved in prevention, whether they be parents, teachers, family doctors and other primary care workers, or simply people who are starting to develop a habit, a compulsion or an addiction.

The information presented in this book is based, to a large extent upon recent advances in experimental and clinical psychology. Our primary goal, however, is not simply to impart precise, scientific information, but rather to provide a way of looking at behaviour which will be of practical help. Changing the habits of a lifetime is an endeavour which requires a fair degree of commitment and motivation, but commitment is not enough. The other essential is a plan of action. An addiction or a compulsion is basically a very strong habit which can be modified if the right strategies are used. But what is the right strategy for a particular person with a particular problem? It is hoped that the ensuing chapters will give readers a clear picture of one well-established and empirically based way in which addictions and compulsions can be analysed, and modified.

Ray Hodgson
Peter Miller

1
BEYOND ALL REASON

Human nature leads at times to behaviour which is often irrational, sometimes preposterous and occasionally bizarre. An irrational fear whether of spiders, or snakes, or of enclosed spaces, can limit an individual's freedom of action as effectively as a physical barrier like the Berlin Wall. Moreover, a mental barrier can continue to operate even though the individual knows that it runs directly counter to his or her best interests.

Nowhere is this more true than in the area of human habits, addictions and compulsions. The heavy drinker or smoker, or the person who compulsively gambles or over-eats, feels compelled to behave in ways that are detrimental to physical and mental health, personal relationships, work and finances. In a recent television programme a heavily addicted smoker illus-

trated this point with alarming clarity. He had ignored his doctor's warnings to give up smoking and slowly developed first sclerosis then gangrene in both legs, which had to be amputated. He smoked continuously as he described the terrible effects of his dependence on cigarettes. Another smoker had undergone a tracheotomy, removal of the windpipe, as a treatment for throat cancer. As a result of his operation he had to breathe through a hole in his throat – yet he continued to smoke by sticking a cigarette into the hole.

How is it possible to understand behaviour like this, seemingly beyond all reason? In the case of dependence upon a drug such as nicotine, alcohol or heroin, what is the balance between physiological addiction – the action of the drug on the body – and the psychological reasons for dependence? And is there any link between compulsive dependence on drugs and other compulsive behaviours in which no drug is involved? Sexual compulsions, for example, may range from those, such as transvestism or fetishism, with relatively minor social consequences, to others, such as exhibitionism, paedophilia and rape, which may carry the most serious legal penalties. Other compulsions, such as washing or checking rituals, may affect only the daily lives of those who suffer from them. What is certain, however, is that compulsive behaviours of all kinds carry with them a high potential for human suffering. In investigating why these behaviours occur, the psychologist paves the way for their effective treatment.

Is my husband an alcoholic?

This is often the first question that a woman asks when her husband is referred for treatment. She wants to know whether he is suffering from a true disease like a cancer or just from a problem, more like a benign lump. This is the wrong way of looking at problem drinking or, indeed, any other 'bad habits', 'compulsions' or 'addictions' such as smoking, gambling or watching TV. A better conception considers a problem to be located along a dimension ranging from slight through moderate to severe. At one end of this dimension we have an annoying habit, such as drinking more than you planned at a party. At the other end of the continuum the habit has developed and spread. It is now difficult to control and is associated with harmful consequences.

We are all creatures of habit and many of our habits are adaptive. That is, they are ways of 'automating' skills that are useful in our daily life. Driving a car, getting dressed, eating, sleeping, walking and talking all involve a complicated series of habits which would be difficult to change – even if we wanted to do so. In fact, survival itself may depend on the strength of a particular habit – looking both ways before crossing a main road, for example. It is only when, for some reason or other, we want to change a strong habit and fail, that it can be labelled 'compulsive'.

The advice given in this book is appropriate for a variety of problems along the whole range of severity from annoying but minor habits up to major compulsions. An adolescent girl with a slight weight problem, a severely dependent alcoholic, as well as a compulsive gambler should all be able to pick up useful hints and find new ways of looking at and solving the problems.

Cut off from the world outside. Unwanted habits can impose limits to individual freedom as real as the bars of a prison cell.

In an American city a man under the influence of PCP, a powerful hallucinogen, hurls himself at a shop window. Why does such self-destructive behaviour happen?

Psychology or pharmacology?

In this book we take the view that *all* habits and compulsions involve psychological, physiological and biochemical levels of explanation. This approach may trouble those who see sharp distinctions between drug taking habits and purely psychological compulsions and therefore between the appropriate treatments. Addiction to a drug, they argue, is not the same as an addiction to gambling. In the first case the appropriate course is to wean the addict away from a physiological dependence, perhaps by use of a less dangerous substitute; in the second, the problem is a psychological one and should be dealt with by encouraging the person to recognize the harmful consequences of gambling and solve associated psychological problems.

In our experience, however, psychological methods of treatment can be very powerful in altering behaviour, even when there appears to be heavy physiological dependence. These methods are founded on extensive research by psychologists into the way human beings learn behaviour and acquire and deploy skills in managing and solving problems. The application of this research to helping with habit problems is a comparatively recent and growing area of endeavour. The results so far encourage us to believe that the methods we advocate will be used to alleviate an ever-widening range of behavioural problems.

Selfwatching, self-management

We have gathered these methods of treatment under the general heading of Selfwatching. This is not to say that there is a fixed set of procedures that will work for all individuals in all cases. Every individual behaves in ways specific to him or her, even though there may be general resemblances between the behaviours of groups. If there is a guiding principle behind the Selfwatching approach, it is that it is possible to encourage people to un-learn unwanted behaviours and learn new ones which allow them to manage their daily lives more effectively. They are taught to identify the factors in their day-to-day experience which support motivation and morale as well as techniques by which to avoid or modify negative influences. The confidence gained from learning and exercising new skills enhances the

Above: Positive reinforcement: the regular association between a particular habit, such as smoking, and a sense of pleasurable relaxation helps the habit to become ever more firmly ingrained.

Left: Counselling sessions help break down the barriers of isolation.

Far left: Drugs are the modern answer to behavioural and medical problems. But drugs cannot deal with the processes that create habits and cause them to persist.

individual's self-image, so that problems are approached in the expectation of success and mastery rather than failure and helplessness. Selfwatching techniques are generally effective because they block, or even set in reverse motion, the processes responsible for creating problem behaviours in the first place.

The reinforcement of habitual behaviour

For a classic description of how habits can develop into compulsions we can do no better than turn to the writings of St Augustine, who became the first archbishop of Canterbury at the end of the 6th century AD. For many years he battled with a sexual compulsion and described its development in the following way:

> 'When desire is given satisfaction, habit is forged and when habit passes unresisted a compulsive urge sets in. By these close links I was held.'

This account should not be interpreted simply as a puritanical view of pleasure. It tallies closely with modern psychologists' views that it is a basic principle of behaviour that, other things being equal, habits are strengthened, or *reinforced*, when a desire is repeatedly satisfied. Those habits most firmly associated with either strong feelings of pleasure or with the avoidance of distress are the most likely to develop into compulsions which damage the quality of our lives. It is not necessarily the length of time they have been practised that is the decisive factor. Putting your right sock on first is a habit which could probably be changed even after a lifetime of practice – no strong feelings are involved. On the other hand, the habitual use of alcohol or other drugs to gain immediate pleasure or relief from distress is much more difficult to stop.

Positive and negative reinforcement

The pleasures of sex, food, drugs and money can all reinforce a habit until it is difficult to resist. Psychologists call this *positive reinforcement*. On the other hand the *avoidance of distress* is an equally important motivational force. The strengthening of a habit which postpones, however temporarily, the experience of pain, anxiety, frustration and other unpleasant feelings is labelled *negative reinforcement*.

Many psychologists and neurophysiologists have explained the relationship between reinforcement and behaviour in terms of activity in the brain itself. They believe that electrical activity in certain areas of the brain is responsible for experiences of pleasure and pain. James Olds, working in the United States, has been one of the pioneers of this approach.[1] In his experiments, laboratory animals (usually rats) have electrodes implanted deep within the brain. They are allowed to press a bar which controls the supply of a small electrical current to the electrodes. Olds found that, when the electrodes are planted in certain areas of the brain, animals would press the bar repeatedly to keep up the electrical stimulation. With other placements of the electrodes, the animals pressed the bar to stop stimulation. It is reasonable to suppose that these electrode locations corresponded to areas directly related to pleasure and discomfort and that similar structures exist in the human brain. If so, it might be these 'pleasure centres' and 'pain centres' which are activated by drugs or distress and so involved in positive or negative reinforcement.

The ABC approach
The conclusions of Olds and others suggest a useful approach to understanding how human habits are formed and reinforced. We can try to trace the sequence of events which begins in the outside world, causes electrical activity within the pleasure or pain centres in the brain, and ends up reinforcing or strengthening behaviour. We can divide this sequence into three sections A, B and C: (A) Antecedent cues, (B) the Behaviour itself, or the whole response of the organism to those cues; and (C) the Consequences which may positively or negatively reinforce the behaviour.

Antecedent cues
Compulsive urges rarely descend out of the blue. They are normally triggered by a series of previous events which, of course, vary considerably from person to person. These events which prompt an individual to behave in a particular way are what we have labelled as *antecedent cues*. Some cues, like hunger, arise from biological events within the body. Others arise from social

At every level of Western society, alcohol is the symbol of good-fellowship. Feeling at ease with others is a powerful reward for those who drink, especially if they are nervous or shy.

experiences such as the influence of friends or family. Others may stem from strong feelings of anger, fear, anxiety or other emotions. *The first step in controlling habits and getting rid of compulsions is to identify the cues which give rise to them.*

These cues often interact in complicated ways. Consider the case of Tom, an alcoholic. Tom started drinking in his teens, but only began to drink habitually and excessively when he joined the Army. From the first, he found Army life very difficult, but soon discovered that by drinking heavily he was able to overcome his natural unsociability and feel that he was one of the lads. Tom learned that it was drink which enabled him to feel relaxed and sociable in company and, becoming accustomed to this relief, found that he experienced a compulsion to drink in the face of *any* social situation. At this stage, Tom could be considered to be *psychologically* dependent on alcohol. During the next five years, however, he regularly consumed a daily bottle of gin and began to experience withdrawal symptoms – trembling fits, nausea and a pounding heartbeat – whenever he attempted to abstain. Tom was now *physically* dependent. The only way he could get rid of his uncomfortable bodily symptoms was by drinking more alcohol.

Above: Habits are triggered by cues which, like road signs, set up certain expectations about the immediate future. Above right: The mere promise of a catch keeps the fisherman hooked!

Undoubtedly the physical symptoms that Tom experienced were real physiological events in his body resulting from the effects of alcohol. But in fact his need to drink arose from two types of antecedent cues. First there were the social cues: Tom had a compulsion to drink whenever he had to face a group of people. Secondly, there were physiological cues: when he tried to stop, he felt awful, and these feelings only fuelled his desire to drink.[2]

Cues, choice and consequences

Antecedent cues act as signals, they give promises or warnings of future consequences. Delicious aromas issuing from the kitchen trigger conditioned reflexes – salivation, changes in the intestinal tract – which tell the waiting dinner guests that it is time to be hungry. Traffic lights at red tell a driver that it is dangerous to proceed. In the same way the prospect of mixing with company signalled to Tom that drinking would be followed by a pleasant uninhibited experience, whereas sobriety would not. In the early stages of physical dependence, the thought of abstaining from drink was a warning cue to Tom that unpleasant consequences – withdrawal symptoms – were likely to follow. In the light of

this analysis, Tom's choice of behaviour – to drink rather than abstain – becomes much more understandable. As we shall see, the fear of unpleasant consequences can be as potent a cue as the expectation of pleasure in triggering and eventually reinforcing habits, addictions and compulsions.

Different types of reward

It is by no means a simple matter to explain how the performance of a particular habit pays off in terms of its consequences. So far we have suggested a pattern whereby the use of a drug, alcohol, to secure pleasant consequences can lead to its continued use to ward off the fear of withdrawal symptoms. But why do people persist in such behaviours when even worse consequences – loss of friends and family, social degradation, even fatal disease – follow? Why don't these consequences help the individual to give up rather than continue the habit? This is a paradox which psychologists have been trying to solve for the last thirty years and there are at least three possible explanations.

The first is simply that *short-term gratification* is more motivating than the prospect of long-term harm. The slimmer who binges on chocolate cake will not experience the consequences in the form of extra pounds until a few days later. In the meantime he or she has the satisfaction of having eaten fully. Less obvious is the principle of *intermittent reinforcement*. Those rows and rows of unlucky people who are addicted to the one-armed bandits in Las Vegas do not hit the jackpot every time they pull a lever. Far from it: they are rewarded only once in a while, yet they keep playing for hours and hours. Similarly, alcoholics and heavy drinkers report that they do not always derive satisfaction from drinking sessions; feelings of depression, anxiety or violent aggression may be reported instead. Yet on occasions they *do* get the feeling of being at one with the world, when the alcohol in their systems seems (to them at least) to transform them into the gregarious, witty and clever personalities they would secretly like to be. Intermittent reward, then, can make us persist in habits just as effectively as immediate reward.

The third explanation involves what

psychologists call *relativity of reinforcement*. A smoker lighting up in a roomful of non-smokers may be acutely aware that his action is disapproved of: he may even feel strong feelings of guilt. However, his justification to himself is that he would feel even worse without a cigarette! The social discomfort he feels is easier to put up with than the discomfort of not smoking – the two discomforts are relative and the first is preferable to the second. The alcoholic feels awful after his first drink of the day – but knows that it would be twice as bad without one. In a very different context, Hilaire Belloc advised children

>   always keep a hold of Nurse
> For fear of finding something worse.

And it is the fear of something worse that can keep the victim of habit firmly enmeshed in the cycle of behaviour.

These three kinds of consequences – reward now, reward sometimes, and the reward of avoiding discomfort – will regularly outweigh all other considerations in reinforcing habitual behaviour. They, rather than any particular drug or the type of behaviour, are the true roots of habits, addictions and compulsions.

Conflict

Victims of compulsive habits typically experience strong feelings of conflict. The slimmer wants to lose weight, but also craves food. The compulsive handwasher wants to stop after one wash in order to get ready for work but also feels desperate to wash again.[3] The problem drinker tries to stop after two drinks – he knows that continuing could be disastrous – but he also wants the good feeling that comes from being drunk. We know from experiments with animals and the reported experiences of humans that conflict can lead to strange feelings and consequences. For example, slimmers who find themselves binge eating often feel themselves to be helpless spectators of their own actions. This experience, called dissociation, seems to be a symptom of the battle between urges to continue and attempts to stop. Dissociated feelings, as we shall see, are linked with anxious and depressed states of mind in which willpower, planning and reasoning are difficult to sustain. In helping

Above: Who's conditioning who? Automatic responses to familiar cues are a feature of animal and human behaviour alike.

Right: Being torn between what you want to do and what you ought to do is difficult. In the face of temptation, positive efforts are needed to boost motivation and morale.

people to overcome habits, then, it is not enough to identify why habits arise and how they are triggered. The individual must be equipped with the necessary skills to survive episodes of conflict, when morale and motivation are likely to be at their lowest ebb.

Associative learning and generalization

Throughout this chapter we have portrayed habits, addictions and compulsions as learned behaviour rather than as simply physical dependence (in the case of drugs) or mental illness (in the case of compulsive handwashing or checking). Actions are learned, we have argued, because they offer rewards, either in the form of pleasure or the avoidance of distress. The rewards for performing a particular action work to reinforce it, a process possibly associated with electrical activity in the brain. We know, also, that once established the reinforcement can outweigh even the bad consequence of a habit, leading to feelings of conflict which sap motivation and morale, so closing the vicious circle on the unfortunate victim. Two further complications can be added to complete the picture – associative learning and generalization.

We spoke of specific environmental cues which trigger habits. Under some circumstances, however, new cues arise as a result of the habit. For example, some drug addicts become so conditioned through repeated injections of heroin that the very process of injection becomes pleasurable. When this state is reached they may even inject water in order to get just a hint of the 'high' produced by heroin. This is an example of conditioning or associative learning. Charles O'Brien and his colleagues at the University of Pennsylvania, have collected evidence to show that the physical symptoms of withdrawal from heroin can also be conditioned by association.[4]

One of O'Brien's patients was a heroin addict who had successfully kicked the habit while in prison. On the day of his release he found himself in a neighbourhood in which he had frequently experienced narcotic withdrawal symptoms while trying to acquire drugs. He was immediately overcome by feelings of nausea to the point of actually vomiting. He bought drugs and the symptoms were relieved. The following day, in his own neighbourhood, he again experienced craving and withdrawal symptoms and again relieved them by injecting heroin. The cycle continued and within a few days he was re-addicted.

In experimental tests with 16 volunteer heroin addicts, O'Brien was able to show this process at work. The addicts were receiving methadone treatment (oral methadone is a less addictive substitute for injected heroin) as a first stage in weaning them off heroin. In this treatment the methadone is used to relieve the symptoms resulting from the withdrawal from heroin. O'Brien arranged for his subjects to be injected with naloxone (a drug which counteracts the effects of methadone) in order to precipitate withdrawal symptoms. Just before the symptoms appeared, the subjects were exposed to a tone and a peppermint odour. After a number of such exposures – ranging from six to eleven – withdrawal symptoms appeared promptly on exposure to the combined tone and odour, irrespective of whether naloxone had been administered or not. Subjective withdrawal (complaints of nausea and feeling cold) occurred in all O'Brien's subjects, while physiological changes occurred in 13 out of the 16. These effects included tears, sniffling, reduction in skin temperature, increased heart rate, increased breathing, increased blood pressure and dilated pupils. So we have clear evidence that even a neutral stimulus can produce withdrawal symptoms and presumably, under certain circumstances, craving. O'Brien and his colleagues have also shown that exposure to drug-preparation procedures (cooking-up rituals) produces withdrawal responses in former addicts.

Generalization

In these examples, repeated pairings of cues (stimuli) with otherwise unconnected physical reactions seem to follow the pattern of the classical conditioned response. It was the Russian psychologist Pavlov who first showed that, through repeated association between two events (the ringing of a bell and the appearance of food) dogs could be made to exhibit the physical symptoms of hunger at the sound of the bell alone.

Another aspect of associative conditioning is called generalization. The alcoholic's craving, normally provoked by withdrawal symptoms such as 'the shakes', may also be provoked when he or she feels shaky for reasons that have nothing to do with alcohol. One of our patients with an obsessional fear of cancer experienced acute feelings of contamination and distress on being shown a photograph of a single cancer cell. Another, with a phobia of snakes, was unable to look at a picture of a snake. In these cases the cues which originally triggered the compulsive behaviour had extended to include events or objects only tenuously related to them. Generalization is most marked in obsessional compulsions, and in Chapter 15 we give some bizarre examples of it.

In this first chapter we have focused upon a relatively simple way of understanding habits and compulsions. We have argued that habits are reinforced by the pleasure or reduced distress that follows their performance. But this conception leads straightaway to a paradox, since it is obvious that compulsions often cause a great deal of suffering. Why aren't the guilt, depression, family rows and liver damage experienced by the alcoholic enough to outweigh the attractions of a drinking binge? We have provided a number of reasons. First, the binge is often immediately followed by a powerful pleasurable experience whereas the suffering appears after a delay. Other things being equal, *short-term reinforcement* exerts the strongest influence. Also, even though most of the time drinking binges may not be at all pleasurable, there may be odd occasions when they are very pleasurable indeed. Habits which are *intermittently reinforced* in this way tend to be very persistent since there is always the hope that this time it will be pleasant. It should be remembered as well that *pleasure is relative*. The guilt and suffering may be very unpleasant but stopping drinking might be even worse. Persisting in a compulsive urge is also made difficult by the state of *conflict* that is usually involved. Conflict causes feelings of helplessness and dissociation which are associated with an inability to exert self control. Then we have *generalization* and *associative learning* which account for the spread of compulsive urges and finally put them beyond all reason.

Of course much else is involved besides. We have outlined just a few of the subconscious processes that lead to the development of addictions and compulsions. But human beings are not simply passive creatures of circumstances and cues. They are able to think, plan, strive to achieve future goals and exert self control. This book is about strategies for strengthening self-control skills and weakening the powerful compulsive urges that can ruin our best laid plans.

Changing behaviour

In recent years psychologists have developed a number of methods of modifying habits, compulsions and addictions. These techniques are designed to deal with three aspects of compulsive behaviour – the antecedent cues, the behaviour itself, and the consequences which reinforce it. In summary, the techniques designed to increase self-control are:

1 Selfwatching

The victim must keep a behaviour diary. In this he or she jots down every instance of the habitual behaviour or compulsive urge, together with the precise circumstance in which it took place. This helps to identify the antecedent cues, the events, thoughts or feelings which precipitate, or at least influence, the behaviour.

2 Self-management

The victim is helped to develop strategies to deal with the antecedent cues. Relaxation training, for example, can be used to combat anxiety – a common cue for many types of compulsive behaviour. Strategies have been developed to cope with depression. The victim is encouraged to rearrange his or her life so that antecedent cues or states are avoided or coped with.

3 Cue exposure

This is a later stage in treatment. The victim is encouraged to confront antecedent cues, and for increasing periods of time, rather than avoid them. The longer resistance can be kept up, the more certain that the antecedent cues will eventually lose their power to precipitate the compulsive behaviour.

4 Developing alternative pleasures

Cravings and compulsions are more likely to be resisted if alternative pleasures are anticipated. Self-help groups, such as Weight Watchers, or Alcoholics Anonymous, can be very helpful in altering the reinforcing consequences of moderation and abstention. Abstaining from drink, or sticking to a weight-control programme receives warm praise in these groups – a counterweight against the reinforcing power of the victim's own activities.

5 Relapse prevention

Many people find it relatively easy to resist a compulsive habit for a short period of time. Even severely dependent alcoholics can go for weeks without a drink; eventually, however, strong cravings start to lead them into temptation. An application of selfwatching and self-management techniques involves learning the skill of anticipating and recognizing tempting situations and developing coping strategies in advance – rather like a pilot practising emergency landing drills in a simulator.

All these strategies are described in more detail in the following chapters. They are not cure-alls – but they have a proven record of effectiveness over a very wide range of problems.

2
SELFWATCHING 1
self-observation

In this chapter we examine some specific examples of how selfwatching techniques can be used to change behaviour. The first step is always to make a detailed assessment of the individual case in order to provide a better understanding of all possible factors that are influencing the problem. Since no two people are ever exactly the same, it is rare that two habit patterns are alike in every respect. While two problem drinkers might consume about the same amount of alcohol, their reasons for heavy drinking might be quite different.

As we have seen, habits develop through the repeated association of certain antecedents and consequences with behaviour. Thus, an individual can best understand his or her own habits by examining circumstances occurring immediately before and immediately after behaviour. We need to know precisely which are the cues which trigger the individual to respond in a particular manner. And we also need to understand the consequences – positive and negative – which follow that behaviour.

The case of Rosemary illustrates this point. Rosemary is a 45-year-old overweight housewife who has a compulsion to eat sweets. She has gained over 50lb (23kg) since her marriage 20 years ago. Her husband jokingly refers to her as a 'chocoholic' but she herself knows that her compulsion is no joking matter. Several years ago Rosemary began to eat sweets every day at about 3:00 pm because she felt fatigued and sluggish in the mid-afternoon. After many repetitions of this association, sweets and fatigue became closely linked to one another. This chain of events resulted in conditioning by association so that feelings of fatigue automatically triggered thoughts of food and feelings of hunger. Fatigue became an *antecedent* of her compulsion. As time progressed, and with further associations, the fatigue→hunger→eating sequence became habitual and occurred without conscious thought or decision. In addition, the act of eating sweets is reinforced by the fact that it does temporarily alleviate fatigue by providing a brief energy boost (by raising the blood sugar level), and also because the sweets taste so good! Human behaviour is most influenced by its short-term, immediate consequences. Because of this fact, pleasant taste sensations have a more powerful effect on Rosemary's behaviour than the guilt and frustration she feels because she cannot control her weight. These negative consequences simply occur too long after the eating episode to do much good. The first few seconds after eating sweets are the most critical. This delay is one of the main reasons why the habits described in this book grow to be so strong. They all are reinforced by satisfying consequences which occur immediately. The compulsive checker feels an immediate sense of relief that nothing is wrong, the drug abuser experiences a sense of relaxation after drug intake and the gambler becomes pleasantly aroused by the uncertainty of his bet.

Four major categories of antecedent and consequent events that influence habits have been identified. These include (1) situations, (2) family and friends, (3) thoughts, and (4) emotions.

Situations

It is difficult to live a normal life without being exposed to situations that trigger thoughts of a habit. The smoker sees a friend light up a cigarette at a cocktail party and is reminded how good a cigarette can taste. The compulsive gambler is triggered by driving past a betting shop on the way home from work. Dieters are bombarded with magazine and television advertisements for food. At least a problem drinker or smoker can remove alcohol and cigarettes from the house. The compulsive eater must confront food if for no other reason than to consume enough to survive. Situational antecedents are everywhere.

Several years ago Dr Miller and his research team set up an experiment to study the influence of situational cues on alcohol consumption.[1] Subjects were asked to sit in a small room and press a lever on a 'drinking machine' during a period of 10 minutes. For every 50 lever presses a 5cc squirt of bourbon mixed with water was dispensed into a small glass. Perhaps this was the first computerized, robot bartender! Subjects were instructed to drink the alcohol as it was dispensed. All participants performed this drink-

ing task twice, under two different stimulus conditions. In one condition, the room contained several alcohol stimuli such as bottles of bourbon and pictures of people enjoying alcoholic drinks. In the second condition, the room was bare, except for a chair and the drinking machine.

The visual reminders of alcohol proved to be a powerful influence on behaviour, causing social drinkers to press the lever much more frequently, and therefore to obtain more alcohol, when these cues were present. Interestingly, alcoholics clearly showed a different pattern from the social drinkers on this test. Alcoholics tended to drink a great deal regardless of the environment. Apparently, the chronic alcoholics in this study often drank alone at home, mainly in response to inner cues such as withdrawal symptoms, or feelings of anxiety and depression. Social drinkers usually drink in situations, such as bars and parties, that contain many visual cues.

In the absence of a concrete reason not to smoke, the influence of others – 'behavioural contagion', as it is sometimes called – can be irresistible. Individuals who want to change habits must find ways of reminding themselves and others of their new patterns of behaviour.

Some situations are not obvious triggers but become antecedents through an associative conditioning process. Every time an individual eats, smokes, drinks, or gambles, the behaviour becomes associated with everything around it. A specific room in the house, the time of day, or an activity such as reading or watching television can be a condition which elicits habits or cravings.

The drinking behaviour of Mr and Mrs Walters became conditioned to certain environmental and time antecedents in just this manner. This middle-aged couple, who lived in the suburbs of a large American city, were in the habit of having cocktails each evening at 6:00 pm. Mr Walters, a hard-working building contractor, enjoyed the relaxation of two or three drinks with his wife after a stressful day. Mrs Walters was employed as an interior decorator. She usually arrived home slightly before her husband and also looked forward to the cocktail time. As soon as

Mr Walters arrived he poured two glasses of whisky and they retired to the sitting room. All these elements – cocktails, relaxing conversation, the sitting room, and 6:00 pm – had become closely linked to one another by repeated association. After reading a newspaper article on alcohol abuse Mrs Walters became concerned over their drinking. Over the past year their cocktail time had become a regular daily event and one or two drinks had grown into four or five. She discussed her concern with Mr Walters and they agreed to try an experiment. They decided to give up all drinking for one week, to find out how important alcohol was to their lives.

On the first day of their personal experiment they returned home from work and sat together in the sitting room, without drinks, to discuss the day. Both of them began to feel quite uneasy and tense. They were amazed to realize that they both strongly craved a drink. In fact, they found it very difficult to relax and concentrate on the conversation. The mere exposure to the situation – sitting room at 6:00 pm – was enough to trigger the craving.

Family and friends

What other people say and do can also trigger habits. Even the mere presence of another person engaging in a similar behaviour is influential. Drs Wayne Glad and Vincent Adesso of the University of Wisconsin investigated this phenomenon, which they termed 'behavioural contagion'.[2] They asked college students who were either heavy or light smokers to sit in a room with other people. One half of the student group shared a room with people who were smoking. The other half were seated with non-smokers. Two observers were watching behind a one-way window to observe the number of cigarettes smoked, the number of puffs, and flicks, and the number of minutes spent smoking. Smoking was indeed contagious in that the presence of other smokers significantly increased the

Four examples of situations where it is difficult not to join in: a junkie's pad, the solicitous fellow-guest who loads your plate, the machismo of the beerhall or just being one of the lads.

amount the students smoked. There was a tendency for this to be more powerful in influencing light as opposed to heavy smokers. This may simply indicate that heavy smokers are more addicted to nicotine and that, therefore, the amount of smoking is primarily governed by internal, physiological cues rather than external, social ones.

Conversely, some people actually smoke less when in the company of non-smokers. A study of the University of Mississippi Medical Center found that light smokers took more frequent and longer puffs when smoking alone than with others. Social interaction with people who were not smoking led to an overall decrease in the total amount of smoke inhaled. Normal social interaction may exert a controlling influence on some smokers (especially if they are talkative) because talking to other people and puffing on a cigarette are incompatible. On the other hand, perhaps light smokers consciously limit their smoking under these circumstances because they are becoming more aware of the desire of many non-smokers to avoid exposure to cigarette smoke. As with the previous study, however, normal interaction with other people exerted neither a positive nor a negative influence on the behaviour of heavy smokers.

Other people can exert a considerable influence on addictions by being 'friendly enemies'. They may directly encourage the addiction or simply make it easier by such comments as 'Oh come on, one little drink won't hurt you.' The drug pusher is the most obvious and sinister friendly enemy although the food, cigarette and alcohol pusher can be just as dangerous. Such people not only trigger habits but also provide positive consequences for them in the form of comments and increased attention. After talking a friend into having a whisky that he really did not want, the alcohol pusher may put his arm around his 'conquest' and say 'That's it, Fred. I knew you'd enjoy it.'

Thoughts
People underestimate the influence of thoughts on behaviour: indeed, they frequently talk themselves into bad habits. In chapter 1 we talked about the feelings of dissociation (also called 'cognitive dissonance') which result when behaviour is inconsistent with beliefs, attitudes or public statements. If, on the one hand, a person believes that smoking is unhealthy and, on the other hand, lights up a cigarette, this demonstrates a state of dissonance. This conflict can be avoided if an acceptable excuse can be

found for smoking. He might say to himself, 'Just *one* cigarette won't hurt me' or 'This is an exception; a special occasion.' He's let himself off the hook. Some people avoid cognitive dissonance by refusing direct personal responsibility for their actions with such statements as 'If it weren't for my stressful job, I could stop smoking easily' or 'I was tense and a strong craving just took control of me.' The excuses you make for yourself actively encourage the behaviour by falsely reducing its significance.

Emotions

Emotions exert a strong influence over learned behaviour. Anger, boredom, loneliness, depression and tension are commonly reported antecedents to addictions and compulsions. Addictive habits triggered by these emotions are reinforced by the emotional arousal that they engender. Addictions become a means of 'letting go', of escaping from the daily routine of life.

Certain patterns of compulsive behaviour – such as binge eating – are particularly susceptible to emotional influences. Stress and depression can precipitate the consumption of large quantities of food at irregular intervals. Professor Albert Stunkard, a renowned obesity expert, notes that as many as 20,000 calories per day can be consumed by a binge eater going through an emotional trauma. That amount is equal to more than the number of calories consumed by the average person in one week.

Self-observation

The influence on habits of these different types of antecedents and consequences must be determined before a programme of change can be established. Most people know very little about the conditions controlling their behaviour. When asked 'What makes you drink, smoke, eat, gamble, or overwork?', they usually reply, 'If I only knew, then I could control myself.' They are exactly right. Unfortunately, no universal test or sudden psychological insight will provide the answer.

The key to self-understanding is self-observation. People must study and analyse their behaviour in much the same way as a medical researcher examines diseased cells under a microscope. The only way to study behaviour is to observe it closely and systematically on a day to day basis. A casual look will accomplish nothing. A scientist could never discover the cure for cancer by looking into his microscope once in a while.

Methods of self-observation

The first chore of self-observation is to decide exactly what should be observed. What is the most essential target behaviour? The element of the habit pattern that is observed must, first of all, be expressed in terms of numbers. For example, a gambler's report on self-observations might consist of the number of minutes or hours spent in the betting shop. Basically, the factors of particular interest are the times at which betting occurred and the frequency and duration of periods of betting per day or per week. In this way the report remains an objective and factual account. Subjective self-analyses such as 'I drank a little more this week than last' or 'My problem is getting worse' provide absolutely no useful

Benjamin Franklin, selfwatcher

One of the earliest recorded attempts at self-observation to understand habits was employed, surprisingly enough, by Benjamin Franklin. This American statesman, scientist, and inventor spent his life striving for self-improvement both for himself and for others. He is especially noted for his advice on the virtues of industry, frugality and thrift that he scattered throughout his *Poor Richard's Almanac*, published yearly from 1733 to 1758. His wise and witty sayings showed a keen understanding of human nature. Such advice as 'Early to bed and early to rise, makes a man healthy, wealthy and wise' and 'He that falls in love with himself will have no rivals' are still with us.

Franklin's rather lofty ambition in life was to live '... without committing any fault at any time'. As might be expected he found this to be easier said than done. As a scientist, however, he reasoned that behaviour as well as the physical elements of nature could be systematically studied and, if necessary, modified.

He carefully devised a self-observation and monitoring plan. Franklin began by listing all of the behaviours for which he was striving. These included the following 13 'virtues':

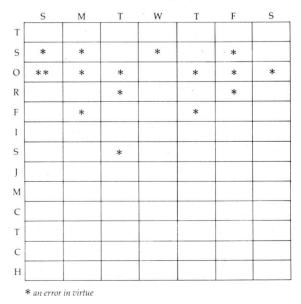

1. Temperance
2. Silence
3. Order
4. Resolution
5. Frugality
6. Industry
7. Sincerity
8. Justice
9. Moderation
10. Cleanliness
11. Tranquillity
12. Chastity
13. Humility

It is interesting to note that Franklin listed these behaviours in positive rather than negative style. That is, he includes temperance rather than drunkenness, frugality rather than extravagance, and tranquillity rather than tension or anxiety. Contemporary behavioural scientists have found this focus on positive behaviours to be a viable one

in the modification of habit patterns.

Once Franklin established his list, he obtained a notebook in which he kept a record of the occurrence of each behaviour. He felt that self-observation was essential to better understand faults. He also wisely noted that 'habit takes advantage of inattention'. A page from Franklin's notebook illustrating one week of self-monitoring is shown in Table 1. As can be seen, he carefully observed *all* of his habits although he concentrated on improving only one per week. Temperance was his goal for this first week. By the end of the 13th week he hoped to have broken all bad habits and attained 'moral perfection'.

An asterisk in a column of the notebook indicated an error in virtue. It is apparent that during this first week Franklin seemed to be having a difficult time in being quiet and orderly. When this happened, he inspected his records closely, trying to figure out what went wrong. In selfwatching terms, he was looking for specific antecedents and consequences.

Self-observation provided Franklin with useful insights into his behaviour. In his autobiography[5] he wrote, 'I was surpris'd to find myself so much fuller of faults than I had imagined'.

	S	M	T	W	T	F	S
T							
S	*	*		*		*	
O	**	*	*		*	*	*
R				*		*	
F		*			*		
I							
S			*				
J							
M							
C							
T							
C							
H							

* an error in virtue

information. On this page we give a selection of target behaviours to be observed for various addictions and compulsions.

In addition, the self-observer must be careful not to try to observe too much at once. Self-monitoring is difficult enough without turning it into a full-time occupation. For example, a smoker who drinks and overeats should decide which of these three habits should be modified first and observe only one at a time. When too many behaviours are being assessed, careful and accurate observation is not possible.

In addition to the *occurrence* of a habit, the antecedents and consequences of that habit must be observed. The person who is self-monitoring must observe the whole sequence of events, from a few minutes before the behaviour has occurred to a few minutes after. The best method is to detail four particular aspects of the conditions which may have triggered the behaviour: the general setting or situation, the number of people who were there, the feelings experienced, and any thoughts which may have been present in the mind at the time. The consequences of the habit must also be observed and catalogued. Care must be taken to observe *objectively* without attempting either to make judgements upon or to assign reasons for what happened. *The antecedents and consequences are the reasons. No other explanation is necessary to modify behaviour successfully.* The importance of this descriptive, scientific, observational frame of mind cannot be overstated. Without it, the monitoring becomes a search for underlying psychological reasons for habits which is nothing but guesswork and speculation, resulting in confusion and frustration. The question during self-observation is not 'Why?' but 'What?', 'When?', 'How?', and 'Under what circumstances?'

Keeping a selfwatching diary

The most efficient way of keeping track of these observations is through a selfwatching diary. This is a so-called behavioural diary – a special type of record which can help to discover patterns among antecedents and habits. In order for this to happen, the diary must be methodical and to the point. Page after page of lengthy narrative describing details of daily experiences may

Watch out for binges! By keeping a record of what you eat and when you eat it, you can stay in control of your eating habits.

Sample target behaviours for self-observation

Problem	Sample Behaviours
Alcohol abuse	Number of drinks per day Amount of alcohol per day Types of drinks per day
Smoking	Number of cigarettes per day Number of puffs per cigarette Amount of nicotine consumed
Drug abuse	Mg. of drugs per day Types of drugs per day Number of pills or injections per day
Sexual deviations	Number of episodes Number of impulses
Compulsions	Number of checking episodes Number of thoughts about contamination
Overweight	Number of calories per day Number of meals/snacks Duration & type of exercise
Gambling	Number of bets Amount of money bet Duration of time in casino or betting shop
Workaholism	Amount of time working Amount of time in leisure activities

be interesting as reminiscence, but it makes the analysis of specific problems very difficult.

Behavioural diaries take many forms. Some people keep records of their behaviour on index cards or small booklets that are handy to carry with them. Smokers are urged to wrap their recording sheets around their cigarettes. One of the best methods of structuring a diary is illustrated by the case of Terry, a 38-year-old government employee who was married with three children. He sought professional treatment for his alcohol problem after his work supervisor expressed concern about his increasing number of absences from work due to 'illness'. Actually, Terry was either drinking or trying to cope with a hangover on those days. The supervisor indicated that any more absences would result in his losing the job. Although Terry's drinking problem had been worsening over the last few years, it had not, until now, affected his work.

At the beginning of treatment Terry, in common with many victims of compulsions and addictions, seemed to have little understanding of factors which influenced his drinking. He could only say that he was drinking quite a bit every

---

Drinking diary

Tuesday, April 14, 1981

Time	Antecedent	Behaviour	Consequence
11:00am	Bar across from work; felt restless, tense and angry at boss	3 beers	Felt more relaxed
12:30pm	Lunch with co-workers	2 beers	No particular feelings - thoughts of 'I can control my drinking with no trouble'. Maybe I really don't have a problem'
5:00pm	Driving past favourite bar on the way home and knew friends would be there - still angry at boss	4 whiskies	Felt relaxed; enjoyed the company of my friends. Friend kept encouraging me to have one more
6:45pm	Arrived home late - wife angry; nagging about my drinking - felt tense and angry but didn't say much	2 whiskies	Became more talkative - expressed my anger but overdid it by yelling and screaming at wife and kids
8:30pm	Felt angry and guilty about my temper outburst - thought 'What difference does it make? I'm just going to get good and drunk. I'll show her who's boss around here'	3 whiskies	Became drowsy; fell asleep on the sofa

---

day because 'I like the taste of the stuff.' He was asked to keep a drinking diary for one week to provide a better analysis of his behaviour. He was instructed to write down after every drinking episode the time of day, number and types of drinks, antecedents, and consequences. This self-observational approach, with specific examples of antecedents and consequent events, was described to Terry in great detail. When recording antecedents and consequences he was advised to consider not only locations and circumstances but also thoughts and feelings. Even though he was somewhat hesitant to 'play these psychological games', he agreed to monitor his drinking. After one week of self-observations his behavioural diary provided a detailed picture of his drinking. One typical day from his diary is reproduced on this page. In reviewing this and other days it is apparent that most of the drinking occurred in the afternoon and evening. The two major antecedents triggering alcohol consumption were (1) feelings of tension and unexpressed anger and (2) social interactions with friends. A third antecedent, becoming more and more important, was a feeling of guilt and remorse over excessive drinking or extremes of inappropriate behaviour during a drinking episode. The reinforcing consequences for drinking seemed to be (1) tension relief, (2) ability to express anger more directly and (3) enjoyable social interactions with friends. As Terry and his therapist began to analyse his diary, he came to understand more about his pattern of drinking and the circumstances which controlled it.

On this basis it was possible to pinpoint certain *high-risk situations* – sets of circumstances in which Terry was most likely to drink. Recognizing antecedent and consequent elements of high-risk situations through self-observation enabled Terry to make predictions about his drinking behaviour. Learning to predict when temptation is likely to be at its strongest is one key to the successful control of habits. It is a bit like predicting financial probabilities in the stock market. If one can observe the factors that control a company's earnings on a day-to-day basis, better control can be exerted over investments. For example, high-risk situations for Terry included:

1. Being angry towards his boss but being unable to express it
2. Feeling tense, particularly in the late morning after a previous evening of heavy drinking
3. Being in a social gathering with friends and feeling under pressure to drink
4. Having an argument with his wife, particularly about his drinking or failure to stand up to his boss.

Based on this analysis it was possible to set treatment goals that best suited Terry's individual needs. Such goals must be designed to provide more effective methods of coping with or avoiding antecedents of drinking. In addition, they must enable him to experience positive consequences of refraining from alcohol, but negative or neutral ones if he persisted in drinking. Along these lines, treatment goals based on Terry's behavioural diary included the following:

1. To develop more direct and assertive ways of expressing anger which are neither too passive nor too aggressive

Frustration can trigger self-destructive behaviour. Sometimes people need to be taught how to assert themselves.

2. To learn methods of physical and mental relaxation and practise them regularly
3. To learn and practise 'drink refusal skills' in order to counter pressure to drink from friends and colleagues
4. To increase positive interactions and decrease arguments and disagreements with wife through marital skills training
5. To enlist the aid of friends and co-workers to reduce the positive social consequences of drinking
6. To learn to control excuses and negative thinking which influence drinking.

Self-observation and the setting of realistic goals are essential in establishing the appropriate groundwork for habit change. The next several chapters will describe specific methods of self-watching needed to accomplish these goals.

Positive benefits of self-observation

Self-observation not only serves as a method of assessment but is also effective in actually changing behaviour. As a person becomes more aware of his behaviour he or she is often able to modify it much more easily. Drs David Watson and Roland Tharp of the University of Hawaii teach their psychology students about self-observation by giving them an assignment to keep records on a personal habit pattern. Students usually choose smoking, studying (usually when they are finding it difficult to study), or eating. The doctors report that, after a few days of self-observation, an occasional concerned student will report, 'I'm sorry, but I cannot work out a plan.' 'Why not?' they ask. 'My problem is that my problem has gone away!' is the reply.[5]

Self-recording tends to change behaviour in a positive direction. For example, during this self-understanding phase smokers smoke about 20 per cent fewer cigarettes than usual, overeaters consume fewer calories, and workaholics get more enjoyment out of life. In fact, Drs Watson and Tharp estimate that in approximately 15 per cent of their clinical cases, systematic self-observation is all the treatment that is necessary.

An example of this phenomenon is provided by the case of a young drug abuser treated at Duke University Medical Center in North Carolina. The patient was a 21-year-old female college student who was taking as many as 30

5mg tablets of dexadrine per day. She had a five-year history of amphetamine abuse. Apparently, one motivating factor was that the student was considerably overweight – she was, 5ft 5in (1.64m) and weighed 260lb (118kg) – and she was using dexadrine to suppress her appetite. To analyse her problem she was asked to record the type and quantity of drugs she took on a daily basis and the times and setting in which they were taken. In addition, prior to ingesting the drug, she was asked to write down her reasons for taking it. After only three weeks of self-observation the patient's drug taking decreased

At home, as at work, bad relationships generate violent and uncontrolled feelings. The development of personal skills – simply being better with oneself and with other people – helps to make permanent changes in behaviour patterns.

Selfwatching: behavioural diaries

Behavioural diaries must be specific if they are to provide useful information. They must be constructed in such a way that they provide a clear record of the antecedents that trigger the habitual behaviour. Here is an example of a smoker's behavioural diary for a typical Monday morning. The selfwatcher is Evelyn M., a 36-year-old divorced real estate agent.

Smoking diary

Monday, February 1, 1982

Time of Cigarette	Craving strength (Rate from 0-5)	Location	Activity	Thought or feeling
7:30am	5	Bedroom	Lying in bed trying to waken	Nothing in particular
8:00am	4	Kitchen	Drinking coffee	Relaxed
8:20am	4	Bedroom	Telephoning office	Thinking about my busy schedule
8:45am	3	Car	Driving to work	Slightly tense ("Will I be able to make that sale today?")
9:20am	4	Office desk	Drinking coffee and doing paper work	Thinking how much I hate paper work
10:00am	2	Office desk	Waiting for clients to arrive	Feeling impatient
10:20am	3	Driving in car	Showing clients houses to buy	Slightly tense
10:50am	3	Driving in car	Showing clients houses to buy	Slightly tense
11:30am	4	Office desk	Talking to clients about the details of house	Feeling excited about the possibility of a big sale
12:15pm	2	Office	Talking to co-worker about my sale	Feeling proud and happy - using cigarette to reward and relax

from about 11 tablets per day to nil. Over the next six months she continued to keep a drug diary and she remained completely abstinent except for four separate days of minimal dexadrine intake. After the first month she was instructed to keep additional records of any thoughts about drugs. These thoughts decreased over time, but more slowly than the drug taking itself. By the end of two months she was relatively free of cravings and thoughts about amphetamines.

In addition to providing information on trigger factors, self-observation gives regular feedback on day-to-day variations in the addiction or compulsion. 'Good' days boost morale and increase motivation: not-so-good days should not be cause for despair, but for renewed determination. At the same time, self-monitoring ensures that a certain amount of time each day will be devoted to thinking about changing behaviour and the reasons for change. Reviewing a daily diary, an overweight person might think, 'Look at that. More than 2000 calories over my limit yesterday. I'll never be able to get into my favourite clothes if this keeps up. Tomorrow I resolve to do better.'

Overweight individuals benefit particularly from this kind of self-confrontation because, under normal circumstances, they usually avoid reminders of their eating behaviour. When not dieting they are poor judges of total calories consumed – usually under-estimating how much they eat. Better to know, objectively, one's calorie intake than to exult or despair over the weight registered by the bathroom scales.

Two variations of self-observation designed to enhance feedback and confrontation have been identified. The first involves *when* self-observation records are kept. Dr Allan Bellack of the University of Pittsburgh asked a group of overweight women to monitor their food intake for several weeks. Half of the women were instructed to write the type of food, quantity, and calories consumed in their diaries *after* they had finished eating. The other half recorded this information *before* eating meals or snacks. The group that made diary entries before eating consumed fewer calories and lost more weight than the other group. The women explained that in writing down calories before they ate, they were made more aware of what they were about to do and consciously consumed less food. Similar information, however effective, provided to the other group could not affect behaviour until the *next* eating episode.

The second method involves the particular information to be recorded. Drs David Abrams and G. Terence Wilson of Rutgers University wondered whether one type of information monitored about a habit might affect the rate of behaviour change more than another. They asked smokers to keep behavioural diaries on one of two aspects of smoking. Half were instructed to record the number of cigarettes smoked per day. The other half were requested to record the amount of nicotine they consumed each day. In the USA the number of milligrams of nicotine per cigarette is printed on cigarette packages, so such records were relatively easy to keep. Nicotine monitoring proved to be much more effective in modifying smoking behaviour. Over a period of four weeks, nicotine monitoring resulted in almost a 50 per cent reduction in smoking while cigarette monitoring reduced smoking by only about 15 per cent.

Conclusions

Self-observation is the first step in the selfwatching approach to altering hard-to-break habits, addictions and compulsions. Keeping a systematic behavioural diary can make a big contribution to understanding the cues which trigger the performance of a particular habit, and the circumstances in which cues are most likely to be present. Basic information of this nature is very important in setting goals and choosing techniques which are most realistic and appropriate for the particular individual involved. Self-observation, however, is more than the basis for continuing treatment. Evidence shows that it has positive effects on its own account, firstly by increasing awareness of the day-to-day pattern of habit and secondly by providing a record of the progress made. Moreover, the more specific the information recorded, the more effective the self-observation method seems to be.

Knowing it can be done, and convincing yourself that you can do it, really will help in keeping up motivation. It worked here! But a habit-change programme must be methodical to be successful – writing it down as you go along will enable you to celebrate progress and bring relapses under control.

3
SELFWATCHING 2
self-management

After a period of keeping and analysing a behavioural diary, specific circumstances that trigger cravings can be identified. The next step is to develop self-control over these temptations by learning to apply appropriate selfwatching techniques.

Most people think of the word self-control as meaning willpower, guts, or inner strength. Giving in to cravings is viewed as a weakness, proof that self-control is lacking. As Oscar Wilde so succinctly phrased it, 'I can resist everything except temptation.'

People also view self-control, quite mistakenly, as an all-or-nothing characteristic, as though some individuals have a lot of it while others have practically none. Supposed lack of willpower can be dangerous since it serves as an excuse for loss of habit control. 'I couldn't help myself', someone may say, 'I was born without

any willpower; it's not my fault.'

In reality, self-control refers to a set of skills that can be learned and developed through practice. An excellent definition is provided by Drs Goldfried and Merbaum in their book, *Behaviour Change Through Self-Control*. They describe self-control as 'a process through which an individual becomes the principal agent in guiding, directing and regulating those features of his own behaviour that might eventually lead to desired positive consequences'. In this light, self-control is best conceptualized as *self-management*. Managing an addiction or compulsion is much like managing a business. Self-management implies an active process of planning ahead and problem solving as opposed to simply suppressing and controlling behaviour. For example, a smoker may think he is demonstrating willpower by standing in front of a cigarette machine in his office building, arguing with himself about making a purchase. Such behaviour shows a definite *lack* of self-control in that the smoker is placing himself in a risky situation and, thereby, increasing the probability that smoking will occur. The self-management approach to such a situation would be to plan a route to the office which avoids the cigarette machine altogether. The tempting circumstances must be recognized and a plan of action developed, *ahead of time*, to avoid it.

How to measure self-management

Dr Michael Rosenbaum[1] of Haifa University in Israel recently developed a test to measure the degree to which some individuals manage their behaviour in a conscious fashion rather than depend on natural 'inner strengths' of willpower and strongmindedness. In developing his *Self-Control Schedule* Dr Rosenbaum included items that sample a broad range of self-management skills (see box overleaf). As you can see, several items make reference to ways in which a person might manage unpleasant emotions (for example 'When I am feeling depressed I try to think about pleasant events'). Others refer to methods used to delay immediate gratification and contend with frustration ('When I do a boring job, I think about the less boring parts of the job and the reward that I will receive when I am finished' or 'When I am hungry and unable to eat, I try to divert my thoughts away from my stomach or try to imagine that I am satisfied'). Other items test the ability to plan alternative solutions to problems (for example 'If I find it difficult to concentrate on a certain job, I divide the job into smaller segments').

Having tested a number of subjects, Dr Rosenbaum wondered whether people who received a high score really did manage their behaviour more effectively than those who scored low. He devised an interesting experiment to determine the answer to this question. After completing the *Self-Control Schedule*, each of 40 subjects was asked to immerse his or her dominant hand in a plastic basin filled with ice and water. The temperature was approximately 1°–2 °C. Subjects were told to hold their hands in the cold water for as long as possible. The 40 volunteers were divided into two groups. An experimental group

Self-management means self-sufficiency. Like this fireman, you can learn to anticipate dangers – and equip yourself to deal with them.

Want a drag, man? To change a habit of any kind, it's good self-management to keep yourself away from temptation for a while.

was taught the use of a self-management technique to help them cope with this unpleasant task. The strategy was simply to imagine pleasant events in order to distract themselves from the sensations of cold and discomfort. The other (control) group was not given any assistance in coping with the task. The results indicated that the subjects who had been given the self-management technique were able to keep their hands in the cold water about two and a half minutes longer than the control group.

The next stage was to evaluate the relationship between the *Self-Control Schedule* test scores and performance on this cold water task. The subjects in both groups were divided into High Self-Controllers and Low Self-Controllers on the basis of their test scores. In the experimental group the High Self-Controllers had an average score of 37.8 and the Low Self-Controllers had an average score of only −6.6. In the control group there was also a wide disparity between the scores of High and Low Self-Controllers. In each group, the High Self-Controllers, as predicted,

Paddling your own canoe – like staying upright on a sail-board – should be thought of as a skill to be learned rather than something only some people can do.

tolerated the cold almost two minutes longer than the Low Self-Controllers.

Encouragingly, then, the distraction strategy seemed to help subjects in the experimental group withstand the cold regardless of their test scores. Everyone seemed to benefit from self-management training. In fact, such training over a period of time would probably increase test scores to a significant degree. The *Self-Control Schedule* is a useful tool in assessing a person's level of self-management and in evaluating improvements as new coping skills are learned.

But what are these skills? In general they can be grouped into four main strategies for self-management.

The Rosenbaum self-control schedule

Each item is simply rated on a scale ranging from +3 to −3, using the code system provided on the test. This rating system varies from 'very characteristic of me, extremely descriptive' to 'very uncharacteristic of me, extremely undescriptive'. Items with an asterisk are expressed negatively so that the + or − value of the rating must be reversed prior to scoring. The average (mean) score on this test for different samples of college students (average age = 22 years) falls between 23 and 27. It is interesting to note that an older sample of subjects whose average age was 50 years scored higher than the students. The average score of the older subjects was 31, indicating more developed self-control skills. Perhaps experience is the best teacher after all!

Directions: Indicate how characteristic or descriptive each of the following statements is of you by using the code given below.

+3 *very characteristic of me, extremely descriptive*
+2 *rather characteristic of me, quite descriptive*
+1 *somewhat characteristic of me, slightly descriptive*
−1 *somewhat uncharacteristic of me, slightly undescriptive*
−2 *rather uncharacteristic of me, quite undescriptive*
−3 *very uncharacteristic of me, extremely undescriptive*

1. When I do a boring job, I think about the less boring parts of the job and the reward that I will receive once I am finished.
2. When I have to do something that is anxiety arousing for me, I try to visualize how I will overcome my anxieties while doing it.
3. Often by changing my way of thinking I am able to change my feelings about almost everything.
4. I often find it difficult to overcome my feelings of nervousness and tension without any outside help.*
5. When I am feeling depressed I try to think about pleasant events.
6. I cannot avoid thinking about mistakes I have made in the past.*
7. When I am faced with a difficult problem, I try to approach its solution in a systematic way.
8. I usually do my duties quicker when somebody is pressuring me.*
9. When I am faced with a difficult decision, I prefer to postpone making a decision even if all the facts are at my disposal.*
10. When I find that I have difficulties in concentrating on my reading, I look for ways to increase my concentration.

11. When I plan to work, I remove all the things that are not relevant to my work.
12. When I try to get rid of a bad habit, I first try to find out all the factors that maintain this habit.
13. When an unpleasant thought is bothering me, I try to think about something pleasant.
14. If I smoked two packets of cigarettes a day, I probably would need outside help to stop smoking.*
15. When I am in a low mood, I try to act in a cheerful way so my mood will change.
16. If I had the pills with me, I would take a tranquillizer whenever I felt tense and nervous.*
17. When I am depressed, I try to keep myself busy with things that I like.
18. I tend to postpone unpleasant duties even if I could perform them immediately.*
19. I need outside help to get rid of some of my bad habits.*
20. When I find it difficult to settle down and do a certain job, I look for ways to help me settle down.
21. Although it makes me feel bad, I cannot avoid thinking about all kinds of possible catastrophes in the future.*
22. First of all I prefer to finish a job that I have to do and then start doing the things I really like.
23. When I feel pain in a certain part of my body, I try not to think about it.
24. My self-esteem increases once I am able to overcome a bad habit.
25. In order to overcome bad feelings that accompany failure, I often tell myself that it is not so catastrophic and that I can do something about it.
26. When I feel that I am too impulsive, I tell myself 'stop and think before you do anything'.
27. Even when I am terribly angry at somebody, I consider my actions very carefully.
28. Facing the need to make a decision, I usually find out all the possible alternatives instead of deciding quickly and spontaneously.
29. Usually I do first the things I really like to do even if there are more urgent things to do.*
30. When I realize that I cannot help but be late for an important meeting, I tell myself to keep calm.
31. When I feel pain in my body, I try to divert my thoughts from it.
32. I usually plan my work when faced with a number of things to do.
33. When I am short of money, I decide to record all my expenses in order to plan more carefully for the future.
34. If I find it difficult to concentrate on a certain job, I divide the job into smaller segments.
35. Quite often I cannot overcome unpleasant thoughts that bother me.*
36. Once I am hungry and unable to eat, I try to divert my thoughts away from my stomach or try to imagine that I am satisfied.

reverse items

Strategy 1: Rearranging the environment

As we have seen, many of the circumstances and situations which take place just before a habit pattern may contribute to its continuation. Thoughts, feelings, social pressures, associations with particular places or times of day can all play their part in triggering addictive behaviour. Of these, thoughts and feelings are best dealt with through the relaxation, assertiveness or thought-control skills discussed in Chapters 4, 5 and 6. In many cases, however, the place/time associations which trigger habits can be neutralized by actively changing or rearranging the circumstances which give rise to them. For example, if drinking coffee triggers the desire for a cigarette, the would-be non-smoker can simply substitute another beverage. Alternatively, coffee could be drunk only under relatively 'safe' conditions, for instance when there are no cigarettes in the house.

Potentially dangerous places and times are best identified through careful analysis of a behavioural diary. Next a self-management plan can be designed to counter their influence. Two cases of problem drinkers treated by Dr Miller show how this can be done. The first involved Robert, a 42-year-old married businessman with two children. He was a compulsive worker who was beginning to drink heavily in the evening after work. The most likely times for him to drink alcohol were immediately after work from 5:30 pm to 7:30 pm and in the late evening before bedtime. As a self-management strategy Robert planned to schedule specific activities during these times that would make alcohol consumption difficult or impossible. For example, several possibilities included:

1. Eating supper immediately upon arriving home from work (Robert lost his craving for alcohol after a meal)
2. Taking his wife and children or his wife alone out to supper, a movie, or shopping
3. Visiting his sister and brother-in-law who never drink alcohol
4. Working with his sons on restoring a 1946 Mercedes that he bought for them.

For later in the evening he planned the following alternatives to drinking:

1. Arranging to have intimate talks with his wife on specific subjects
2. Scheduling evening exercises from 10:30 pm to 11:00 pm (Robert seldom felt like drinking after exercise)
3. Practising relaxation and meditation for 20 minutes before bedtime to reduce tension and make him sleep better.

Good self-management is learning to avoid loneliness (left) when cravings are likely to be at their strongest. Plan to fill dead time with other activities – whether useful (centre) or simply fun (right).

With the help of his wife, Robert rigidly scheduled his evenings with these activities for three full weeks. After this amount of time he began to enjoy his alternative activities and gradually his habitual pattern of evening drinking dissolved.

The second case involved Leonard, a 49-year-old travelling salesman who drank excessively only when he was away from home on business trips. These trips frequently led to drinking binges of several days' duration. Leonard's behavioural diary revealed that heavy drinking was most likely to occur (1) when he was alone in his hotel room during the time from his arrival in the town in the afternoon until the evening or next morning when he would call on his customers and (2) when he was with a customer or group of customers at dinner and they were ordering drinks.

His self-management treatment involved several elements. He was instructed to arrange his schedule so that he would arrive for business meetings very close to the time that the meetings were scheduled. If the meetings were at 10:00 am he was to arrive early in the morning rather than the previous evening. Since much of his travelling was within a small county area, he could arrange to wake early and drive to his destination. When possible he was instructed to con-clude his business in one day and return home the same evening. With proper planning this schedule proved to be quite easy to follow.

Whenever possible Leonard was to excuse himself from cocktail gatherings, using further work or fatigue as a reason. When dining with customers he was to order his 'drink' first, asking the waitress to bring him coffee or tea. Leonard had found that when others ordered alcoholic drinks before he had a chance to order, he felt somewhat intimidated and was more likely to ask for alcohol.

He was also advised to plan enjoyable activities for the hours during his business trips when he might have free time. For example, he enjoyed reading mystery novels but never seemed to have enough time at home. Reading a novel during a two-hour break on his trip served as a pleasant alternative to drinking and also satisfied the same basic purpose – to escape temporarily from his work and responsibilities and to relax.

With vigilant planning and scheduling Leonard learned to control his drinking. He developed a pattern of never drinking alcohol during business trips and drank only an occasional beer with friends at social functions.

Basically, then, incompatible activities must be scheduled at times when the addiction or com-

Self-reward works to reinforce progress in a habit-control programme – but special treats should be reserved to reward specific targets successfully achieved.

pulsion is most likely to occur. These activities should be as enjoyable as possible and be capable of preventing the habit. A dieter might enjoy a brisk stroll during a time of day that was previously associated with eating snacks. It is difficult, although not impossible, to walk quickly and eat a packet of biscuits at the same time.

Strategy 2: Modifying the consequences of behaviour

Behaviours can also be modified by changing their consequences. A positive habit can be rewarded, while a negative habit can be punished. Self-rewards or punishments must occur soon after the behaviour in question if they are to be maximally effective. Everyone rewards and punishes himself every day although

seldom systematically enough to have much impact. After accomplishing a difficult task a person may be rewarded with the thought, 'I really worked hard on that project. Now I think I'll relax and go to a movie tonight.'

Investigators at the University of Pennsylvania designed an innovative self-reward procedure for dieters. At the beginning of a weight control programme they instructed participants to buy a quantity of pork fat (suet) equivalent in weight to their total amount overweight. The dieters were asked to store this fat in their refrigerators and to imagine that it represented their own excess body fat. As the participants lost weight each week they were told to remove an equal weight from the suet and throw it away. This proved to be a very popular and effective method. It was important for the participants to store the fat in such a way that it could be seen each time they opened the refrigerator.

Rewards can also take the form of special gifts or favourite activities. Self-restraint in the face of the temptation to fall back into old habits can be rewarded with spending time at a favourite hobby, buying a new record, book, or article of clothing, going to a movie or a play, or taking time to relax. A gambler interested in music might buy a new record or attend a concert at the end of each week during which he has managed to avoid making a bet. Such reinforcers, however, must be provided only when progress is being made and withheld at other times.

Dr Michael Mahoney[2] of Pennsylvania State University has found that the method by which a person rewards himself is quite important in terms of the effectiveness of that reward. He devised a research plan to answer the question of *what* should be rewarded – the achievement of a specific goal or an ongoing pattern of behaviour. For example, is it more effective to reward oneself for attaining a particular goal, such as losing 20lb (9kg), or for daily changes in habit such as eating fewer calories or exercising more often?

To provide an answer, Dr Mahoney conducted a study on weight reduction using a total of 49 men and women who were at least 20 per cent overweight. Subjects were randomly assigned to one of four treatment conditions: (1) Self-Reward for Weight Loss, (2) Self-Reward for Habit

Improvement, (3) Self-Monitoring, and (4) Delayed Treatment (the control group). Members of the first two groups were required to pay a deposit of $35 for the programme, a sum which was later used for self-reward purposes.

During the first two weeks subjects in the first three groups were required to keep a behavioural diary, recording weight, quantity and nutritional quality of food eaten, and situational determinants of eating on a daily basis. These records provided a baseline from which changes resulting from treatment could be compiled. After these two weeks, treatment recommendations were provided. The Self-Monitoring subjects were instructed to continue their behavioural diaries. At weekly weigh-ins they were also provided with recommended goals for weight loss and eating habit changes. In addition to keeping a diary, Self-Reward for Weight Loss subjects were advised to reward themselves for attaining their weekly weight-loss goals. The Self-Reward for Habit Improvement subjects were asked to reward themselves for attaining their weekly habit-change goals, which might include eating 1000 calories per day or eating more slowly. The rewards consisted of envelopes containing cash and gift certificates from local stores. These envelopes were made available after each weekly weigh-in and subjects were free to reward themselves according to the established guidelines. The Delayed Treatment subjects received no treatment and simply served as a control group. Treatment continued for six weeks with a follow-up after 12 months.

Dr Mahoney found that the Self-Reward for Habit Improvement subjects not only lost more weight than the other groups but also kept the weight off for a longer period of time. These differences were especially clear at the one year follow-up. At that time 70 per cent of the subjects who rewarded themselves for changes in habit either had maintained their weight losses or had lost even more weight. The percentages for the Self-Reward for Weight Loss, Self-Monitoring, and Delayed Treatment groups were 40 per cent, 37.5 per cent, and 40 per cent, respectively. Reward for weight loss was no better than not having any treatment. Rewards, then, *must* be based on improvements in behaviour and not on the ultimate results of behaviour change.

Self-punishment – fining yourself a small amount of money, denying yourself a favourite television programme – can also play a part in habit control. But don't be too hard on yourself!

If self-reward can help modify addictive behaviours, what about punishment? Can a person change his habits by punishing his behaviour? The simplest form of self-punishment involves giving up a pleasurable activity. For example, if a smoker were to smoke a cigarette he might punish himself by not watching a favourite television programme.

Dr S. Axelrod, of the State University of New York at Buffalo, has devised a system of fines for smokers. He reported the case of a long-term smoker who had been smoking about one packet of cigarettes per day. During the first week of treatment the smoker was limited to 15 cigarettes per day. For each cigarette that exceeded the limit, he was instructed to tear up a dollar bill. The limit was decreased by one cigarette every

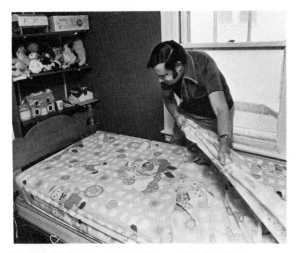

Household chores make suitable penalties for slips in your programme.

five days until the smoking rate was zero. The smoker was obviously a very thrifty individual since he never exceeded his limit once during the entire treatment process. Sometimes the mere threat of punishment is enough to control the behaviour.

Another case of self-punishment has been reported using an ingenious arrangement between a husband and wife. The wife decided that housework was so unpleasant that she could use it as a punishment in her weight-reduction plan. Her husband agreed to make a list of all of the household chores and to divide them equally into 'his' and 'hers'. Each did an equal number of chores each week. The wife started on her diet and weighed herself once a week. If she had lost weight during the week they continued sharing the chores as usual. However, if she had gained weight she had to do his chores in addition to her own until her next weekly weigh-in. Needless to say, she lost weight and the programme was a tremendous success.

Which is the most successful method – reward or punishment? Generally, the use of reward by itself or a combination of reward and punishment is preferable to punishment used alone. Self-punishment strategies can have undesirable side effects. Suppose that an exhibitionist or a drug abuser withheld a favourite activity, such as

going to see close friends, as a punishment for engaging in compulsive behaviour. Such a punishment might result in loneliness, depression and feelings of isolation which, far from curbing compulsive behaviour, could very easily trigger further episodes. Self-punishment, then, must be used carefully so that it does not interfere with adaptive, healthy behaviour. In our opinion a self-management plan emphasizing frequent self-reward for habit changes together with a carefully controlled minimum of self-punishment would be most effective in most cases.

Strategy 3: Self-control through thought control
Self-control skills can also be used to control secret, or *covert*, thoughts that trigger habit problems. In 1965 Dr Lloyd Homme described these thoughts as *covert operants* (*coverants* for short), and argued that coverant thoughts and images could be altered by techniques similar to those used to modify overt behaviours. In other words, he viewed *thought* modification in the same way as *behaviour* modification and began to formulate conditioning techniques of thought control.

Many of his techniques were based on a rule of conditioning known as the Premack Principle. Simply put, the principle states that, given two different behaviours, the one that occurs more frequently will reinforce the one that occurs less frequently. One behaviour can be used to increase the probability of another behaviour or thought. For example, suppose that a person has a very negative self-concept and constantly reminds himself of how inept and inadequate he is. The goal is to improve that person's idea of himself by encouraging positive rather than negative thoughts. According to the Premack Principle the frequency of positive thoughts will be increased if those thoughts are scheduled to occur just prior to a common habit such as using the telephone or drinking tea. The person would be advised to dwell on a positive thought such as 'I am a kind and considerate person' immediately before answering the telephone or making a telephone call. A person who uses the telephone a great deal will gain considerable practice in positive thinking by this method. After many repetitions, positive thoughts begin to come to mind automatically more frequently throughout the day.

Drs John Horan and R. Gilmore Johnson of Michigan State University were anxious to test the application of Dr Homme's coverant techniques to habit control.[3] They were particularly interested in studying a motivational procedure referred to as the Ultimate Consequences Technique. This method is intended to counter the fact that the immediate, short-term consequences of addictive behaviour are usually positive and, hence, reinforce the habit. Long-term negative consequences – developing cancer as the result of smoking, for example – can potentially influence behaviour, but in the normal course of events their impact is minimal. The influence of long-term consequences can, however, be heightened by developing an immediate connection with the behaviour via thought processes.

Two types of thoughts about consequences can be used to accomplish this goal. First, *negative* consequent thoughts are those related to the undesirable aspects of a habit problem. Patients are instructed to imagine the long-term negative consequences that would occur if their habit con-

A useful image for would-be non-smokers: each individual has managed to pack the daily consumption of a cigarette smoker, a cigar smoker and a pipe smoker into his mouth. Glamorous, it ain't.

Talking to yourself can be good for you

Recognizing and controlling thinking patterns that lead to the loss of control is crucial in dealing with habits, compulsions and addictions. Negative thinking, self-doubts and excuses must be identified as saboteurs and challenged by more appropriate, goal-oriented thinking. By listening carefully to what you are telling yourself or even thinking out loud when confronted with temptation, you can catch yourself in time to reprogramme your mind.

The following are excerpts of self-talk by a gambler having trouble with his resolve. Once he becomes aware of his 'uncontrolled' self-talk he should counteract it by using the more 'controlled' self-talk listed below.

'Uncontrolled' Self-Talk

1. I just don't have the willpower to give up gambling.

2. I get so few pleasures out of life. I deserve to gamble.

3. One little bet won't hurt me.

4. If it weren't for the tensions on my job I could control my habits a lot easier.

'Controlled' Self-Talk

1. There's no such thing as willpower, just poor planning. If I use the selfwatching techniques I've learned I *will* be successful.

2. In the long run gambling is no pleasure for me. I end up in debt and with problems with my family.

3. Oh, yes it will. I've said that hundreds of times and I've never been able to stop after one bet. I'm a compulsive gambler and I must stop completely.

4. A lot of people have more tension than I do. Besides, I can teach myself to relax and cope with my job better.

tinued forever or worsened. Such thoughts as 'I would die sooner', 'I would lose my family', 'I would lose my job', 'I would become more and more depressed', or 'I would develop a chronic disease and become an invalid', are included in this category. Second, *positive* consequent thoughts are those related to the desirable aspects of habit control. Patients are asked to consider the long-term positive results of changing their habits. Such thoughts as 'I would have a strong sense of accomplishment', 'I would have the recognition and approval of others', 'I would live longer and have more energy and stamina', or 'I would advance in my career' are included in this category.

The more these long-term consequences are kept in mind, the more they influence current cravings and behaviour. The goal, then, is to find the best method of encouraging thoughts about these consequences.

Drs Horan and Johnson devised an experiment to examine this problem. They recruited 96 overweight college women to participate in an experimental weight-control programme. The women were randomly assigned to one of four treatment groups. Group 1, the *Delayed Treatment Condition* served as a control and did not actually receive treatment until the experiment was over. Group 2 was given a *Dietary Treatment*: subjects were put on a diet of 1000 calories per day and encouraged to count calories. Group 3 was provided with a *Scheduled Ultimate Consequences Treatment.* Members of this group were helped to identify pairs of negative and positive thoughts contrasting the consequences, in the long term, of continued weight gain with the benefits of keeping to an ideal weight. For example, a sample pair consisted of 'shortened life span' – 'clothes fitting better'. Once these pairs were established these subjects were asked to think of them at least seven times per day.

Group 4 was exposed to an *Experimental Ultimate Consequences Treatment.* As in the previous treatment group, these subjects were also assisted in identifying negative-positive pairs of long-term consequences. However, these subjects were asked to make a positive plan to think of the consequences throughout the day. To accomplish this, they were first asked to think of specific events that usually occurred at least

seven times each day. One example was 'sitting down on a particular chair'. Subjects were then instructed to think of the pairs of consequences every time the target event occurred.

Over eight weeks of treatment the investigators found that the subjects in Group 4 who had used the Premack conditioning principle reported twice as many thoughts of consequences as subjects in Group 3 who did not use the conditioning procedure. The Premack approach also had a marked effect on weight loss. In Group 1, the non-treatment group, only 5 per cent of its members lost at least one pound per week or more for eight weeks. Based on this criterion the diet group had a success rate of 20 per cent. Group 3 had a similar success rate of only 21 per cent. Group 4, however, showed a success rate of 52 per cent, more than twice that of Group 2 or 3. In addition, the women who reported having the most thoughts about long-term habit consequences tended to lose the most weight.

Thus, motivational thoughts can be increased and strengthened by associating them with behaviours which typically occur frequently from day to day. Simply trying to concentrate on these thoughts more often does not seem to be sufficient. In addition, the more thoughts of this nature, the more easily a habit is changed.

The use of *emotional* imagery can enhance the impact of these consequences even further. In this procedure, rather than simply thinking of these consequences at appropriate times, individuals are asked to imagine them vividly, as if they were occurring at the present moment. They are told to visualize the consequences and to experience all of the accompanying sensations and emotions that would exist if the consequences were actually happening. In a sense, people are asked to project themselves into the future and actually experience the long-term results of their behaviour at first hand.

In addition, it is helpful to imagine that the addiction or compulsion has already been totally conquered. The person who is compulsively neat and tidy might visually and emotionally imagine what life would be like if he could see dirt on his hands and not be the least bit bothered by it. A keen imagination and frequent repetition are the keys to the successful use of this technique.

Strategy 4: Self-management as restraint

A basic self-management skill involves the ability to restrain oneself; to resist temptation and delay gratification. Temptations are bound to occur from time to time. When these situations arise the first rule of restraint is immediately to impose a 10-minute delay on any decision regarding the temptation. This simple strategy allows enough time for several self-control factors to come into play. First, cravings to succumb to the temptation may simply subside by themselves after a few minutes. Second, the delay prevents impulsive actions and decisions made under the emotional stress of a craving and allows for a more logical, rational analysis of the decision. Third, it allows an individual to 'think ahead', comparing the longer term consequences of succumbing to the temptation with the benefits of overcoming it successfully.

Distraction can also be a powerful tool of restraint. Thoughts or images about the temptation itself should be avoided by substituting daydreams or fantasies about constructive, pleasurable events. A practical course of action may be simply to walk away from the situation, alternatively, to become involved in an interesting activity that demands attention and concentration. In this way the discomfort of restraint is soon forgotten.

It's just a matter of practice . . .

Making self-management work

Avoiding or changing the environmental cues which trigger habits, substituting new rewards for changed behaviour, and combating negative thoughts which tend to precipitate cravings are all effective techniques for managing and modifying habitual behaviour. They must be applied and practised systematically (although not obsessively!) on the basis of patterns of behaviour revealed by a selfwatching diary. It is very useful to have the help of a therapist to advise on the most practical course of action and to come up with ideas on planning self-managing routines. But even without the help of a therapist, the techniques outlined in this chapter really will help people to maintain and reinforce changes in their behaviour.

4
SELFWATCHING 3
facing up to reality

Cue exposure

We have talked about avoiding temptation by self-management – changing your lifestyle, identifying danger zones, taking evasive action and so on. But one cannot spend the rest of life making long detours to avoid temptation. There comes a time when the enemy must be confronted by facing up to all those cues that signal danger. Dealing with compulsion by exposing oneself gradually to temptation is a fairly new technique that has been tried with great success. It has come to be known as 'cue exposure'. The strategy involved is well demonstrated by the following case of strong compulsion that responded readily to this approach.

A compulsion to wash

In 1970, Barbara was referred to the Institute of Psychiatry in London to try out a new method in the treatment of compulsions.[1] She was 37 years old and suffered from the irrational and very strong compulsion to wash her hands after touching door-knobs, money, telephones, in fact almost anything that could have been touched by someone who might be carrying germs. She lived in constant fear of contamination. Her cleaning compulsion had started to be troublesome when she was 21, at about the time when her best friend had died of tuberculosis.

Because washing was so time-consuming, she would avoid many activities which most of us perform without giving a thought to germs or illness. Rather than move around the house, she lived in one room which she kept 'safe' by repeated cleaning – always followed by hand-washing. She would scrub and wash her hands over and over again and sometimes had to ask her husband to carry her away from the sink in order to make sure she did not re-contaminate herself. She turned lights on with her shoulder and opened doors with her toes. Her little boy was not allowed to crawl or walk around the house for fear of germs – he was kept in his playpen all the time. Because he was so confined, he was never able to crawl but he learned to walk in his small prison.

Barbara's problem was very severe. Yet after only three months of 'cue-exposure' treatment, she was able to report: 'I am now able to live again. I started to do things and touch things without panic and I kept on improving every day, until I was normal again. I can now mix with other people, sit on all chairs and use all tables. My son is now allowed to touch animals and I don't have a compulsion to wash his hands every few minutes. I can use public toilets and let my son use them. My son now goes out into the garden and picks flowers, touches trees and digs away to his heart's content. I have cleaned the house from top to bottom without excessive handwashing and I don't have to wipe every-thing with disinfectant.' Her return to normality amazed her. She had, in her own words, been 'released from the chains' which had bound her for 16 years.

Cue exposure on trial

The treatment that helped Barbara, and is now helping many others throughout the world, is based upon a very simple principle. *If you deliber-ately expose yourself to temptation and then resist the urge to yield to it two very beneficial things happen. The next time you experience the same temptation it will be easier to resist and the urge to yield will gradu-ally go away.*

The first stage of Barbara's treatment involved drawing up a list of the tasks which provoked her compulsion to wash. Then she was encouraged to practise exposing herself to 'contamination', carrying out more and more difficult tasks, yet resisting the temptation to wash excessively.

Compulsive cleaning is much more than a need to have everything in the house spick and span. It is a debilitating urge triggered by anxiety and linked to the mechanisms that create habits and addictions.

During the first week in hospital she was able to handle a suitcase full of 'contaminated' items brought from her home – most of these had been hidden away in a cupboard and she had never dared to go near them. She then spread the 'con-tamination' to her room, bed, locker, toilet bag, clean underclothes, and to the rest of the hospital ward. During the first session she burst out cry-ing, but even when feeling terrible, she was encouraged to keep going, to continue carrying out very difficult tasks. She was taken to the local general hospital where she 'contaminated' her-self by touching chairs and walls in the waiting room. During the second week similar exercises were repeated. At each stage she was able to resist a strong urge to wash excessively. During the third week her son and husband joined in the daily therapeutic programme. Barbara spread the 'contamination' to her son, his toys and his clothes; she played with him, she prepared all his meals and she even changed his nappies without excessive washing. After 21 daily sessions she was discharged.

A senior nurse with extensive experience of this type of treatment then accompanied her to her home, which was 200 miles from the hospi-tal, and helped her to continue similar exercises in her home environment. A few months later she was almost free from the compulsion to carry out washing rituals, and two years later she was still improving.

The essential feature of this type of treatment is prolonged exposure to cues which provoke the compulsion while at the same time resisting the urge to carry out compulsive behaviour. The basic psychological processes and psychological treatment involved have been investigated by many different research institutions in Europe and the United States and this research demonstrates that cue exposure is a very successful method of modifying compulsions.

A wide range of compulsive disorders – including checking, drinking and masturbation – are now routinely treated by the cue-exposure method. Twenty or thirty sessions in diverse situations and different moods are usually sufficient to extinguish a compulsion. But do the effects last?

Long-term effects of cue exposure

A study, carried out by Rachman, Hodgson and Marks, involved 20 patients, all chronically handicapped by compulsive rituals, which also affected their families severely. Three weeks of relaxation treatment brought no change in their compulsive behaviour. But three weeks of cue exposure brought about a dramatic change in most cases: 15 patients reported themselves either 'improved' or 'much improved'. After six months this figure had dropped to 13, but after two years it had risen again to 15, a success rate of 75 per cent.[2]

Further studies have now been carried out in the United States, Germany and Australia. They demonstrate conclusively that, for many people, this approach does produce large changes in long-standing, persistent compulsions.

Learning to cope in the real world, with a little help from a friend.

Away with alcohol craving

Hodgson, Rankin and Stockwell, working at the London Institute of Psychiatry, have been investigating the possibility of applying cue-exposure treatment to addictions as well as compulsions. It seems that a severely dependent alcoholic's compulsion or craving to drink can also be modified by prolonged cue exposure.

In one test, hospitalized alcoholics were given a priming dose of four or five double vodkas and then asked to sit in a room for an hour with an open bottle of vodka or whisky. One glass was already poured and they were asked to smell and taste this every 15 minutes. They were told that this was designed to reduce their craving and increase their willpower. They were also told that nobody would stop them drinking, but that if they did give in to the urge to drink this would not help them in the long run.

Despite feeling high levels of craving, most of these severely dependent alcoholics were able to resist drinking. After repeated exposure to these cues their cravings were virtually extinguished – most of them did not have to struggle to resist temptation. Though cue exposure was only one component of their overall treatment, this simple experiment nevertheless shows that a compulsion to drink can be modified in exactly the same way as a compulsion to check or wash.

Learning to resist temptation

The sense of lack of self-control that accompanies a compulsion or addiction is in itself highly disturbing, as the case of Colin, a patient at the Maudsley Hospital, London, demonstrates. In Chapter 1 we cited St Augustine's description of his own sexual temptations: '. . . when habit passes unresisted a compulsive urge sets in. By these close links I was held.'

Colin was in the grip of the same compulsion as St Augustine, the compulsion to masturbate. Colin himself saw the problem as a major one; it interfered with his work and with sexual intercourse, and he regarded it as abnormal. He desperately wanted to get rid of the feeling of compulsion and regain his self-control.

He masturbated every day, and sometimes twice a day, usually at work or when alone in the house, or late at night when his wife was in bed. As a preliminary to treatment, Colin was asked

You can't have other people making decisions for you for the rest of your life.

to keep a selfwatching diary, which he conscientiously did. From Colin's diary, it became clear that his masturbatory urges were associated with the following major stimuli and situations:

- being criticized at work
- seeing an attractive girl in the street on the way home
- feeling depressed
- being alone in the country on a summer's day
- being in the house alone
- coming home after walking through Soho
- being in any situation which would normally elicit a slight erection
- seeing a crucifix
- watching his sexy neighbour in her garden
- looking at pornography.

One situation in particular will be discussed here since it was abnormal and disturbing to him. Ever since adolescence he had been preoccupied with a fantasy of Christ on the cross. One of his earliest sexual memories was of having an erection when looking at a sculpture of the crucifixion. Subsequently, throughout adolescence, this fantasy repeatedly linked itself with masturbation. Alone at home he would often lie on his bed, picture the crucifixion, and masturbate. He regarded masturbation as normal under certain circumstances (for example, in the country 'when overwhelmed by nature'), and so the goals of treatment, as he saw them, were to eliminate masturbation to the crucifix fantasy and to pornography, and to control masturbation in other situations – in other words to eliminate the feeling of compulsion.

To this end Colin was encouraged to obtain an erection in many different situations and told that he must resist masturbation both during his sessions at the Maudsley and between sessions, if the treatment was to be successful. He was encouraged by assurances that self-control would become easier as treatment progressed.

During the first two weeks Colin received four one-hour treatments. Each session consisted of approximately 40 minutes spent looking at pornographic literature and 20 minutes concentrating on the crucifix fantasy. The presence of a therapist made self-control much easier and so, on the third and fourth sessions, Colin was left alone for most of the time. After the fourth session he felt that the treatment might be helping but that self-control, particularly over the crucifix fantasy, was more difficult at home.

The next 10 sessions were therefore held in his home and included watching his next-door neighbour in the garden and imagining attractive girls who had recently caught his eye. The aim was to confront him with situations likely to provoke his compulsion and then to inhibit masturbation and prevent ejaculation. To increase the strength of Colin's self-control, the therapist began to leave him alone for increasing lengths of time. Up to this stage Colin was told to resist masturbating between sessions but not to deliberately tempt himself. For the last three sessions he was left alone and the therapist began and ended the session by telephoning him. In addition, Colin was told to deliberately tempt himself between sessions by walking through Soho (London's red-light district), looking into the windows of pornographic bookshops. He was also asked to seek out and look at images of crucifixion.

Colin kept a diary which the therapist read before each treatment session. He was told that making an accurate record of his feelings at least twice a day would help the treatment, but was warned against giving false impressions just to please the therapist. During the seven weeks before treatment, Colin was masturbating on average six times a week. During treatment, and also one year after treatment, he was only masturbating once a week. He pointed out that his compulsion fluctuated during the one-year follow-up period. He occasionally masturbated compulsively, but never to the extent he had before treatment.

Why does cue exposure work?

Strong habits, addictions and compulsions are often the result of a wish to avoid a disagreeable feeling or situation. This even applies to some trivial habits that we do not really wish to change. For example, Bernard Levin, writing in *The Times* in 1973, calculated: 'I have eaten at least 7,000 tons of digestive biscuits in my time, solely because the prospect of eating a digestive biscuit seemed to me more inviting than sitting down and hitting the keys of the typewriter.'

Psychologists have been studying avoidance behaviour in humans and animals for more than 50 years on the assumption that many types of fearful and compulsive behaviour are basically examples of excessive avoidance. An example of the behaviour on which this assumption is based is shown by a typical experiment in animal psychology. A rat is put into two interconnected boxes, one black and one white; an electric shock is applied to a grid on the floor of the black box. The rat quickly learns to avoid the black box. Subsequently, every time it is placed in the dangerous box, the rat responds to the colour cue by moving to the white box. Once this avoidance behaviour or compulsion has been learned it persists, even after the shock leads have been disconnected, for thousands of trials. The most efficient method of curing the rat of its compulsion is to oblige it to stay in the black box and discover that it is no longer dangerous. This example of *reality testing* is sometimes used by psychologists as a model of cue exposure treatment. Of course animal avoidance cannot be equated exactly with human compulsion but is used as an analogy or model.

Compulsive behaviour and addictions are often thought of as strategies of avoidance because the person involved can be trying to avoid either expected anxiety or expected frustration. For example, Barbara expected to feel extremely anxious during exposure to 'dirty' cues, but she found the discomfort less than she expected. Cue exposure could be said to have cured her of her compulsion because it allowed her to *test reality*. She found that failure to wash her hands after every 'contamination' did not necessarily lead to panic and depression, and she therefore became less worried when she did not wash.

Similarly, one of the alcoholics treated by Dr Hodgson and his colleagues, felt a compulsion to continue drinking after a priming dose of four double vodkas because he expected to experience unpleasant withdrawal symptoms if he stopped at that stage. The cue-exposure treatment described earlier showed him that these expectations were false and he therefore found it much easier to control his drinking.

Self-management using cue exposure

In the previous chapter we discussed methods of avoiding temptations. Now, by suggesting that compulsion can be banished by cue exposure we are apparently giving contradictory advice. The truth is that both approaches can be effective, but they need to be adopted at different stages in the fight. Stage 1 involves avoiding dangerous cues altogether and stage 2 entails gradual exposure to increasingly dangerous cues.

The problem drinker, for example, should completely abstain for a month at least, avoiding fellow drinkers, drinking situations, stressful events – all cues which prime the desire to drink – and should refuse to go to dinner with friends who exert inordinate pressure on guests to drink. It's important to find pleasurable and/or useful ways to fill the time. Reading the latest bestseller, going to the cinema, mending the car, playing tennis, joining a neighbourhood group may not be everyone's idea of fun, but most people can find something to interest them. Whatever the personal plan of campaign, the first aim should be to avoid temptation and to deal with any hints of craving before the compulsion can take hold.

The second stage should involve a planned and gradual progression up the rung of a ladder, or *hierarchy*, of dangerous situations or tasks. Our problem drinker, for example, should

Right: If this construction worker can get used to working 500 feet up, you should be able to get on top of things too!

Far right: Looking good enough not to eat. Learning to walk by the fattening foods with a smile is better than having to keep out of the supermarket – so keep concentrating on how you want *to look on the beach next summer.*

Step by step: Beating temptation through cue exposure

A problem drinker or an addict may find it easy enough to remain abstinent while in hospital. This is because he or she has been cut off from the temptations and cues which prime compulsive urges. Relapse often occurs very quickly after leaving hospital, as everyday stresses and temptations take their toll of confidence and determination. In order to achieve a long-term recovery the person at risk must learn how to show self-control even in the most tempting of circumstances. Deliberate exposure, on a step-by-step basis, to powerful cues can certainly help to reduce their ability to affect one's behaviour. Here's how one problem drinker was helped to get his drinking under control. As a first step, he was asked to rate a number of tasks for difficulty on a scale of one to ten. The plan was that he should tackle the tasks in ascending order of difficulty. Here are the tasks, with his rating of difficulty given in brackets:

Drinking a glass of beer with my wife and
    then stopping (4)

Watching TV with a glass of whisky within
    reach, but without drinking it (5)

Thinking about drink when feeling bored at
    Sunday lunchtime (5½)

Staring at the drinks cabinet late at night
    when unable to sleep (6)

Walking past my old haunts in Soho (London)
    at opening time (6½)

Staring at the drinks cabinet when feeling
    tense (7)

Giving myself a taste for whisky by swilling a
    little around my mouth (8)

Carrying a small bottle of whisky in my pocket
    over the weekend. Taking a sniff but not
    drinking (9)

Drinking 2 pints of beer with my drinking
    friends and then stopping (9½)

His treatment plan was to be abstinent for three months during which time he would carry out the series of tasks, repeating each one until he felt reasonably confident that he could face the next. When craving started to mount he was asked to say to himself 'If I can ride the craving, like a surfer, the craving will eventually subside. Until that happens I will just let the craving do what it wants. I won't fight it but I won't drink either.' There were a few hitches along the way. For example, he did have a few unplanned drinks on one occasion when he couldn't sleep and he did drink the glass of whisky on two occasions while watching TV. When this happened he was asked to say to himself 'That just proves that I have a problem with this situation but I can render it powerless if I practise and practise, by rehearsing it in my head, and then in reality.' Despite these lapses, this individual reported that the cue-exposure method was very helpful in maintaining control over his drinking problem.

deliberately go into a party, or go into a bar, first when feeling happy and relaxed, then when feeling anxious or miserable. A slimmer might start by having morning coffee in the local patisserie or eating just one digestive biscuit with afternoon tea. Each situation successfully negotiated in this way increases the person's sense of self-control.

Planning a hierarchy
If you intend to do battle with your problem using the cue-exposure approach you need to plan a hierarchy of tasks, working along these lines:

1. Keep up the selfwatching. Try to identify the situations, moods, thoughts, people, sights and sounds that act as cues or signals
2. Decide which cues are the least and which the most dangerous for you
3. Construct a list of specific tasks which will expose you to these cues in a graduated way, starting with the least dangerous.

Unless you have the help of a psychologist or counsellor experienced in this approach, you must progress very slowly up the hierarchy. To begin with you will probably feel anxious or frustrated, so be prepared to talk yourself out of temptation. Have some arguments lined up ready to help you cope. For instance, say to yourself:

1. 'I will probably feel some discomfort, but if I resign myself to that the discomfort will not seem as bad as expected.'
2. 'If I get on with my life and get involved in some other activity, the urge will go away.'
3. 'If only I can resist now, I'll be chipping away at my problem once and for all. I'll feel short-term discomfort, but it'll be worth it in the long run.'

Whenever you successfully complete a task, be sure to remember the experience and use it to help you in the future. One of our alcoholic patients who was aiming at total abstinence took great heart from one such experience. Once he

started drinking he would usually continue to drink for days or weeks, but on a particular occasion after only one night on the bottle, he surfaced next morning and decided to stop and observe himself. This strategy paid dividends. He did feel great initial discomfort, but it faded away before lunch and he spent the rest of the day happily pottering about in the garden. He remembered this episode and brought it to mind whenever he craved a drink. Success breeds success, and the memory of each temptation effectively resisted can definitely reinforce self-control.[3, 4]

The story so far
At the heart of the selfwatching approach to habit control are self-understanding through self-observation, self-management and self-control through progressive exposure to the cues which previously set off a particular habit. All the techniques we have described have been systematically tested in the field and have been shown to work effectively. To those who criticize them as over-simplified we reply that, through them, many victims of severely compulsive behaviour – like Barbara – have been helped to live normal lives again. Moreover, the very simplicity of the techniques makes them non-threatening and easy to use. They provide clear-cut and sensible ways by which people can re-assert control over their daily lives.

But in order to persevere with these techniques, emotional attitude is very important. Feelings of anxiety and depression are closely associated with relapse into self-destructive habits and addictions. At the root of such feelings lie fear of consequences, fear of failure, or the inability of the individual to assert his or her interests against social pressure from business colleagues, friends or family. Hand-in-hand with techniques designed to modify specific behaviours must go methods of maintaining morale and motivation in the face of untoward circumstances. This area is the subject of the next two chapters.

5
ANXIETY
and how to beat it

Along with problem behaviours of any kind we commonly find general feelings of anxiety and depression. It is hard to tell whether feelings like these are the cause or result of compulsive behaviour: a better way of talking about them is to say that these feelings *pervade* compulsions, they are present, in one capacity or another, at every turn.

A high proportion of problem drinkers, for example, cite the relief of anxiety as the main reason for using alcohol. In a study by Gloria Litman, anxiety, especially in the face of social situations, proved to be a prime cause of relapse in alcoholics. A similar justification is offered by dependent users of opiates and psychotropic drugs such as cannabis (marijuana). Equally, most people who have become addicted to tranquillizers such as Valium or the barbiturates, began by taking these drugs for their intended purpose, the alleviation of anxiety. In compulsive behaviours in which drugs are not involved, feelings of anxiety are again a commonly reported factor. This is true of gambling and over-eating, and especially so of cleaning and checking rituals. Anxiety is also strongly associated with sexual compulsions. But what exactly do we mean by anxiety?

Real and imagined threats
Feelings of anxiety are associated with certain physical symptoms which are the body's natural reaction to a perceived threat. This response – usually called the 'flight-or-fight response' – is common to all mammals, whether rats, monkeys or humans. Special glands, the adrenals, secrete substances designed to mobilize strength and energy by increasing the heart rate, the blood flow to the muscles, the rate of breathing and so on. These changes prepare the animal to attack the threat – or flee from it.

In humans the fight-or-flight response works perfectly well whether the threat is real or imaginary. People who report feeling anxious may know, rationally, that there is nothing to be worried about: yet they still experience the physiological symptoms – racing heart, trem-

bling, breathlessness, sweating. Worse still, with no obvious threat, there is nothing to attack and no clear direction in which to flee! At such moments the mechanical performance of some action – lighting a cigarette, pouring a drink – may offer a temporary release from the physical tension brought about by the fight-or-flight response, and thus provide strong reinforcement for the particular action.

As we have said, feelings of anxiety commonly accompany habits, addictions and compulsions. Coping strategies that help to defuse anxiety are likely to be effective in modifying compulsive behaviours overall. But anxiety does not operate simply at one level as the following example illustrates.

Anxiety: a state and a trait

Michael is a successful business executive but he is also very anxious. Most days he worries about the meetings that he will have to attend and the people that he will have to meet. He often gets the feeling that these interactions will not go well and occasionally he experiences intense anxiety when involved in a protracted discussion with critical or assertive colleagues. During these

attacks he perspires freely, his heart races, he not only feels restless but appears so to others and he experiences tension in his forehead and stomach. His thoughts on these occasions are usually to do with the impression that he is giving to others – 'they must think I'm neurotic', 'I bet they'll talk about me later.' Sometimes during an attack he will excuse himself and leave the room for a minute. During the past six months he has slipped into the habit of taking 20mg of Valium before going into a business meeting.

When Michael is involved in a threatening business meeting he is in a *state* of anxiety. We can also say that he is an anxious person. Psychologists might refer to this personal characteristic as trait-anxiety, meaning that he is prone to anxiety. *Trait-anxiety* refers to the predisposition whereas *state-anxiety* refers to anxiety at a particular time. When Michael is fishing and feeling totally relaxed he is low on state-anxiety but he is still high on trait-anxiety since he has experienced anxiety states frequently in the past and will more than likely be similarly predisposed in the future.

Anxiety is not just a state of mind or a beating

heart. It is a response of the whole person to a perceived threat. Michael was displaying anxious behaviour and thinking, and his body was clearly over-reacting at a physiological level. The figure shows the interaction of these three processes. If anxiety is to be countered then the whole system of integrated responses has to be changed.

Coping skills and the appraisal of threat

Notice in the figure that anxiety is triggered by a *perceived* threat. For many people business meetings are very enjoyable but for Michael they constitute a threat. His past experience of distress and his keen desire to make a good impression influence his appraisal of these situations. It is perceived threat that leads to his anxieties, not some objective characteristic of the situation.

To most people a cocktail party, for example, will be either enjoyable or boring but *not* an event likely to provoke anxiety. For others it may present a considerable ordeal. The socially anxious person will worry about saying the wrong thing, doing the wrong thing and creating the wrong impression. The abstaining alcoholic may see the event as a very strong temptation

We all suffer from anxious moments – what we feel as anxiety is the body's natural reaction to threatening events. But, as the diagram shows, anxiety can feed on itself to become a constant state of mind.

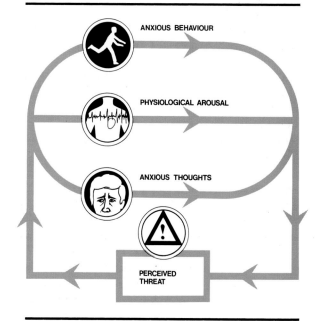

and will worry about the craving that might build up before, during and after the party. The anxious person's appraisal of the situation as threatening is very closely related to worry about the ability to cope with it. If the alcoholic could work out a way of coping with craving that proved to work in a wide variety of social surroundings, then a party would no longer be a threat.

The view of anxiety shown in our figure has led psychologists to argue that coping skills should be developed to counteract all three of the anxiety response systems. At the behavioural level, Michael has to learn how to respond to aggressive colleagues, at the physiological level he has to learn how to relax, and at the thinking level he must be able to see things in a different light. The strategies explained later in this chapter cover all three anxiety response systems.

Life events and anxiety

Anxiety may arise because events are misinterpreted – seen to be more important than they really are. But what of events that really are serious and, in some cases, unavoidable? Most of us know of someone who started smoking again after a stressful experience. Such life events have been implicated in anxiety states, drug dependence and compulsive behaviour, as well as in heart attacks, ulcers, arthritis, allergic reactions and depression. This is hardly surprising in view of the radical readjustment that such events can entail.

Consider the consequences of divorce, for example. At least one of the parties concerned is likely to end up alone, perhaps dealing with children and financial worries, needing to make a new circle of friends, and fraught with feelings of rejection and inadequacy. In this state he or she is likely to display anxious behaviour, physiological arousal and anxious thoughts. Each day will become a threat.

As we have emphasized, the sense of threat is determined by appraisal of the situation and a stressful event for one person could be a blessing for another. Termination of employment, for instance, is known to be a factor involved in excessive drinking, but for a commercial traveller with a drink problem, it could be a chance to develop a hobby, landscape a garden and get

away from the stress and temptations to drink involved in his work. In spite of this caveat, it would seem that people in many different cultures and environments, of many different religions and races, do tend to be put under stress by similar life events.

Thomas Holmes and Richard Rahe of the University of Washington Medical School have developed a questionnaire called the Social Readjustment Rating Scale (SRRS)[1] to investigate the events which the majority of people consider to be stressful. Their research was based on clinical interviews, medical histories, and a series of studies with more than 5000 patients. They were able to identify 43 life events or changes in lifestyle that were associated with stress and disease. These included marriage, divorce, death of a spouse, new living conditions and a wide variety of personal, social and economic changes requiring some degree of readjustment. They then asked a larger number of people in different societies to rate the events according to the degree of readjustment entailed by each. The box opposite lists the 15 events which American subjects judged to require the greatest amount of readjustment, compared

Anxiety and stress are directly implicated in a wide range of addictions and compulsions, as well as in physiological conditions such as heart disease, arthritis and allergic reactions. But it is possible to quieten our anxious feelings.

with rankings given by European and Japanese subjects.

Most of these life events cannot be avoided. They are sources of anxiety for many people throughout the world. If drug dependence and other compulsions are to be controlled then some way of coping with this unavoidable anxiety is essential.

Behavioural Strategies

The most powerful behavioural approach to anxiety is to attack it head-on. In Chapter 4 we have described the way in which compulsive urges can be reduced through repeated, prolonged exposure to the cues that provoke them. There is now a mass of scientific data[2] to confirm the common-sense view that the same applies to anxiety. A cat phobia will disappear if the phobic person gradually works up a hierarchy of 20 difficult tasks ranging from looking at pictures of cats, via stroking a kitten, to picking up a cat. A fear of being assertive can be dispelled if assertive behaviour is practised, again moving up a hierarchy of confrontations, from the least to the most difficult. There is no doubt that this kind of desensitization can reduce anxiety and alter the

Ratings of stressful life events

Fifteen major life events were marked in order of seriousness by American subjects (column 1). Columns 2 and 3 show how European and Japanese people ranked the same events.

Life event	American	European	Japanese
Death of spouse	1	1	1
Divorce	2	3	3
Marital separation	3	5	7
Jail term	4	2	2
Death of close family member	5	18	4
Personal injury or illness	6	8	5
Marriage	7	4	6
Being fired from job	8	9	8
Marital reconciliation	9	7	15
Retirement	10	17	11
Change of health of family member	11	20	9
Pregnancy	12	6	13
Sexual difficulties	13	15	10
Addition of new family member	14	13	23
Major business readjustment	15	11	12

beliefs and associations which contribute to it. The planning and execution of a progressive series of exercises needs patience and courage but with the help of the strategies described in this chapter there is a high probability of success.

First of all it is necessary to identify the particular cues that provoke anxiety. Watching out for fluctuations in the level of anxiety and pinpointing the provoking events should be all that is needed, but the fear-survey schedule presented in this chapter can also help in allowing you to identify those factors which are likely to be disturbing. The anxiety cues could be situations, activities or thoughts. When they have been identified, a hierarchy should be developed for the list of cues.

A good example of this kind of 'in vivo' exposure was reported by Christensen, Arkowitz and Anderson[3] of the Psychology Clinic, University of Oregon. Radio and newspaper advertisements, class announcements and signs posted on campus asked for volunteer subjects to take part in a project designed to increase dating frequency, skill and comfort. A total of 75 males and 70 females volunteered for the programme. From this pool of subjects, 30 males and 30 females with the lowest dating frequency were selected for the experiment.

The 'treatment' was not exactly complicated and did not need years of training or a personal analysis to execute. The male volunteers in the treatment groups were simply provided each week with the name of a female volunteer. Different matches were made, one per week, for a period of six weeks. Each pair was asked to regard the date as an opportunity for finding out and practising social skills. With the fear of the unknown, and of rejection, removed, the volunteers showed a clear improvement in confidence and social relationships.

Whether or not other techniques are used, one essential ingredient of the successful self-help strategy is graduated exposure to anxiety-provoking situations. In 1919 Freud commented that 'one can hardly ever master a phobia if one waits till the patient lets the analysis influence him to give it up . . . one succeeds only when one can induce them through the influence of the analysis to . . . go about alone and struggle with the anxiety while they make the attempt.' We now know that 'in vivo' exposure is an effective form of treatment on its own without psychoanalysis or any other form of prolonged psychotherapy.

Left: The simple process of getting to know other people can be fraught with anxiety – or as easy as one, two, three . . .

Right and below: The fight-or-flight reaction builds up tension in the body. This tension can be released constructively in violent activity – athletes deliberately 'psych' themselves up for a big effort.

Meditational techniques can calm anxiety and damp down the bodily symptoms – increased heart-rate, shallowness of breathing, muscular tension – that go with it. A deliberate, progressive relaxation of the muscles and a conscious effort to breathe deeply, at a measured pace, have proved effective in defusing the human body's alarm system.

Physiological relaxation

The fact that physiological arousal prepares us to flee or to fight, leads to the first method of producing physiological relaxation, which has many other benefits besides. Running, jumping, jogging, climbing, digging, dancing and swimming can all release the tension that prepares us for action. Exercise is useful in other ways in dealing with the compulsions described in earlier chapters, but it should not be seen simply as a hobby or one way of losing weight. It is also a powerful way of physically releasing the 'flight or fight' response.

The second method, usually called *muscle relaxation training*, has a long history in medicine, clinical psychology and psychiatry. Back in 1929 Edmund Jacobson reported his discovery that by systematically tensing and relaxing various muscle groups, and by learning to attend to the resulting relaxation response, muscular tension can be gradually reduced and this has a marked effect on anxiety. Since then, many investigations have demonstrated the usefulness of this technique in the treatment of physiological arousal, insomnia and tension headaches.[4]

Apart from these scientific investigations there are numerous glowing reports from clinicians which attest to the beneficial effects of relaxation. Consider, for example, the experience of David, one of our patients with a gradually developing drinking problem. He is a 64-year-old retired automotive designer who used alcohol to relieve boredom and to induce sleep. Since his retirement he had experienced insomnia almost every night, but then he found that drinking before going to bed relaxed him sufficiently to get off to sleep. Because of a medical problem, however, David had to give up drinking completely. It was not until this happened that he realized how dependent on alcohol he had really become. Without his nightcap his insomnia returned in full force. He was therefore given taped relaxation instructions to play each evening before retiring and after just a few nights the cassette worked so well that he would fall asleep half way through. In fact, one night he actually fell asleep in the short pause between switching on the tape and the first word of the relaxation instructions.

It is worth noting, in the context of the pharmacology vs. psychology debate, that the most important biological cause of insomnia is drug-related. Many insomnias are maintained by the very drugs prescribed for treatment. The problem with most sleeping pills is that their regular use for more than a week or two can lead to tolerance, at which stage the drug can no longer have a soporific effect. However, a very severe 'rebound insomnia' is experienced if the drug is stopped. When this type of dependence occurs the problem should be solved by gradual withdrawal of the medication and the use of some kind of relaxation training. Instructions for muscular relaxation are given later on in this chapter.

Meditational techniques

The use of techniques of muscular relaxation is based upon the theory that anxiety can be reduced by dampening down one important *peripheral* component of the physiological response system. Another approach which sometimes proves even more effective than muscular relaxation involves a process which is right at the centre of our being. That process is attention. *Meditation* has a history stretching back thousands of years but it has only recently been scientifically investigated as a result of the increasing interest in transcendental meditation, or TM. Since 1970 there has been a considerable amount of research into the effects of TM and many of the claims of meditators have been confirmed.[5] In particular it has been shown that physiological arousal is reduced. TM is a technique involving the mental repetition of a nonsense word for twenty minutes, once in the morning and again in the early evening. It is claimed that this simple procedure calms the mind and deactivates the 'flight–fight' response.

Dr Herbert Benson, one of the scientists involved in an early study of TM, has attempted to demystify meditation by providing the following simple instructions for achieving relaxation.[6]

1. Sit quietly in a comfortable position.

2. Close your eyes.

3. Deeply relax all your muscles, beginning at your feet and progressing up to your face. Keep them relaxed.

4. Breathe through your nose. Become aware of your breathing. As you breathe out, say the

Meditation and the body

Most investigations have shown that TM has a very beneficial effect on the physiological, biochemical and psychological measures of anxiety. However, there are few experimental comparisons of the effects of TM and other techniques, such as muscular relaxation, with subjects being randomly assigned to the two treatments. In some studies that do not use random assignment meditators are compared with volunteers who do not meditate. But then there are some problems interpreting the results. There is always the possibility that the successful meditators are people who are better able to relax in the first place even before the training. Nevertheless, the results are very suggestive. For example, Paul Corey of the University of Colorado Medical Centre in Denver tested people who had learned meditation and also a control group of people who were going to learn it the next day.[6] Physiological measures were taken before and during meditation or relaxation. Meditation had a very clear effect on physiological measures which was not observed in subjects who were untrained. For example, heart rate during meditation decreased by 7.6 beats per minute in the meditators with no significant change in the control group.

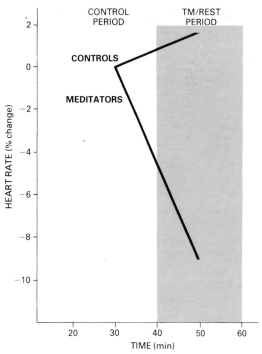

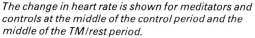

The change in heart rate is shown for meditators and controls at the middle of the control period and the middle of the TM/rest period.

word, 'ONE', silently to yourself. For example, breathe in . . . out, 'ONE'; in . . . out, 'ONE'; and so forth. Breathe easily and naturally, *not* deeply.

5. Continue for 10 to 20 minutes. You may open your eyes to check the time, but do not use an alarm. When you finish, sit quietly for several minutes, at first with your eyes closed and later with your eyes opened. Do not stand up for a few minutes.

6. Do not worry about whether you are successful in achieving a deep level of relaxation. Maintain a passive attitude and permit relaxation to occur at its own pace. When distracting thoughts occur, try to ignore them by not dwelling upon them and return to repeating 'ONE'. With practice, the response should come with little effort. Practise the technique once or twice daily, but not within two hours after any meal, since the digestive processes seem to interfere with the elicitation of the Relaxation Response.

Using this method he studied the effects of relaxation breaks on blood pressure in a work setting. In this study, four groups of subjects were given different relaxation instructions. Group A was taught the simple meditation technique described above. Group B was instructed just to sit and relax. Group C received no instructions and Group D were subjects who didn't volunteer but later agreed to be tested before and after completion of the study. Groups A and B were advised to take two 15-minute relaxation breaks every day for eight weeks. Significant decreases in blood pressure occurred only in Group A.[7]

The gradual accumulation of scientific evidence during the last ten years strongly suggests that meditation can reduce physiological arousal and must therefore be considered as one possible approach to self-control. If a person under stress can control physiological reactions then there is a greater likelihood that drug dependence and other compulsions can also be brought under control.

Cognitive approaches
Patterns of anxious thinking are the third leg of our anxiety triad – behaviour, body arousal and

There is a strong Western interest, both popular and scientific, in the meditational traditions of the East (right and below). The biofeedback machine (bottom right) monitors some key body rhythms – alpha and theta electrical waves in the brain, the electrical conductivity of the skin and variations in body temperature – which indicate the degree of relaxation. The person connected to the machine receives direct feedback on the effectiveness of his relaxation techniques.

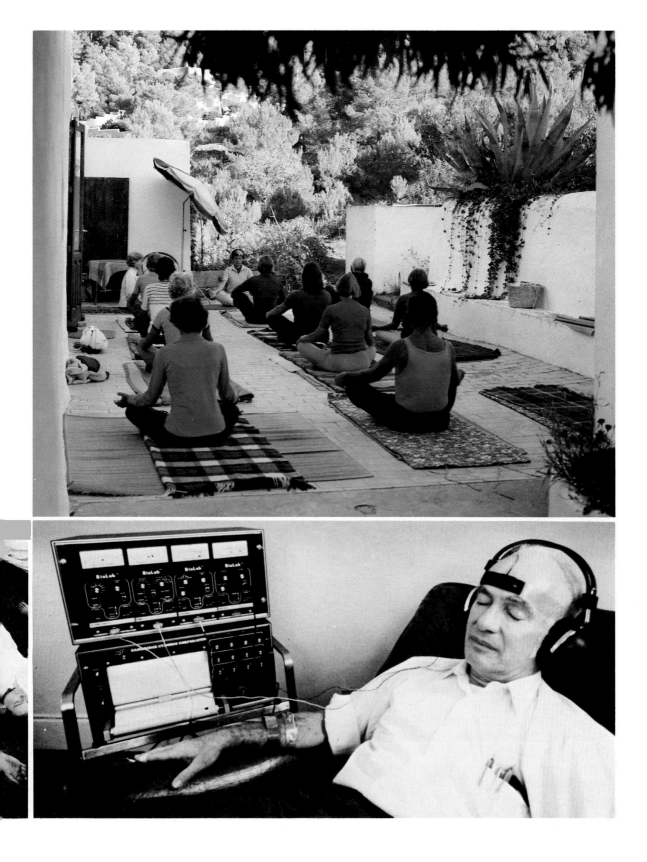

ways of thinking. The anxious person worries that a tragedy is about to occur. If a realistic appraisal of the situation shows that this is an unlikely possibility, then that person has a blinkered view of the situation and by hook or by crook, the blinkers have to be prised off. Alternative ways of viewing the world must be tried and tested.

For example, a 48-year-old woman had been drinking daily for six months, in order to reduce her anxiety at work. She was the supervisor in a small dressmaking business and was in charge of 12 women. One of her main problems had always been a tendency to blush. Consequently, she was very anxious when other people stared at her during a conversation, or when she gave a talk or a demonstration, listened to a complaint or gave orders. She had discovered that alcohol released her from this anxiety. Before going to work she would gulp down a quarter of a bottle of vodka and then took another two drinks at lunchtime.

She was asked to imagine herself in the work situations that made her anxious and identify the automatic thoughts that were part and parcel of her fears. The following were the strongest:

- I will blush and the girls will think I'm weak. Only teenagers blush.
- How can I give orders if they think I am a nervous wreck?
- Will I faint? I did faint once when I was very nervous.
- I won't be able to talk fluently and spontaneously. You have to have a quick answer if you are a supervisor.

It was first explained to her that these thoughts could be misconceptions, based upon her idiosyncratic view of the world, and she was encouraged to try out alternative interpretations for each of the four anxious thoughts. She found the following statements believable and they made her feel less anxious when she thought about work:

- I might not blush. If I do the girls might not notice.
- Many nervous people get on very well with other people. Being nervous means being conscientious. All I do is blush, this doesn't mean that I am a nervous wreck.

- I've been nervous many times and I haven't fainted. If I do pass out, so what. Nobody will hate me for fainting.
- If I slow down and talk hesitantly it doesn't matter. People seem to like me and a bit of stammering won't make much difference. They will just accept it as part of me.

The day after this exercise she plucked up the courage to go to work without drinking. Six months later she was still coping without her morning tipple and was sure that she had mastered the problem. Almost every day, before going to work, she would go over her four coping thoughts. At work, when she felt 'that a blush was about to blossom forth' (her words) she would say to herself: 'come on you little blush, do your worst. You don't worry me.'

Frustration and anger

Anger is the 'fight' rather than 'flight' response to stress. Frustrated anger – with a superior at work, with a spouse – can often trigger off a bout of self-destructive behaviour. As William Blake wrote:

> I was angry with my friend
> I told my wrath, my wrath did end
> I was angry with my foe
> I told it not, my wrath did grow.

Worse still, violent uncontrolled anger can become an habitual response to petty frustrations. Like other destructive habits the short-term reward – a sudden release of tension and frustration – masks the longer-term negative consequences. However, there is good evidence that the kind of relaxation and thought-control strategies that are effective in reducing interpersonal anxiety work equally well in helping people to deal with anger. The evidence comes from the work of Raymond Novaco, a psychologist at the University of California. His clients had intense problems with controlling anger. Several

A performer overcomes stage-fright by rehearsing the performance so many times that it becomes second nature. We can improve our own performances by rehearsing techniques and procedures to overcome anxiety.

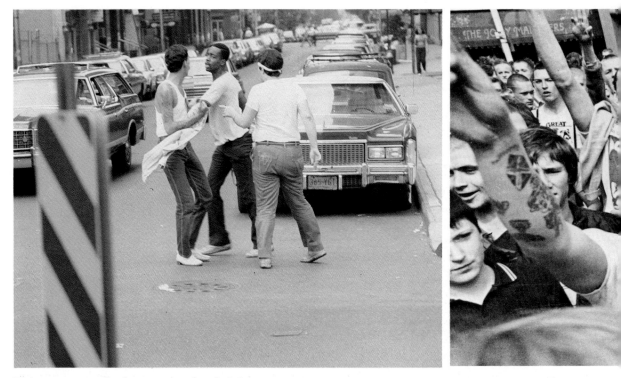

Violent anger can offer the same reward as alcohol – a sense of release from normal inhibitions.
Among young British skinheads, the expression of anger has become entrenched as a group style.

had physically assaulted others; one kicked in a glass door at an ice cream parlour when refused service, another hurled a brick through a car window, and another decorated objects with blood from his fists after he had intentionally smashed them into a wall. Novaco found that training in the use of both thought control strategies and muscular relaxation was better than either on its own.[8]

To test his programme he compared the effectiveness of various anger and impatience regulation techniques among 34 volunteers. His criteria of 'success' were greater tolerance to anger-provoking situations, and greater control over the way anger builds up. Novaco's training programme had four major components: learning about anger and how it arises; identifying the circumstances that trigger it off; drawing a distinction between useful anger and anger that achieves nothing; and working on ways of coping with conflict and stress. In a situation likely to provoke irritation or anger, the person is instructed to relax as much as possible and then

rehearse a series of thoughts such as 'Easy does it. I can work out some way of handling this', or 'Just stick to the issues and don't take it personally', or 'There's no point in getting mad. This is just a work situation.' An internal pep talk of this kind helps the person to establish self-control. If he feels his anger starting to build up he says to himself, 'Time to take a deep breath', or 'He probably wants me to lose my temper', or 'I'm going to relax and deal with this constructively.' Novaco's trainees were also asked to keep an 'anger diary' in which they recorded outbursts of anger, along with their causes and consequences.

Dr Novaco compared his thought-control relaxation procedure with (1) relaxation training by itself, (2) thought-control treatment by itself, and (3) a control group receiving neither thought-control nor relaxation training. In each case except the last, six training sessions were given. Before and after treatment participants were asked to rate their probable reaction, on a five point scale, to 80 anger-provoking incidents.

The muscular relaxation response

This relaxation technique involves very simple steps and takes a total of 20 minutes or so to complete. People have found it useful in dealing specifically with feelings of anxiety and nervousness – but it is also a helpful way of relaxing after a tiring day. For the best results you should choose somewhere comfortable and fairly quiet where you can lie down. It is important to complete the exercises without falling asleep, although you may wish to sleep at the end of the relaxation period itself.

First of all, loosen any tight clothing and remove your shoes. Now lie down. During the exercises you will progressively relax each part of your body, beginning with your toes and finishing with your face.

The same instruction applies to every part of your body. You might care to learn it by heart. It is:

Tense the relevant part of the body. Hold that tension for a count of 5. As you count, try to increase the tension. 1, 2, 3 – tighter – 4 – a little tighter – 5.

Take a deep breath and let the tension go as you breathe out. Repeat the word to yourself: 'Relax. Relax. Relax.'

Now close your eyes, and concentrate on each part of the body in turn. Tense and relax repeating the instruction above at every stage.

Toes Curl your toes and tense them vigorously. Relax.

Calves Point your toes towards your face and tense calf muscles. Relax.

Buttocks Push your buttocks against your chair, sofa, bed, floor. Relax.

Abdomen Tense your abdomen as though you were expecting a punch in the stomach. Relax.

Chest Tense your chest by pushing the palms of your hands together. Relax.

Shoulders Tense your shoulders by shrugging them as high as they will go. Relax.

Throat Tense your throat by pressing your chin down on your upper chest. Relax.

Neck and head Press your neck and head against the back of your shoulders. Relax.

Face Scrunch your face up as tightly as possible. Relax.

Now, still with eyes closed, feel for the feedback your body is giving you – a sense of heaviness and warmth, perhaps even a tingling sensation. Finally, go back to each part of your body and simply tell it to relax five times. Do not tense your muscles. Try to feel for a deepening of relaxation. As you repeat the word 'relax', allow the mind to empty itself of any lingering thoughts. When you have worked back from your toes to your face, the exercises are at an end.

Police officers are trained to be confident in their ability to size up and handle a potential flare-up.

In addition to this 'anger inventory', anger-provoking situations were acted out, so that angry behaviour, blood pressure, galvanic skin response, and self-ratings of angry feelings could be assessed. The anger diaries provided additional information on how each participant coped with real-life aggravations.

To cut a long story short, a combination of cognitive and relaxation techniques appears to have clear advantages over either technique separately. Whatever the factor measured – self-control, skin response, blood pressure – the combined approach was more successful. Relaxation training on its own produced some improvement in anger management, but thought control techniques enabled this improvement to be maximized.

In summary, there are a number of tried and tested ways of reducing anxiety involving behavioural and thought-control strategies as well as relaxation techniques. These methods are designed to change a person's appraisal of threat. Professor Richard Lazarus of the University of California makes a very useful distinction between primary and secondary appraisal of threat. A policeman arresting a drunk might expect to be attacked (primary appraisal) but is not worried because he has confidence in his ability to deal with the assault (secondary appraisal). Similarly, most of us expect to be anxious in a wide variety of situations (primary appraisal) but many feel that they can cope with the stress (secondary appraisal). The strategies described in this chapter are directed towards the alleviation of primary appraisal of threat by altering expectations and encouraging secondary appraisal by the development of coping skills.

LIFTING DEPRESSION

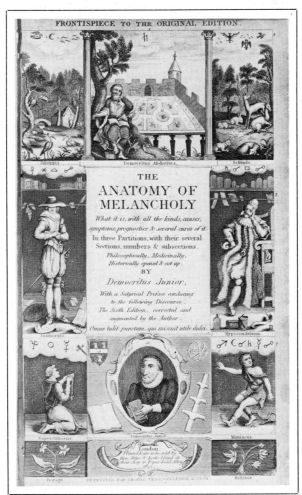

Title page of Anatomy of Melancholy, *by the English author Robert Burton (1577–1640).*

In 1973 a report on depressive disorders by the National Institute of Mental Health in the United States concluded that depression accounts for 75 per cent of all psychiatric hospitalizations, and that during a given year 15 per cent of all adults between 18 and 74 may suffer significant depressive symptoms. Most people experience mild depression from time to time and would like to work out a coping strategy for themselves. Of great importance in the present context is the fact that depression is very closely associated with addictions and compulsions, especially problem drinking, overeating and obsessive-compulsive problems such as excessive hand-washing, checking and tidying. The ability to cope with the slings and arrows of outrageous fortune is a skill that can neutralize a large number of antecedent cues associated with compulsive habits.

What is depression?

There is now widespread agreement that depression is characterized and can be recognized by the following group of signs and symptoms covering behaviour, physiology and subjective experience.

1. Sad, apathetic mood (dysphoria)
2. Negative self-concept (self-reproach, self-blame)
3. Desire to hide, to stay away from others

4. Loss of sleep, appetite, and sexual desire, but sometimes a tendency to sleep an abnormally great amount
5. Shift in activity level, to become either lethargic or agitated
6. Recurrent thoughts of death or suicide
7. Difficulty in concentrating.

We should also add that in those people who suffer from a compulsive habit there is also evidence of impaired control. Just as depression makes it very difficult to initiate any activity, so, it would appear, depression reduces self-control generally, with the consequence that compulsive urges are difficult to resist.

The following eloquent description of a depressive episode will give some indication of the depths of despair, helplessness and inactivity which are typical of this unpleasant state.

> I was seized with an unspeakable physical weariness. There was a tired feeling in the muscles unlike anything I had ever experienced. A peculiar sensation appeared to travel up my spine to my brain. I had an indescribable nervous feeling. My nerves seemed like live wires charged with electricity. My nights were sleepless. I lay with dry, staring eyes gazing into space. I had a fear that some terrible calamity was about to happen. I grew afraid to be left alone. The most trivial duty became a formidable task. Finally mental and physical exercises became impossible; the tired muscles refused to respond, my 'thinking apparatus' refused to work, ambition was gone. My general feeling might be summed up in the familiar saying 'What's the use'. I had tried so hard to make something of myself, but the struggle seemed useless. Life seemed utterly futile.[1]

Apart from such changes in behaviour and the perception of experience, scientists have identified biochemical changes which occur during periods of depression, and a number of reasonably successful anti-depressant drugs have been developed. But drug therapy for depression is not the complete answer since many people refuse to rely on drugs and, furthermore, of those who do try them only about 60 per cent

Depression is one of our most common illnesses. It accounts for 75 per cent of all psychiatric hospital admissions in the United States.

respond at all, of whom 50 per cent tend to relapse when the drug therapy is terminated.

A number of psychologists and psychiatrists have argued that in order to ameliorate and prevent depressive episodes the psychological core of the syndrome must be treated. According to Aaron Beck[2] this core is characterized by hopelessness or 'generalized negative expectancies'. In a similar vein, Martin Seligman[3] has gathered a mass of data to support the view that 'learned helplessness' is the main psychological problem that has to be uprootd. But even though there are identifiable psychological problems it is still possible that these are caused by a biochemical imbalance. It has been argued that treating the psychological symptoms would therefore be like treating the experience of pain without attending to the broken leg. Fortunately, there is now convincing evidence that a psychological approach to treatment, based upon the work of Aaron Beck, is as good as, if not better than conventional anti-depressant drug therapy. This evidence will be described later in the chapter.

The psychological approach

This is based upon the assumption that a person prone to depression suffers from misconceptions in three areas. The self, individual experiences and personal prospects for the future are perceived in very negative ways and this so-called 'cognitive triad' results in self-blame and self-depreciation. A depressed person takes the blame when things go wrong and believes that other people, or simply lucky chances, are responsible when everything goes right. Any failure is interpreted as a sign of worthlessness but a tendency to be perfectionist means that experiences of failure are common. Inactivity and apathy results from a feeling of helplessness, 'nothing I do can get me out of this state', as well as a deeply ingrained pessimism about the future: 'I will fail whatever I try'; 'I will never be able to keep a friendship going.'

Depression is linked to these negative misconceptions rather than to the events themselves. 'Men are disturbed not by things but the view that they take of them' (Epictetus). Behavioural, physiological and cognitive responses are influenced by 'perceived helplessness' and the feedback from these three response systems seems to

The Beck depression inventory

A core of symptoms associated with depressed feelings appears in most cultures across the world. The severity of depression can be easily measured by rating scales completed either by the therapist or by the individual concerned. This self-rating questionnaire was designed by Dr Aaron Beck. The individual concerned is asked to select from each of 21 items one of four sentences which most accurately sums up his or her feelings for the previous 7–14 days. The sentences are coded 0, 1, 2, 3 – which are also the marks for each one. At the end of the questionnaire the marks are added up. The possible score ranges from 0 to 63: 0 to 9 is normal; 10 to 18 is mild; 19 to 25 is moderate; 26 to 35 is moderate to severe, while above 36 indicates severe depression. 46

On this questionnaire are groups of statements. Please read each group of statements carefully. Then pick out the one statement in each group which best describes the way you have been feeling the *PAST WEEK, INCLUDING TODAY!* Circle the number beside the statement you picked. If several statements in the group seem to apply equally well, circle each one. *Be sure to read all the statements in each group before making your choice.*

1 0 I do not feel sad.
   1 I feel sad.
   2 I am sad all the time and I can't snap out of it.
   3 I am so sad or unhappy that I can't stand it.

2 0 I am not particularly discouraged about the future.
   1 I feel discouraged about the future.
   2 I feel I have nothing to look forward to.
   3 I feel that the future is hopeless and that things cannot improve.

3 0 I do not feel like a failure.
   1 I feel I have failed more than the average person.
   2 As I look back on my life, all I can see is a lot of failures.
   3 I feel I am a complete failure as a person.

4 0 I get as much satisfaction out of things as I used to.
   1 I don't enjoy things the way I used to.
   2 I don't get real satisfaction out of anything anymore.
   3 I am dissatisfied or bored with everything.

5 0 I don't feel particularly guilty.
   1 I feel guilty a good part of the time.
   2 I feel quite guilty most of the time.
   3 I feel guilty all of the time.

6 0 I don't feel I am being punished.
   1 I feel I may be punished.
   2 I expect to be punished.
   3 I feel I am being punished.

7 0 I don't feel disappointed in myself.
   1 I am disappointed in myself.
   2 I am disgusted with myself.
   3 I hate myself.

8 0 I don't feel I am any worse than anybody else.
   1 I am critical of myself for my weaknesses or mistakes.
   2 I blame myself all the time for my faults.
   3 I blame myself for everything bad that happens.

9 0 I don't have any thoughts of killing myself.
   1 I have thoughts of killing myself, but I would not carry them out.
   2 I would like to kill myself.
   3 I would kill myself if I had the chance.

10 0 I don't cry any more than usual.
    1 I cry more now than I used to.
    2 I cry all the time now.
    3 I used to be able to cry, but now I can't cry even though I want to.

11 0 I am no more irritated now than I ever am.
    1 I get annoyed or irritated more easily than I used to.
    2 I feel irritated all the time now.
    3 I don't get irritated at all by the things that used to irritate me.

12 0 I have not lost interest in other people.
    1 I am less interested in other people than I used to be.
    2 I have lost most of my interest in other people.
    3 I have lost all of my interest in other people.

13 0 I make decisions about as well as I ever could.
    1 I put off making decisions more than I used to.
    2 I have greater difficulty in making decisions than before.
    3 I can't make decisions at all anymore.

14 0 I don't feel I look any worse than I used to.
    1 I am worried that I am looking old or unattractive.
    2 I feel that there are permanent changes in my appearance that make me look unattractive.
    3 I believe that I look ugly.

15 0 I can work about as well as before.
    1 It takes an extra effort to get started at doing something.
    2 I have to push myself very hard to do anything.
    3 I can't do any work at all.

16 0 I can sleep as well as usual.
    1 I don't sleep as well as I used to.
    2 I wake up 1–2 hours earlier than usual and find it hard to get back to sleep.
    3 I wake up several hours earlier than I used to and cannot get back to sleep.

17 0 I don't get more tired than usual.
    1 I get tired more easily than I used to.
    2 I get tired from doing almost anything.
    3 I am too tired to do anything.

18 0 My appetite is no worse than usual
    1 My appetite is not as good as it used to be.
    2 My appetite is much worse now.
    3 I have no appetite at all anymore.

19 0 I haven't lost much weight, if any, lately.
    1 I have lost more than 5 pounds.
    2 I have lost more than 10 pounds.
    3 I have lost more than 15 pounds.
    I am purposely trying to lose weight
    by eating less. Yes ____ No ____

20 0 I am no more worried about my health than usual.
    1 I am worried about physical problems such as aches and pains; or upset stomach; or constipation.
    2 I am very worried about physical problems and it's hard to think of much else.
    3 I am so worried about my physical problems that I cannot think about anything else.

21 0 I have not noticed any recent change in my interest in sex.
    1 I am less interested in sex than I used to be.
    2 I am much less interested in sex now.
    3 I have lost interest in sex completely.

validate the perception of helplessness. If we are disturbed by our interpretations of events, then we have to work out alternative interpretations which can put our minds at rest, as Alfred Adler has suggested:[4]

> ... there is probably something of a mistake always involved when we take particular experiences as the basis for our future life. Meanings are not determined by situations but we determine ourselves by the meanings we give to situations.

Leaving aside drug therapy to modify the physiological response system, there are two main ways of changing perceived helplessness and associated misconceptions. The first involves making small changes in *behaviour* in order to put our interpretations to the test. The cue exposure approach described in Chapter 4 provides a good example of this method of modifying expectations. The second involves the search for alternative conceptions through *cognitive approaches* such as self-questioning. Both approaches are illustrated in the following case.

Charles was a civil servant, rather a perfectionist, who considered himself to be compulsive about checking his work, checking for dirt on his clothes and tidying at home. His compulsion was very much worse when he was depressed and his depression was intensified by problems at work. He was over-worked partly as a result of his checking and slowness but also because he could not discuss the situation with his superiors. Whenever he considered this line of action he worried about possible criticism.

Charles was persuaded that he might be able to change his view of his work situation by both a behavioural and a cognitive strategy. First he was to try, *as an experiment*, letting his boss know that he was over-worked. He should then cope with the ensuing criticism by neutralizing the thought *'I am a failure'* with an alternative such as 'my boss is irritated because I've created an additional problem for him to deal with, but after all he is my boss and that is his job'. This strategy worked perfectly. His boss was not critical but just a little brusque and Charles was able to think of a number of alternative interpretations of his boss's behaviour.

Like a hermit crab within its shell, the depressive withdraws into a solitary world.

Altering behaviour and thinking of alternative interpretations of events sounds simple in principle, but in practice neither of these most reasonable approaches is plain sailing for the person who is already depressed. Sailing is a skill which has to be learned and only becomes 'plain' after many simple component skills are practised until they become second nature. The same applies to the skill of coping with depression. The procedures described in the following pages must be repeatedly practised before their efficacy can be evaluated.

Altering behaviour

'Boredom is a vital problem for the moralist, since at least half of the sins of mankind are caused by the fear of it' (Bertrand Russell). Inactivity follows directly from an underlying assumption which is almost always a misconception. The depressed person believes that there is no activity that will make him feel better and therefore it is pointless to try to get moving. There are no infallible means of 'snapping out of it' but there are ways of gradually coaxing the spirit back to life. The most important precursor of any voluntary change in behaviour is a reason for making the change.

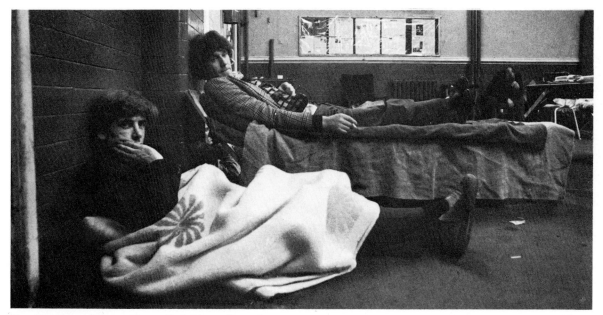

Negative views of the world are reflected in apathy and inactivity, which in turn ensure that the negativity remains unchallenged.

Increasing activity

The depressed person is held back by a whole network of negative beliefs, especially assumptions about the negative consequences of his own actions. These assumptions have to be modified if depression and compulsions are to be prevented. Aaron Beck has argued that:

Acting against an assumption is the most powerful way to change it. The action is tied to the patient's assumption. The therapist suggests that the patient who is afraid to make mistakes seek out situations in which there is a high probability of his making mistakes. He proposes that the patient who feels compelled to be with others force himself to be alone. The patient who places the highest value on acceptance is urged to go to places where the probability of being accepted is slight. The patient afraid of making a fool of himself is asked to do something outlandish.

There is strong scientific support for this behavioural approach to psychotherapy. We would add that in our experience clients nearly always report back: 'I was a little worried but it wasn't as bad as I thought it would be.' For this

reason the depressed person should take seriously the view that action can break up the assumptions that lead to inactivity. For example, Pamela was a bored, depressed housewife with drinking problems. She hadn't been able to develop an interest in any activity since her children had drifted away from home. In addition to hankering for her former role as a mother, she suffered because her husband was so successful. He worked long hours and spent at least one week each month abroad, pursuing his business interests behind the Iron Curtain. At the age of 48 Pamela had little to do but watch television and keep the house tidy. Furthermore, she could not get rid of the thought that her active life was coming to an end. It took quite a while to convince her that the answer to her problem did not lie in either a complex analytical approach, such as the uncovering of a repressed memory of childhood, or in tablets, and that suicide was not the answer. When she finally accepted that small changes in her behaviour could lead to large changes in her basic assumptions she planned for herself a 'commando course' using the guide lines described in this chapter. Within six months, in spite of self-doubts and awful feelings of depression along the way, she was a busy

Escaping from the trap of depression can be a struggle.

woman again with many interests including golf and participation in Alcoholics Anonymous. She had more confidence in her own abilities and looked forward to a life spent developing her own skills, especially her new-found ability to help others.

Understanding the rationale

Before starting on such a programme depressed persons must be convinced that activity can contribute towards a cure. They must therefore understand the rationale underlying the approach and then look at themselves as subjects for an experiment. Activities must be tested to assess their effects, just as a doctor might try out a course of penicillin to treat an infection. Action of any sort can divert attention away from self-defeating ruminations. Friends and relatives will tend to react more positively as the depressed person becomes active. Most important, however, is the fact that action is the best way of testing the reality of those pessimistic assumptions. The belief that 'everything I do makes me feel awful' will not be shaken by days and weeks of inactivity. On the other hand, there is a possibility that some change for the better will occur after a gentle swim or an hour spent helping an old friend mend his fence.

Try the experiment

What activity will produce feelings of mastery and pleasure for a particular person at a particular time? There is a solution to this question and the very pursuit of a solution could be part of the answer. Like detective work or science, the overall strategy should be to formulate and test very specific hypotheses such as the following:

- Activities involving a little physical exercise might alter my mood.
- I used to be an amateur naturalist. Perhaps walking through a wood for an hour will stimulate my mind and my curiosity.
- I've withdrawn from other people during the last four years. I'll try to reverse this process. I might feel better if I visit a friend tomorrow.

By carefully noting the effects of each course of action, the depressed person can identify activities which make him or her feel better than others. This approach substitutes constructive selfwatching for the negative introspections of the depressed state of mind.

Selecting activities

It is sometimes very difficult to make a list of potentially pleasurable activities, especially when thinking is slow, confused and negative, as it is likely to be during a period of depression. Beck and his colleagues used the following list to help generate ideas.

> What types of things did you enjoy learning before you got depressed? (For example: sports, crafts, languages)
> What types of day trips did you enjoy? (For example: to the sea, to the mountains, to the country)
> What types of things do you think you could enjoy if you had no inhibitions about them? (For example: painting, acting in a play, playing the piano)
> What did you enjoy doing alone? (For example: long walks, playing the piano, sewing)
> What did you enjoy doing with others? (For example: talking on the telephone, going to dinner with a friend, playing handball)
> What did you enjoy doing that costs no money? (For example: playing with my dog, going to the library, reading)
> What did you enjoy doing that costs under $5.00? (For example: going to a movie, riding in a cab, going to the museum)
> What did you enjoy doing when money was

no object? (For example: buying a new suit, going to New York, going out for a nice dinner)
What activities did you enjoy at different times? (For example: in the morning, on Sunday, in the Spring, in Autumn).

Activities should be selected which are likely to bring immediate pleasure. They should be graded according to difficulty and the easiest ones tried first. By gradually moving up a hierarchy from short, easy tasks to more difficult ones, it is possible to get moving without a great deal of effort. However, the advice of Ellis and Harper should be borne in mind when willpower is required:

It takes more than self-talk. In the final analysis, you often would better literally force yourself, propel yourself, push yourself, into action. Often, you can make yourself – yes, make yourself – undertake specific acts of courage: beard an employer in his office, ask a very attractive person to dance, take your idea for a book to a publisher. And keep forcing yourself into action long enough and often enough until the action itself proves easier and easier, even enjoyable.[5]

Scheduling activities

One strategy which many people use when the going is rough is to plan and timetable activities in great detail. Beck and his colleagues encourage their clients to do this for each day's activities and to write down what they plan to do during each hour. Often fear of failure leads to the rejection of this approach and so the following principles have to be remembered:

- No one accomplishes every plan, so don't feel bad if you don't complete everything.
- In planning it is essential to state what kind of activity will be undertaken, not how much will be accomplished.

There are also two ways of making it easier to accomplish a plan. The first involves *mental practice* and the second involves *short-term goal setting*.

Just as a computer needs a programme to guide its operations towards a specific goal, so we need a clear plan or *image* to guide behaviour. When feeling very depressed our minds are so bewildered and obsessed with negative thoughts that there is very little room for these plans and images. It is therefore necessary to make room. There is also a strong tendency to avoid thinking, planning and imagining. This avoidance must be overcome. A person undertaking a first swim for ten years should mentally go over every little detail in order to ensure that the plan is clear and any possible problems are anticipated.

Short-term goal setting is a version of the Alcoholics Anonymous philosophy of 'one day at a time': any task which seems overwhelmingly difficult should be broken down into more manageable parts and the focus of attention should be on the next few hours, even the next few minutes, rather than the next week. Professor Bandura and a colleague working at Stanford University have demonstrated that slimmers who have set themselves weekly goals do not lose as much weight as those who concentrate upon the next few hours[6] and do not burden themselves with the thought of too much effort. This principle can be used very flexibly depending upon the problem and person. If an alcoholic believes that he could be abstinent for three weeks, but not for life, then his target might be to go for three weeks without a drink, at which time goals would be reconsidered. Of course, this is a normal self-control strategy that many people use when facing a difficult task. A writer might be tempted to give in if he allowed himself to dwell on the enormity of the task that faces him. Instead he sets himself a more manageable goal, a specific number of words a day, perhaps.

Mastery and pleasure

Scheduling activities should not be carried out blindly as a way of filling in time. They are part of a systematic selfwatching strategy designed to increase self-knowledge and modify misconceptions. In particular, it is vital to look for those activities which give feelings of pleasure or a sense of mastery, since it is misery and helplessness that have to be counteracted. One effective way of monitoring the positive effects of various activities is to devise a weekly schedule and give each activity a score out of ten for resulting experiences of mastery and pleasure. No matter how small the sense of achievement, any activity with positive effects should be followed up.

The commonsense guide lines outlined above should help to counteract the inactivity which is one of the characteristic symptoms of depression and also disprove some basic misconceptions. Another way of coping with depression is to attack negative assumptions directly by first identifying the assumption and then searching for alternative interpretations.

Getting rid of a negative bias
Most events can be appraised in a number of different ways, depending upon the mental set or the basic assumptions of the people involved. A door bell ringing will be interpreted one way by a mother whose motorcyclist son is late home from work and in another way by her lodger who is expecting his girlfriend to call round. A loud grating noise during a transatlantic flight will terrify the person with a fear of flying, who immediately thinks of holes being ripped in the fuselage and engines and wings dropping off. The air hostess, however, is unperturbed since she supposes that the pilot is testing the landing gear.

People who frequently get depressed suffer from a negative bias in their appraisal of events, especially when their own ability and worth is involved. Very often their pessimistic interpretation of events is made on the basis of insufficient evidence and involves a number of logical errors, including the following examples described by Beck:

Arbitrary Inference A conclusion drawn in the absence of sufficient evidence or of any evidence at all. For example, a woman views herself as a poor mother because she can't breast feed her baby.

Selective Abstraction A conclusion drawn on the basis of just one out of many elements in a situation. A wife feels that her husband's affection is waning, in spite of a great deal of contrary evidence, because he decides to go into the office every Saturday morning.

Over-generalization A sweeping conclusion drawn on the basis of a single, possibly trivial event. An adolescent boy feels that he is disliked

Beating depression means working a little harder at finding ways to enjoy yourself, whether alone . . .

. . . or in company. Either way, exercise restores muscle tone and mental energy.

by the opposite sex because he is told by one girl, on one occasion, that his breath smells.

Magnification and Minimization Errors in evaluating the significance or magnitude of an event that are so gross as to constitute a distortion. Having to wait half an hour in a doctor's surgery is seen as a personal insult (magnification). A very good pianist considers his skill to be worthless because he never made the grade as a concert pianist (minimization).

In order to counteract irrational negative thinking like this, and so prevent depressive episodes, the first essential is for the individual to learn how to break out of these logical errors in his or her own thinking. Firm action must be taken to clear the way for a realistic appraisal of day-to-day experience.

Uncovering automatic thoughts

During any activity there is always in the shadows of our minds a stream of automatic thoughts which are closely related to our mental state at the time. They are very difficult to catch, but if they can be brought to the surface and identified they provide important information about the background assumptions that influence our everyday behaviour.

For example, a depressed woman experienced the following background thoughts as she asked a librarian to reserve a book on psychology.

– She probably thinks I am not quite normal because I want a book on psychology.
– I wish I could speak spontaneously in this type of situation.
– I'm so slow and hesitant.
– That man is listening to us. What is he thinking about me?

This kind of 'thoughtless thinking' that influences our moods is a prime candidate for selfwatching. Collecting a large number of automatic thoughts gives some indication of basic assumptions, just as a sampling of the Earth's crust allows the geologist to build up a picture of rock formations and mineral deposits. Thoughts can be noted down during the day when you feel uncomfortable or distressed. Alternatively a period of time can be set aside to

meditate upon a particular problem and to watch for those fleeting thoughts which contribute towards the appraisal of the problem.

A depressed 54-year-old widow with a weight problem used this latter technique to try to understand the relationship between her obesity and her depression. She imagined herself in the nude and also in various situations involving her family and friends. The following thoughts gradually surfaced.

– My dead husband would be shocked if he could see me now.
– I long for the youthful beauty that I had until I turned 40.
– My husband was a marvellous man. I wish I was slim and he was with me.
– My legs are going. I feel like a rusty car.
– My children don't understand my compulsion to eat. They think I am just greedy.
– I don't care what my children think, or do I? Yes I feel rejected.
– I wonder if I am diabetic?

After recording these thoughts, she was able to get some understanding of her depression which made very good sense to her. Basically she felt rejected by her family and unhealthy. She also felt regret. At the time when she was slim she had been young, attractive, very much in love and a good mother. Now she was fat, old and on the scrap heap. She was certainly fat (which she could do something about) and getting on in years, but the feeling of being rejected turned out to be a misconception based upon very little evidence. By appraising her feelings realistically, she was in a better position to concentrate her energies fruitfully on a weight-control programme.

Modifying misconceptions

Beck has listed some of the basic assumptions which are associated with depression. The following are common examples:

– In order to be happy, I have to be successful in whatever I undertake.
– To be happy, I must be accepted by all people at all times.
– If I make a mistake, it means that I am inept.
– I can't live without you.

Finding new interests will bring you into contact with people again.

- If somebody disagrees with me, it means he doesn't like me.
- My value as a person depends on what others think of me.

A depressed person does not examine or doubt such views. They are as essential to the personality as being male or female, but they can more easily be altered. The plan of campaign is as follows:

- focus upon one assumption at a time
- search for alternative interpretations
- find an alternative that makes sense and has a beneficial effect upon mood

To see this approach in action, consider the following case history. A 31-year-old unmarried woman suffered from cleaning compulsions. It took her at least two hours to get ready for work and frequently she had difficulty curtailing her washing rituals. She identified the following assumption that was linked to her feelings of helplessness and depression:

> I can't get married until I get rid of my compulsions. No man would fancy me and it is not fair on the man.

She was then asked to question this assumption, come up with a number of alternatives, and give them ratings from 0 to 5 to indicate how strongly she believed in each one. The following list was produced with ratings in brackets.

- I can be happy even if I don't get married (1)
- I would make a very good housewife in spite of my compulsions (4)
- Actually I am obsessively house-proud and some men are probably looking for my type of person (4)
- By practising interrupting my compulsive cleaning, I might be able to get it under control in the next few years (2)
- Other people get married even though they have disabilities that are worse than mine (5)
- I am a sympathetic person and could make the right man very happy. Surely this is more important than my washing problem (3)

During the ensuing months she successfully used the alternatives 2, 3 and 5 to cope with feelings of helplessness whenever she caught negative automatic thoughts about herself and marriage floating through her mind.

The scientific evidence

A number of procedures have been described which are designed to increase activity and loosen up the rigid negative beliefs which underlie depression. They should be tried, not only because they sound reasonable and are based upon current theories of depression, but also because there is evidence that they work.

In 1977 Beck and his colleagues published the results of a controlled trial in *The Journal of Cognitive Therapy*.[7] The study compared the psychological approach we have outlined with the use of an anti-depressant drug of proven efficacy (imipramine). Moderate to severely depressed out-patients were randomly assigned to the drug therapy or the psychotherapy treatment and were seen once or twice a week for 12 weeks. Analysis of the data revealed several interesting findings. First, the psychological treatment group improved more rapidly during the first few weeks. Secondly, 79 per cent of the psychological-treatment group showed marked or complete remission of symptoms compared to only 23 per cent of the drug-therapy patients. Finally, follow-up studies at three and six months showed substantially fewer relapses in the psychological-treatment group.

A second study was carried out in the United Kingdom by Ivy Blackburn and Steven Bishop of the Brain Metabolism Unit in Edinburgh.[8] The study was entitled *Is there an alternative to drugs in the treatment of depressed ambulatory patients?* In it, Blackburn and Bishop demonstrated that psychological treatment of the kind described in this chapter is better than drug therapy for the type of depressed patient who is usually given anti-depressant drugs by a general practitioner. The following is one of their case examples:

M.L. was a 32-year-old female trained nurse, married to a church minister, with three children aged 9, 7 and 3 years. The first episode of depression occurred 2½ years ago, and was treated with amitriptyline, Valium and marital therapy. The current episode of 2 months duration included two severe suicide attempts (overdoses). The patient was admitted to hospital and assessed for the treatment trial. She was allocated to cognitive therapy and discharged after 1 week when treatment started. Her main symptoms were: (1) Affective: depressed, irritable, anxious; (2) Physical: sleeping difficulty, poor appetite, loss of weight, physical exhaustion, loss of libido; (3) Behavioural: inactivity, crying; (4) Cognitive: feeling of failure, hopelessness, guilt about children and husband, concern about parents and husband.

This patient was treated for a total of 12 weeks. Her discussions with the therapist revealed certain themes and feelings which dominated her daily life. Examples included excessive tidiness, a lack of assertiveness, constant feelings of inadequacy and fears of losing control over herself and her life. At home she often felt angry with and jealous of her husband, and entertained constant doubts over their marriage. At work, her excessive concern for detail led to ever-increasing pressures as she slipped behind schedule.

M.L. began her therapy by reading *Coping with Depression* (Beck and Greenberg) and discussing the contents. Next, she was helped to plan activities for each day, with special emphasis on pleasant and enjoyable undertakings. These plans were carefully limited to her ability to cope with them. After each day, she was encouraged to focus on the experiences which had given her the greatest sense of mastery and pleasure. At the same time, her difficulties in expressing anger and refusing burdensome extra commitments were met by teaching her ways of expressing her feelings more directly.

An important element in her therapy was to help her identify the automatic negative thinking which was reinforcing her sense of inadequacy and failure. She was asked to write down thoughts and emotions experienced at particular times of day (see box). To counteract these thoughts, M.L. was taught a series of rational

Situation	Emotion	Automatic thought	Rational response	Outcome
Waking up	Sad (100%)	I can't cope with anything (100%)	I can cope as I did yesterday, by taking one thing at a time (30%)	Belief in automatic thoughts (50%) Sadness (50%)

Depressed people must be persuaded to take a chance – the reality – like that of the skydiver – is usually less terrifying than the prospect. The reward is a sense of growing mastery over the self and the world.

responses to them. As a measure of their success, she gave a percentage rating to the power of the negative thought both before and after the rational response. In the example below, the rational response reduced feelings of sadness and inadequacy by 50 per cent.

From all this work, M.L. came to recognize that certain self-imposed rules were governing her existence and, at the same time, condemning her to failure. These were:

1. Showing anger is wrong and unChristian.
2. One must be perfectly clean and tidy at all times.
3. One must try to do God's perfect will.

Through discussion, M.L. was asked to think about the consequences, disadvantages of consciously disobeying these rules. Thus prepared, she tested disobedience in real life (*e.g.* by expressing anger, or avoiding a piece of housework), recording the outcome and her feelings. She found the consequences to be, in reality, less serious than she had feared.

Gradually, M.L. recovered. Measured on the Beck Depression Inventory, her score fell from 29 to eight. A year after treatment, M.L. remained well, indicating that a psychological approach to the treatment of depression is at least as effective as anti-depressant drug treatment.

Conclusions

The selfwatching techniques we have described in this chapter have been developed primarily to combat depression. As a state of mind, depression is not always associated with compulsive behaviour, although it might be described as a compulsive and systematic misinterpretation of reality. But individuals who are the prisoners of addictive and compulsive behaviours very often think in depressive ways, seeing themselves as helpless failures, unable to change their lives. In this frame of mind, a person setting out to change a habit or compulsion is likely to interpret any initial difficulties as yet further evidence of failure and to lose all hope of eventual success. So psychological strategies against depression in general are likely to be effective against particular behaviours. And on the evidence we have that indeed seems to be the case.

7
SOCIAL AND MARITAL CONFLICT

Difficulty in coping with interpersonal conflict can be a major factor in triggering addictions and compulsions. Such conflict can take several forms. The most direct interpersonal influences arise from stressful encounters with friends, relatives, or colleagues at work, which generate feelings of tension, agitation, or anger. The following situations fall into this category:

A dieter is told by her husband as she goes to the kitchen for tea, 'Now make sure that you don't eat anything in there. You know you don't have any willpower.' Her husband's comment aggravates her and in an aggressive reaction she quickly devours two large scones.

A gambler confides in a close friend, telling him his innermost, personal feelings, and then discovers that the friend joked and

laughed about this conversation at the local pub. He feels totally dejected and betrayed and goes off on a five-day gambling spree to forget his troubles.

A drug addict is wrongly accused of a mistake at work that someone else was responsible for. Rather than stand up for his rights he remains silent, feeling victimized, helpless, and angry. This episode precipitates an evening of heavy cocaine use.

In each of these cases the individuals involved either lacked the interpersonal skills needed to confront the problem directly or felt extremely anxious and inhibited about confrontation. Many situations such as these require well developed qualities of assertiveness. Assertiveness refers to the appropriate expression of personal rights and feelings. This includes the ability to disagree with another person; to say 'no' when tempted to eat, drink, or smoke; to express anger and dissatisfaction; or to provide constructive feedback to others.

Dr Miller and his colleagues have demonstrated how crucial the lack of assertiveness can be to alcoholics. In one study male alcoholics and non-alcoholics were asked to role-play a series of staged social encounters requiring assertive responses. Scenes were described to each subject and, with a research assistant playing the part of a friend, relative or co-worker, he was to respond as he would if actually confronted with the situation in everyday life. After his response, the research assistant reacted with an antagonistic remark requiring further assertiveness. A sample encounter follows:

Description:	You had to work late at the office tonight. You are proud of the fact that you have not had a drink in a month. You have no desire to drink. You feel tired from your long day. As you enter the house your wife greets you at the door and says in an angry tone:
Research Assistant:	'Where have you been all this time?! You've been drinking again. What do·you have to say for yourself?'
Alcoholic Subject:	'But . . . ah . . . no. I had to work late.' (Sounding tense and defensive)
Research Assistant:	'Oh, stop making excuses. I can always tell when you've been drinking.'

All subjects were also exposed to a relaxed conversational period on another day to provide a control phase. After each series of procedures, subjects were given the opportunity to drink alcohol. The alcoholic subjects drank significantly more alcohol after the assertiveness encounters than after the conversations which did not involve stress. They demonstrated a marked inability to handle confrontations and evidenced a great deal of anxiety when the encounters were completed. The non-alcoholics drank moderately, responded to the encounters directly and calmly, and did not drink more after the assertiveness encounters. In fact, they tended to drink less.

The ability to cope with social pressure to revert to old habits is also an important interpersonal skill. Dr Alan Marlatt and his colleagues at the University of Washington estimated that 27 per cent of all relapses for smokers, alcoholics, drug addicts, gamblers, and compulsive eaters are triggered by pressure from other people in social situations.

In addition, marital relationships constantly require interpersonal and communication skills.

Ritual boredom or domestic bliss?

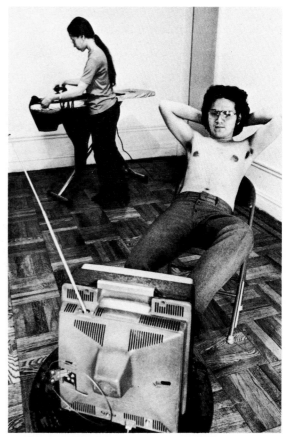

Learning a new skill is never as daunting as it at first appears to be.

If such skills are lacking, marital discord is more likely. In turn, such conflict can precipitate addictive and compulsive behaviour. Unfortunately, these behaviours simply exacerbate marital problems and a vicious circle is established.

Spouses can exert a negative influence in subtle ways. They often make comments that unwittingly sabotage the habit controller. Dr Richard Stuart, in his book *Slim Chance in a Fat World*, describes an experiment in which he analysed these spouse interactions. He instructed women who were participants in a weight control programme and their husbands to tape record family conversation during the evening meal. The results were somewhat startling. First of all, husbands were *seven* times more likely than their dieting wives to discuss food. Husbands were *four* times more likely than their wives to offer food to their spouse. These offers of food occurred in spite of the fact that over 90 per cent of these husbands expressed a strong desire for their wives to lose weight. Finally,

husbands were over *twelve* times more likely to criticize their wives' eating behaviour than to praise it. These comments can exert a profound influence on the dieting spouses' behaviour that, in the long run, can slowly undermine motivation.

Learning social skills

Procedures have been developed to teach methods of coping with (1) situations requiring assertiveness, (2) social pressure, and (3) marital discord. The theory behind this training in social skills is that if an individual were to learn ways to cope with troublesome interpersonal situations more effectively, a major stimulus for addictive and compulsive behaviour would be eliminated. In addition, the ability to deal more efficiently with others results in increased self-esteem, self-value, and feelings of social competence.

Assertiveness training

Assertiveness training typically follows a straightforward teaching procedure which is illustrated by the following case.[1] The individual concerned was a 34-year-old divorced man with a 10-year history of drug and alcohol abuse. His history involved a series of work situations in which he 'started at the bottom' and, because of diligence and competence, quickly moved up the ladder. During the few weeks or months that he was working his way up, he was able to stay away from drugs and alcohol. However, as soon as he was promoted to a position of responsibility, he reverted to his addictions and promptly lost his job. At the beginning of his treatment he related the fact that a few weeks previously he had accepted a position as a night clerk in a small hotel. On the basis of his excellent performance he was promoted to assistant hotel manager. He had reverted to drug and alcohol abuse within the past few days because of an inability to handle responsibilities, caused by a marked lack of assertiveness. The patient was likeable, friendly, and hard-working but could not make decisions easily or deal with other people effectively.

An analysis of his current problem revealed that his drug and alcohol abuse had been triggered specifically by three episodes:

1. His inability to confront housekeeping

Assertiveness test

How assertive are you in dealing with others? Are you direct, open, and expressive or do you let other people take advantage of you?

Answer *Yes* or *No* to each of the following items. Then examine each item to see how you might be more assertive. A *Yes* on items 1, 4, 5, 6, 9, 12, 13, 14, 15, 16, 17, 18, 19, 20, 21, 23, 24, 25, 27, 28, 29, 30 and a *No* on items 2, 3, 7, 8, 10, 11, 22, 26 indicates assertive behaviour. Rather than being a global trait, assertiveness seems to depend on the situation and who you are dealing with.

Assertiveness inventory

Yes or No

___ 1. When a person is blatantly unfair, do you usually say something about it to him?

___ 2. Are you always very careful to avoid all trouble with other people?

___ 3. Do you often avoid social contacts for fear of doing or saying the wrong thing?

___ 4. If a friend betrays your confidence, do you tell him how you really feel?

___ 5. If you shared living quarters, would you insist that he do his fair share of the cleaning?

___ 6. When a shop assistant attends to someone who has come in after you, do you call his attention to the matter?

___ 7. Are there very few people with whom you can be relaxed and have a good time?

___ 8. Would you be hesitant about asking a good friend to lend you a small sum of money?

___ 9. If someone who has borrowed a small amount of money from you seems to have forgotten about it, would you remind this person?

___10. If a person keeps on teasing you, do you have difficulty expressing your annoyance or displeasure?

___11. Would you remain standing at the rear of a crowded auditorium rather than looking for a seat up front?

___12. If someone keeps kicking the back of your chair in a movie, would you ask him to stop?

___13. If a friend keeps calling you very late each evening, would you ask him not to call after a certain time?

___14. If someone starts talking to someone else right in the middle of your conversation, do you express your irritation?

___15. In a plush restaurant, if you order a medium steak and find it too raw, would you ask the waiter to have it recooked?

___16. If the landlord of your apartment fails to make certain necessary repairs after promising to do so, would you insist upon it?

___17. Would you return a faulty garment you purchased a few days ago?

___18. If someone you respect expresses opinions with which you strongly disagree, would you venture to state your own point of view?

___19. Are you usually able to say 'no' if people make unreasonable requests?

___20. Do you think that people should stand up for their rights?

___21. Do you protest verbally when someone pushes in front of you in a line?

___22. Are you inclined to be overly apologetic?

___23. A friend unjustifiably criticizes you. Do you express your reaction openly?

___24. Are you able to contradict a domineering person?

___25. You hear that another person is spreading false rumours about you. Would you go to him directly to correct the situation?

___26. Do you usually keep your opinions to yourself?

___27. Are you able to openly express love and affection?

___28. Do you tell your friends you care for them?

___29. Do you take the initiative to cut telephone calls short when you are busy?

___30. If after leaving a shop you notice that you have been given short change, do you go back and point out the error?

---

personnel about their inadequate cleaning of the hotel rooms

2. His inability to refuse to buy unnecessary items from salesmen who pressured him

3. His inability to deal with unreasonable complaints from hotel guests

Six typical work-related situations were chosen for assertiveness training. The following is one example:

A guest comes to you complaining that his room was not cleaned very well by the house-

*Taking pleasure in the company of others and joining in the
fun are social skills we develop from childhood onwards.*

keeping staff. You check other rooms and find
that they have not been cleaned properly. You
mention this to the maid and she says 'I cleaned
the rooms as well as I can. I'm too busy to be as
neat as you would like.'

Prior to training the manager was requested to
role-play these scenes with the aid of a treatment
assistant to determine his typical manner of
responding. In the above scene he became very
anxious, looked at the floor, and sounded uncer-
tain and apologetic. His reply was 'I . . . ah . . . I'm
sorry to have to ask you this . . . ah . . . but . . .
would you think about . . . ah vacuuming these
rugs a little more. Don't get me wrong. The
rooms look great but . . . ah . . . some of the guests
think the rugs are a little dirty.' The patient
explained that he felt inhibited because he did
not know exactly how to express himself and was
afraid he might make people angry or hurt their
feelings. In real life the outcome of this particular
situation had been that the patient had cleaned

several of the rooms himself, had resented
having to do it, had felt extremely angry about
allowing himself to be put into this position, and
had bought a bottle of whisky as soon as he
finished work that evening.

Training consisted of repeatedly rehearsing
these situations with the patient and providing
him with specific instructions on appropriate
assertive responses. Role-played rehearsals
were videotaped to provide the patient with
feedback on his behaviour. Initially, he was
instructed to focus on eye contact, looking
directly at the person to whom he was speaking.
Although direct eye contact during such encounters initially caused him considerable anxiety, he
eventually felt quite comfortable and relaxed
after several rehearsals with treatment assistants. He was also advised of appropriate voice
tone and facial expressions. The patient had a
tendency to speak too softly, with little
emotional expression. Due to anxiety he often
smiled during assertive encounters. Such

behaviour significantly reduced the effectiveness of his authority. Several direct assertive responses were rehearsed, such as 'Sally, these rooms are still quite dirty. I want you to reclean Rooms 321 and 322 immediately. Let me know when you're finished so I can check them.' By means of a technique known as *modelling*, the therapist provided several examples of such responses by role-playing several scenes himself. The patient then practised, with the therapist providing feedback on the appropriateness of his responses.

Gradually, the patient improved until he had successfully learned assertiveness skills and felt comfortable in applying them. His drug and alcohol abuse ceased as he tried out his new assertiveness and found it to be successful. He was amazed to discover how he slowly gained the respect of those who worked for him and how they began to respond differently to him. As he became more socially competent he also began to feel much more confident and self-assured.

Basically, then, the ability to increase assertive behaviour involves several elements. First, one must identify problem areas in communicating with others. Second, one must decide upon the most appropriate ways – verbal and non-verbal – to express oneself in order to convey the message. Then, each component must be practised in situations that are as close to the actual encounter as possible. For example, people often practise formal speeches in front of family members or even a mirror, but fail to consider the applicability of the same technique in preparing for general conversation and interpersonal situations.

While such rehearsal is rather stilted and mechanical at first, it quickly becomes quite realistic. As the basic responses are practised, learned and applied, they soon become incorporated into the individual's behavioural repertoire and occur without hesitation. Repeated rehearsals also condition people emotionally so that they feel less and less socially inhibited and anxious.

Refusal training

Many reasons exist for problems in dealing with social pressure to indulge cravings. Most of us are social beings who want to be well liked by others. We try to accommodate others' wishes as much as possible without allowing them to take advantage of us. Because of these feelings, the simple act of saying 'no' to temptations offered by others can be quite complex. The thought processes that complicate this issue might include the following patterns:

– How can I refuse to drink with Jim? After all, he's been a good, steady customer for years. He expects me to drink with him. If I don't, it'll make him uncomfortable and I might lose business.
– Marge went out of her way to make that dessert for me tonight. If I don't have any, it might hurt her feelings. She's been upset lately, anyhow. I don't want to make things worse for her.
– I don't want to be a stick-in-the-mud tonight. What will my date think if I don't drink? He'll think I'm dull and will never want to go out with me again.

Such excuses mistakenly over-emphasize the importance of one person's habits in the attitudes and feelings of another person. They demonstrate a rather immature way of thinking in which responsibility is avoided because it is transferred to the other person.

Dr David Foy,[2] of the University of Mississippi Medical Center, has developed a technique known as *refusal training* to teach people to be less intimidated by social pressure. This procedure has been used successfully with overeaters, smokers, alcoholics, and drug addicts. For example, Dr Foy taught alcoholics to handle such remarks as 'One drink won't hurt you', 'A *real* man should be able to handle his liquor', and 'Just have one; it'll make you feel better.' Refusal responses are usually taught just as assertive responses are, using role-playing, behavioural rehearsal, modelling, and videotape feedback.

The components of an effective refusal response include:

1. Direct eye contact
2. Serious and expressive voice tone
3. An attempt to change the subject of the conversation
4. Offering an alternative. For example, a dieter may say, 'No, thank you, I don't care for

When saying 'No' means having to say goodbye to old friends.

dessert. I would like a cup of that excellent coffee of yours.'
5. Requesting the 'pusher' to refrain from such pressure in the future. One possible approach might be: 'John, I've given up alcohol completely. It would help me a great deal if you just never offered me another alcoholic drink again.'

Practising this refusal response through role playing, or even in the imagination, allows individuals to plan their remarks and to feel more sure of themselves when social pressure arises. After successfully refusing temptation a few times, such remarks become second nature and involve few conscious thought processes. In addition, after one or two assertive refusals, other people simply cease to apply pressure. They have learned that it will not do any good.

Marital interaction skills
Deficiency in marital skills frequently goes hand

in hand with an addictive habit pattern. Marital problems lead to tension, anger, and motivational apathy, all of which make habit control extremely difficult. Improved marital interaction skills have been shown to increase the likelihood of successful habit change. While the training programmes differ slightly, depending on the couple and the nature of their problems, the following case illustrates the use of training in assertiveness, problem-solving skills, positive interactional skills, and behavioural contracting (a method of scheduling a successful plan of change between two people).[3]

Harold was a 49-year-old married man whose alcoholism eventually needed hospital treatment. His history of alcohol abuse extended over 10 years. Up to the time he went into hospital he had been drinking between one pint and one quart of vodka per day. Because of a benevolent employer he was able to keep his job as a packer in a glass container company.

Harold's marriage of 29 years, however, was in

Breaking out of the circle of accusation, anger and defensiveness is crucial to kicking the habit.

trouble. Marital conflict triggered episodes of alcohol consumption and, in turn, excessive drinking worsened the problem. His wife Edna had tried a number of techniques to cope with her husband's drinking including threatening, protecting, nagging and ignoring. None of these manoeuvres proved to be effective.

During initial interviews, Harold and his wife agreed that improvements in marital interaction could definitely help the drinking problem. They recognized that their current problems revolved around Harold's excessive drinking and general lack of responsiveness to his wife, her subsequent nagging, and a general lack of positive interaction between the two.

Based on these initial interviews, and observations of the couple conversing together, the following treatment goals were established:

1. To increase the couple's ability to express themselves directly and to solve mutual problems more efficiently

2. To increase positive communication patterns (most of their comments to one another were either negative or neutral)

3. To eliminate conversations regarding negative incidents in the past, thus enabling the couple to become more positively oriented towards solving present problems

4. To provide each partner with skills needed to increase more desirable behaviour in the other, so that the use of threats and coercion would be eliminated

Skills necessary to attain these goals were taught during weekly training sessions using a male and a female therapist. For example, the therapists provided examples of how the couple might negotiate Harold's taking Antabuse daily (Antabuse is a medication which prevents alcohol intake because the two compounds mixed together result in nausea and other unpleasant physical reactions) if his wife refrained from nagging. The therapists role-played these negotiations, demonstrating compromise ('I'll agree to take Antabuse each day if you'll agree to stop discussing my past drinking problems') and the use of direct, assertive problem-solving skills – offering concrete, practical solutions, for example. The couple were asked to practise these negotiations on their own. Their interactions were videotaped so they could view them with the therapists and gradually improve their communication. The couple were initially encouraged to increase very simple, non-verbal, positive communications such as looking at one another while speaking, smiling more frequently, listening attentively, and touching one another. Simple positive statements such as 'I feel good when you say that' or 'You look very attractive today' were encouraged and reinforced by the therapists. Repeated instructions, periodic encouragement, practice, and videotape feedback fostered these new behaviours quite rapidly.

Harold and Edna were also instructed to practise the discussion of marital problems requiring assertiveness, paying particular attention to eye contact, emotional expression, compromise, and requests for the partner to alter specific behaviour patterns. These new skills were rehearsed repeatedly with feedback being provided by the therapists.

The couple used these new skills to solve mutual problems, at first during the training session and finally, at home alone. For example, one difficulty arose because they were frequently asked by their son and daughter-in-law to care for their granddaughter. While they loved the child dearly, they felt that the parents took advantage of their kindness. In the past, discussion of this problem led to extensive arguing and Harold would leave the house to drink with his friends. When discussing the matter after training the couple agreed that they would limit their 'babysitting' service to their own convenience and that Harold would assist his wife in caring for the child. In fact, during the session Harold expressed the fact that he enjoyed playing with the youngster during her visits but did not do so because he felt his wife preferred to spend time alone with the child. Edna was unaware of her husband's feelings on this matter and appreciated his offer of assistance.

Behavioural contracts

Behavioural contracts are simple agreements between individuals which provide specified rewards for particular kinds of behaviour. Many people have found them helpful in dealing with target problems within a relationship: a contract both sets out the problem objectively and helps to sharpen awareness in the people concerned of the complex interchange that takes place over apparently very simple matters.

```
The undersigned, Mr & Mrs H.L., enter into the
following Agreement with each other.  The terms
of this Agreement include the following:

1.  During this weekend Mrs L. agrees not to
    mention any of Mr L.'s past drinking
    episodes or possible drinking in the future.

2.  Mrs L. will be allowed one infringement of
    this Agreement per day provided that she
    stops what she is saying immediately upon
    Mr L.'s reminding her of this Agreement.

3.  On Friday, Saturday and Sunday afternoons or
    evenings Mr L. agrees to take Mrs L. out to
    the shops, or dinner, to a movie, or for a
    drive depending on her choice.

4.  Mrs L.'s Agreement to refrain from
    mentioning her husband's drinking problem is
    binding only if Mr L. fulfils his Agreement
    stated under term number 3.

5.  Mr L.'s Agreement to take Mrs L. out each
    day of the weekend is binding only if Mrs L.
    fulfils her Agreement stated under term
    number 1.

6.  The terms of the Contract are renewable at
    the beginning of each day so that failure of
    one partner to fulfil his or part of the
    Agreement on any one day breaks the Contract
    for that day only.


Mr L.


Mrs L.


Witness
```

In an attempt to set these changes on a broader footing, behavioural contracts were written for the couple at the end of each weekly session. These contracts, signed by each partner, specified one or two behavioural goals to be accomplished during the weekend, when Harold went home from the hospital. In the sample contract above you can see that Edna agrees not to mention her husband's drink problem or any topic related to alcohol. Experience had shown that such remarks often triggered

Exchanging bad habits for new ones – looking good and feeling fit.

drinking episodes. In return Harold promises to take his wife out to dinner, or to the cinema. This was because, during discussion, it had emerged that one of Edna's long-standing complaints was that they rarely went out as a couple. After each weekend visit, the couple discussed with the therapist the failure or success of the particular contract. On the occasions that they had failed to comply with the terms of the contract, the reasons for failure were reviewed in detail and, in the light of the discussions, a new contract was framed for the following weekend.

After Harold was discharged from hospital the couple continued with these training sessions for six months, at first biweekly, then on a monthly basis. The result of the treatment has been that Harold has remained completely abstinent from alcohol for nine months and has taken Antabuse each day. Both parties report a much more positive, enjoyable marital relationship. They go out together once a week and frequently sit together in the evening to discuss mutual goals, interests, and concerns. They both feel closer to one another than they have ever felt before. Harold

expressed a firm commitment to continue his abstinence from alcohol. 'After all,' he remarked as he glanced at his wife, 'We both have a lot to live for.'

Social support

Support and reinforcement from family members and friends is an important factor in habit change. Support and encouragement can come from already existing family and social structures or from groups specifically designed for that purpose. Alcoholics Anonymous, Synanon (for drug abusers), Overeaters Anonymous, TOPS (Take Off Pounds Sensibly) and Gamblers Anonymous are but a few of the self-help groups which systematically reward behaviour change.

Drs Mahoney and Mahoney studied the influence of social support in a group of participants in a weight-control programme at Pennsylvania State University. Group members were followed up for two years. They found that cooperation and encouragement from family and friends were strongly linked with successful weight loss.

Dr Kelly Brownell and his colleagues, having studied the problem of obesity for several years, were well aware of the importance of encouragement from family and friends in the regula-

---

How to help others help you

Since other people have such a great influence on successful selfwatching, here are some tips on how to encourage relatives and friends to provide appropriate support.

1. Ask them to take your efforts seriously – no joking or teasing
2. Tell them not to advise you on how to change your behaviour
3. Request them to avoid monitoring your progress or checking up on you
4. Ask them to recognize and praise your efforts at change
5. Encourage them to ignore temporary setbacks and never criticize momentary 'slips' in control
6. Tell them exactly what they should *say* or *do* to help you
7. Remind them that *you* must be in charge of your life
8. Ask them to be positive and encouraging

tion of eating patterns. They wondered if they might be able to devise a treatment strategy to use spouses as positive therapeutic agents. They reasoned that if family members can sometimes act like 'friendly enemies' they can also learn to be cooperative, helpful modifiers of behaviour.[4]

To test out their ideas they recruited 29 overweight men and women to participate in a special weight control programme. All patients were married and the average weight in the group was 208lb (95kg).

Patients attended ten weekly sessions during which nutritional education, exercise management, and behaviour modification were emphasized. Women were placed on a 1200 calorie per day diet and men were permitted 1500 calories. Spouses of all patients were strongly encouraged to lend their support and attend the weekly meetings. Patients with spouses who agreed to cooperate were randomly assigned to one of two treatment groups.

Group 1 was called the *Cooperative Spouse –*

Couples Training group. Spouses attended all meetings and were given a wide range of written material on nutrition and habit change. Each spouse was asked to help by putting into effect in his or her own life the same changes in daily routine suggested to the patient. The spouses were not expected to diet (indeed, they were not overweight) but they were asked to eat more slowly or eat only at scheduled meal times, just as the patients were. Spouses were also instructed to help distract the patient during times when temptation was high. For example, they might suggest a walk or a game of cards. They were also to refrain from offering food and from bringing high calorific food into the house. Finally, they were trained to be supportive and positive in their attitudes and to reward progress with praise and enthusiasm. Critical remarks were to be avoided. Couples were instructed to keep joint daily behavioural diaries to monitor the eating habits of each partner. The entire programme focused on mutual effort and support.

Group 2 was known as the *Cooperative Spouse – Subject Alone* group. This group was included to determine if simply having a co-operative spouse, without the aid of special training, would be enough to help the dieter achieve his or her goal. Members of this group received the same programme as those in Group 1. Spouses were expected to lend support, but were not given training in how to behave.

Those whose spouses refused to participate in helping them were assigned to Group 3, the *Non-Cooperative Spouse – Subject Alone* group. Group 3 members received weight-control treatment that was identical to that of Group 2.

Left and above: a supportive environment and friendly assurances make it easier to cope with anxiety and accept responsibility for our own behaviour.

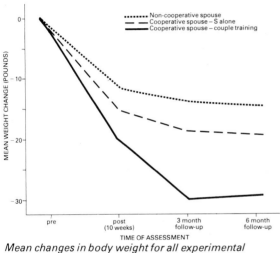

Mean changes in body weight for all experimental conditions at post-treatment and the 3-month and 6-month follow-ups.

Measures of body weight and weekly habit change scores (calculated from the behavioural diary information) were evaluated immediately after the ten weeks of treatment and again at follow-ups of three months and six months. The results are quite astonishing. The table shows the average weight change in pounds for each group. Overall, patients whose spouse underwent the couples training far exceeded the weight losses of the other patients. Their success was especially pronounced at the longer follow-up assessments, after direct therapeutic support had ended. Six months later, patients in Group 1 had lost an average of 30lb (13.6kg) as compared to only 19lb (8.6kg) and 15lb (6.8kg) for Groups 2 and 3 respectively. Since all groups had

exactly the same basic dietary and behavioural treatment, it is apparent that systematic spouse support had a tremendous impact on success rates.

While the patients in Group 2 lost slightly more weight than those in Group 3, they did not lose nearly as much as the patients whose spouses were trained to help them. Good intentions from spouses are not enough. They must know how, when, and where to provide appropriate support and must be willing to view their dieting spouses' efforts as a partnership.

Beware of the habit supervisor

Active involvement from a family member or members, however, refers to positive, supportive help in which the main responsibility for change lies with the individual with the addiction. By trying to help too much some spouses become 'habit supervisors'. A 'supervisor' is a spouse who feels that he or she must design someone else's habit change programme and then remain in control of its implementation. Their attempts at control actually hinder progress. The spouse who is being controlled begins to feel resentful and will eventually rebel and revert to bad habits out of spite. These supervisors must be confronted directly. They usually are unaware of their negative influence and feel they are simply providing 'support'. An example of a supervisor husband and how his wife dealt with him is provided by the case of Stanley and Ruth.[4]

Stanley and Ruth live on Long Island and have been happily married for 33 years. Ruth, 56, is a rather short – 5ft 3in (1.58m) – thick-set woman who has had a weight problem for about 15 years. As a young woman she was described by her friends as 'petite' and was often complimented on her slender figure. Her weight problem bothered her a few years ago, but she gradually became resigned to the fact that she was overweight and probably always would be. As a wife, mother, and grandmother she enjoyed preparing good food and eating it as well. Since her eldest son and his family lived close by, she kept on hand a steady supply of cookies, cakes, fudge, and brownies for her two grandchildren. She nibbled constantly, tasting the results of her culinary skills.

Stanley had been concerned about Ruth's weight for several years. He had difficulty in understanding her plight since he had always been as skinny as a rail and able to eat anything he wanted. He was convinced that Ruth had no willpower and that the only way she would lose weight was for her to be strictly supervised. He realized that she resented anybody telling her what to do, but he felt he knew what was best for her. After all, she had been on every diet imaginable, but had never stuck to any of them for more than a few days.

In addition to her weight problem, Ruth hadn't been feeling well. She had been having dizzy spells and periodic pains in her chest, and finally went to the doctor. Having completed Ruth's physical examination, the doctor asked to speak to Ruth and Stanley together. He told them that Ruth had very high blood pressure,

and with her weight and family history of heart problems, she was a prime target for a stroke or heart attack. He impressed upon them the absolute necessity of Ruth's losing weight and keeping the weight off. He spoke sharply, deliberately frightening both of them to ensure that they took him seriously.

As a result of the doctor's warning Ruth was determined to lose weight. Although he didn't mention it, Stanley was just as determined to take charge of Ruth's weight-reduction programme. Soon after Ruth began her diet, Stanley started to examine her plate at each meal and calculated the exact number of calories. He kept a running account of his figures in a notebook. At the end of each day he lectured Ruth on what he considered to be the 'mistakes' she was making on the diet. 'The way I figured it,' he would say, 'you were a hundred calories over your limit today.' At first this amused Ruth. At least, she was amused until Stanley began to intensify his supervision. He brought home diet books for her to read. He cut articles on dieting out of newspapers and magazines to give to her. He began planning their menus and accompanying her to the supermarket to make sure she bought only what was on the list. He would not allow her to bake any more cakes and pies.

Ruth found herself getting more and more irritated with Stanley's help. She had begun the diet with a great deal of enthusiasm, but eventually felt as if she were being treated like a two-year-old. She resented Stanley's interference and began eating out of spite. She ate secretly when he was out. She would sneak cookies into the house and hide them away until an opportune moment when Stanley wasn't around. Her motivation to lose weight was completely shattered. The more she ate the stronger her appetite became. Of course she was concerned about her health, but the threat of a heart attack seemed remote. 'It won't happen to me,' she thought.

An incident at a local restaurant convinced Ruth that she couldn't go on in this way. She and Stanley were out with close friends, celebrating Stanley's birthday. Ruth was giving her order to the waitress, trying to be careful about calories, when Stanley loudly interrupted her, saying: 'No, no, Ruth, that's all wrong. Miss, I'd better order for my wife. She'll just have a salad with no dressing and broiled fish with no butter.' Stanley then turned to their friends and said, 'Ruth has absolutely no willpower. I have to treat her like a child when it comes to food.' Everyone had a good laugh except Ruth. She was so embarrassed and hurt that she didn't know whether to burst into tears or throw something at Stanley.

That evening after Stanley went to bed she had a long talk with herself. She knew she *had* to lose weight but Stanley was driving her crazy! She decided to settle the matter once and for all.

Early the next morning at breakfast Ruth pointed out to Stanley what he was doing to her.

Ruth: 'Stan, I've got to talk to you about my diet.'

Stanley: 'Good. I've been meaning to talk to you about the way you were ordering at the restaurant last night, I—'

Ruth: 'Now, wait a minute, Stan! That's just what the problem is. I am *not* a baby. I do *not* need you to order for me. Look, honey, I know you're trying to help me, but your constant supervision of my diet is backfiring. I resent it. In fact, I sneak foods just to spite you.'

Stanley: 'You *what*?'

Ruth: 'Now, let me finish! You are *embarrassing* me and making me feel like a child. I realize that I haven't had control over my eating in the past. But this time, if you'll help me, I can do it. Maybe I should say "if you *don't* help me". Stan, you're just too much involved.'

Stanley: 'Ruth, I'm just trying to help.'

Ruth: 'I know that. But you're *not* helping. The more you supervise me, the more I eat. It's not working.'

Stanley: 'Well, what do you want me to do?'

Ruth: 'I *must* be in charge of my own diet. I do think it would help me to weigh in at the doctor's office once a week. I need to report to *somebody*. I think that'll help me. I would rather that you weren't involved, Stan. Just encourage me and praise me when I'm doing well, but ignore anything else.

Even if I happen to eat a little bit too much of something. When you mention it, I just eat more. Let's take last night, for example. Your remarks were uncalled for. Will you promise to help me?'

Stanley: 'Okay, we can try it your way. I guess I didn't realize what I was doing to you.'

Ruth: 'Now, Stan, let's make sure we understand each other. Let's lay down some ground rules. First, no counting my calories. Second, no more articles or books on dieting. Third, *I'll* plan my meals, *not you*. Fourth, no ordering for me when we're out. Fifth, no comments about my diet to anybody else. If I want to discuss my diet, *I'll* bring it up, not you. Of course an encouraging remark from you once in a while would be really helpful. Make *positive* comments, not negative ones. Tell me how well I'm doing or how much thinner my face looks. Is it a deal?'

Stanley: 'Sure, it's a deal. I was just worried about you. I'll do whatever you say as long as it helps you lose weight.'

Conclusions

Learning to deal more effectively with others is an important element of habit control. Assertiveness – the appropriate expression of personal rights and feelings – is an essential social skill. It is especially useful in contending with social pressure from others who sometimes, inadvertently, establish a circumstance in which relapse is more likely.[5]

Friends and family members can play a critical role in habit control through their comments and actions. Such influences, both positive and negative, can be extremely subtle. To ensure success, friends and family must recognize exactly how they influence the habit controller. In addition, they must avoid sarcastic, critical and negative comments and focus on positively reinforcing habit changes. They must be actively involved in changing their own behaviour and in helping the addict cope with temptations.

8
TOBACCO
the well-cured killer

The use of tobacco has a long history throughout the world. Apparently, tobacco was common in America long before it was available in Europe. In 1613 John Rolfe sent the first shipment of Virginia tobacco from America to England. Rolfe later married the Indian princess, Pocahontas.

Over the years attitudes regarding the use of tobacco have been mixed. Sir Walter Raleigh enjoyed it and popularized pipe smoking in England. King James I disliked the odour of what he called 'sot-weed' and forbade its use. Unfortunately, his edict had little impact. The 17th-century Chinese took a deadly serious approach to the problem by decapitating anyone caught smoking! Cigarette smoking actually did not become universally popular until the mid-19th century when French and British soldiers adopted the habit from Turkish officers during the Crimean War.

Smoking has been a popular pastime ever since. In 1968 about 69 per cent of men and 43 per cent of women in the United Kingdom smoked. While cigarette smoking is a declining habit in the United States, there are still more than 50 million smokers out of a total population of 216 million. Over the past several years there has been a gradual decline in smoking in all population groups, with the exception of young women.

Effects on health

In the early 1960s scientists began to discover how detrimental are the effects of smoking on health. In the United States alone it has been estimated that cigarette smoking is responsible for 325,000 deaths per year from cancer and diseases of the heart, lungs and circulatory system. Approximately 90 per cent of lung cancer cases are related to smoking. In fact, the risk of developing lung cancer is ten times greater for cigarette smokers than for non-smokers. Now that the habit of smoking has increased considerably among women, the number of women who die of lung cancer has risen by 400 per cent over the past 30 years. Cigarette smoking has also been linked to coronary heart disease, stroke, chronic bronchitis, and emphysema, a chronic

Craftt Tugend und würckung deß hochnutzbarlichen Tabacs, durch: A.B.C. gezogen feingröblich

Der best Tabac der ist hie feil,
Kompt her bey kauff ieder ein theil.

Ich brauch Tabac, und befindts gut,
Truck net die fluß, reinigt das blut

Kam ich gleich hab Bier oder Wein
Muß Tabac doch getruncken sein.

Man sagt zu viel sey ungesundt.
Das merck ich iezt zu dieser stundt.

Mein Naß die ist verstopffet sehr
Brauch Schnupff Tabac daß ich sie leer.

Der Schnupff Tabac purgiret gut,
Verseiht wann was entfahren thut.

Außbündige Alamodo Bauchpurgation Causirt Durchlauff Effectuirt Fartzen Groltzen Husten Juchzen Kotzen Lufft in hosen, Murmeln im leibe Nissen, Operirt Qualificirt Rotz, Schnupffen Speyen Tabac Vertreibt Wütigkeit Xantho Yn Zahnen.

Of coughs and coffins: today's dire warnings (right) contrast sharply with previous praise for the curative properties of tobacco (above).

lung disease causing difficulty in breathing. While cigar and pipe smokers who do not inhale are less at risk from lung cancer than cigarette smokers, their risk of developing cancer of the oesophagus, larynx, or mouth is just as great.

What is it about tobacco that makes it so harmful? Actually tobacco contains several types of particles and gases that are hazardous to health. Nicotine, for example, acts as a stimulant which raises blood pressure and heart rate, causing the heart to work harder, and in large doses it is poisonous. Small particles of tar have been identified as the major cancer-causing agents in cigarette smoke.

Although most smokers are unaware of it, carbon monoxide, a poisonous gas, is found in 1 to 5 per cent of cigarette smoke. Carbon monoxide robs the blood system of oxygen and has been implicated in damage to the foetus among pregnant women who are smokers. It also damages circulation and leads to the development of cholesterol deposits on the walls of the arteries. Narrowed or clogged arteries pave the way for

More people die of primary lung cancer each year. Vivid section of cancerous lung showing tumours (top). Smoking is adopted as a sign of adulthood (middle) and for women as a sign of liberation (above left). The social rituals of smoking are the hardest to give up (above right).

severe medical emergencies such as heart attacks and strokes. Smoke also contains hydrogen cyanide and nitrogen oxide which are toxic to the lining of the bronchial tubes and lungs and are believed to be associated with chronic lung disease and emphysema.

Why do people smoke?

If cigarettes are so dangerous, why do people smoke? The reasons for taking that very first cigarette are often quite different from those involved in the maintenance of the habit. Smoking generally begins in adolescence, between the ages of 12 and 21 years. Most people smoke their first cigarette simply out of curiosity. Peer pressure and a desire to impress others is often involved. Teenagers want to appear 'grown up' by emulating the habits of adults. Young women, for example, may consider cigarettes to be an important element of their self-image. Cigarette manufacturers reinforce this notion through such advertisement slogans as 'You've come a long way, baby', implying that smoking demonstrates an aspect of liberation for women.

Psychological reasons for smoking

As smoking continues, it quickly becomes a strong habit and other factors come into play. The many elements involved in the conditioning of the smoking habit have been described by Drs Ikard, Green, and Horn in the *International Journal of the Addictions*.[1] In fact, these reasons for smoking have been incorporated into a *Why Do You Smoke?* test provided to smokers by the American Cancer Society and the American Lung Association.

The first of these reasons involves a sense of increased stimulation or energy. Such stimulation is a natural result of nicotine in the body. Many smokers report a physical and emotional boost from smoking especially when they are bored or restless. A cigarette and a cup of coffee (both of which stimulate the central nervous system) provide a sense of 'recharging the batteries' after a couple of hours of monotonous work.

Another reason for smoking involves the satisfaction of handling or manipulating cigarettes. Smokers seem to derive much pleasure from the ritual of their habit. The process of taking a cigarette out of its pack, handling it, lighting it, and taking the first long puff becomes very satisfying. Each smoker seems to have an automatic, individualized ritual that is repeated over and over again.

Some smokers report that they gain a strong feeling of relaxation or reduced tension from smoking. It is interesting that smoking can have either a calming or stimulating effect depending on the emotional state and situation of the smoker. Many smokers, however, regard cigarettes as tranquillizers in times of stress. Dr Miller treated a patient, George, who successfully quit smoking for five years. One day his son was involved in a serious, but not fatal, automobile accident. Without thinking, George bought a pack of cigarettes, opened it hurriedly and lit one, taking several puffs. He described the incident as follows:

> I was completely unaware of what I was doing. I felt so tense and upset; all I could think about was the relief and temporary relaxation I'd have. It's as if I were in a daze. I actually forgot or suppressed the fact that I am now a non-smoker.

In this case, the past associations between relaxation and smoking were so great that they manifested themselves five years later. Fortunately, George obtained no pleasure from the few puffs and successfully avoided further smoking.

Many heavy smokers experience strong physical cravings for cigarettes. They are actually 'hooked' or addicted to smoking in two ways. First, there is the psychological dependence on cigarettes. Cigarettes are used in coping with life from day to day. The thought of going for even a few hours without smoking is terrifying to a heavy smoker. The second factor is a real, physical addiction to nicotine. Attempts to give up, or even cut down, are accompanied by physical withdrawal symptoms similar to those experienced by drug addicts. The significance of nicotine addiction will be discussed later in more detail.

Finally, smoking is a strong habit that can occur automatically, without involving much conscious decision. A two packets a day smoker puffs on a cigarette at least 300 times during the day, or over 100,000 times per year. The following sequence of events was reported by Eileen, a 52-year-old school teacher who had been smok-

Why teenage girls begin to smoke

If smoking is so harmful why do people start in the first place? Smoking is certainly not initially pleasurable. A person's very first cigarette is an unpleasant and often painful experience.

Because of the rapid increases in smoking among teenage girls, surveys have focused on their reasons for taking up this habit. Comments from 12- to 18-year-old girls who were asked, 'Why did you smoke your first cigarette?' shed light on this subject.

Valerie (age, 15 years)
'All of my friends smoke. I felt like an oddball. I was spending the night with my best friend, Betty, and she encouraged me to try one. I choked at first but liked the way I looked with a cigarette. I remember standing in front of the mirror posing with the cigarette. I felt more a part of my group.'

Judy (age, 16 years)
'I just wanted to try it out. I wanted to see what smoking was all about. I'm just like that, anyway. I

like to try new things. I believe in having fun *now* and forgetting about the future.'

Jackie (age, 13 years)
'Believe it or not, I think I started smoking just because my parents told me not to. I don't like people telling me what to do. Even the government thinks they can regulate our lives.'

Paula (age, 14 years)
'I tried it on a dare. The first one was terrible but then I started to enjoy smoking. There's nothing wrong with it, anyway. Everything you do these days seems to give you cancer. I don't believe all those health warnings. Besides, I'm young. Those things won't happen to me.'

Just as these remarks indicate, most teenage girls begin smoking at the encouragement of friends. Girls who smoke also tend to be outgoing, rebellious, and strongly influenced by peer pressure and are little influenced by the consequences of their behaviour.

Here are some statements made by people to describe what they get out of smoking cigarettes. How often do you feel this way when smoking? Circle one number for each statement. Important: ANSWER EVERY QUESTION.

		always	frequently	occasionally	seldom	never
A.	I smoke cigarettes in order to keep myself from slowing down.	5	4	3	2	1
B.	Handling a cigarette is part of the enjoyment of smoking it.	5	4	3	2	1
C.	Smoking cigarettes is pleasant and relaxing.	5	4	3	2	1
D.	I light up a cigarette when I feel angry about something.	5	4	3	2	1
E.	When I have run out of cigarettes I find it almost unbearable until I can get them.	5	4	3	2	1
F.	I smoke cigarettes automatically without even being aware of it.	5	4	3	2	1
G.	I smoke cigarettes to stimulate me, to perk myself up.	5	4	3	2	1
H.	Part of the enjoyment of smoking a cigarette comes from the steps I take to light up.	5	4	3	2	1
I.	I find cigarettes pleasurable.	5	4	3	2	1
J.	When I feel uncomfortable or upset about something, I light up a cigarette.	5	4	3	2	1
K.	I am very much aware of the fact when I am not smoking a cigarette.	5	4	3	2	1
L.	I light up a cigarette without realizing I still have one burning in the ashtray.	5	4	3	2	1
M.	I smoke cigarettes to give me a 'lift'.	5	4	3	2	1
N.	When I smoke a cigarette, part of the enjoyment is watching the smoke as I exhale it.	5	4	3	2	1
O.	I want a cigarette most when I am comfortable and relaxed.	5	4	3	2	1
P.	When I feel 'blue' or want to take my mind off cares and worries, I smoke cigarettes.	5	4	3	2	1
Q.	I get a real gnawing hunger for a cigarette when I haven't smoked for a while.	5	4	3	2	1
R.	I've found a cigarette in my mouth and didn't remember putting it there.	5	4	3	2	1

1. Enter the number you have circled for each question in the spaces below, putting the number you have circled to question A over line A, to question B over line B, etc.

2. Add the 3 scores on each line to get your totals. For example, the sum of your scores over lines A, G, and M gives you your score on Stimulation – lines B, H, and N give the score on Handling, etc.

Totals

A ____	+ G ____	+ M ____	=	____	Stimulation
B ____	+ H ____	+ N ____	=	____	Handling
C ____	+ I ____	+ O ____	=	____	Pleasurable Relaxation
D ____	+ J ____	+ P ____	=	____	Crutch: Tension Reduction
E ____	+ K ____	+ Q ____	=	____	Craving: Psychological Addiction
F ____	+ L ____	+ R ____	=	____	Habit

Scores can vary from 3 to 15. Any score 11 and above is high; any score 7 and below is low.

ing more than forty cigarettes per day for 30 years. In describing a typical day in her life, Eileen reported that on Monday she woke up at her usual hour of 6:30 am. She immediately reached for her first cigarette. No conscious decision was involved – her behaviour was simply a reflex action. Then she got out of bed, went to the kitchen and prepared a cup of coffee. As soon as she poured the coffee, it was time for another cigarette. Eileen cannot remember a time when she ever drank coffee without a cigarette. This association was so strong that the mere sight or smell of coffee would trigger a physical craving for a cigarette. The same was true of talking on the telephone, an activity which also triggered the desire to smoke.

The strength of her smoking habit was demonstrated on that Monday by the following episode. She was talking to another teacher during a break in her schedule at school. She lit a cigarette, took a few puffs and then rested it on an ashtray so that she could find some papers in her purse. After a minute she again became involved in her conversation and took out a second cigarette, lit it and inhaled deeply. Only after several puffs did she glance down at the table and notice what she had done. The habit of lighting up was so automatic that she had completely forgotten that she had done so only a minute earlier.

Most people smoke for a combination of reasons. However, some people are likely to smoke specifically to relax and reduce tension while others smoke almost entirely out of habit. Recognition of the major reasons for smoking is necessary in order to determine the most appropriate plan of action which will overcome this habit successfully. The smoker using cigarettes to ease tension must learn more appropriate methods of stress management such as relaxation, meditation or exercise. The habitual smoker would be successful in giving up after fully analysing the circumstances (coffee breaks, for example) which are strongly associated with smoking and trigger the cravings. In this way it is possible to find out how to rearrange the environment or circumstances which underline the habit (e.g., reduce coffee drinking for a few weeks by substituting water or soft drinks) to foster the conditioning of new associations.

Smoking advertisements ironically associate smoking with rugged good health and the freedom of the open country . . . (top). Breathing in other people's tobacco smoke can also be dangerous to health (above).

The tolerance questionnaire

1. How many cigarettes a day do you smoke?
   0–15   16–25   26 +
2. What is the nicotine yield per cigarette of your usual brand? (For a list of brands and their yields see page 107.)

   | 0.3–0.8gm | 0.9–1.5gm | 1.6–2.2gm |
   | (Low to medium) | (Medium) | (Medium to high) |

3. Do you inhale?
   Never   Sometimes   Always
4. Do you smoke more during the morning than during the rest of the day?
   No   Yes
5. How soon after you wake up do you smoke your first cigarette?
   More than 30 min   Less than 30 min
6. Of all the cigarettes you smoke during the day, which would you most hate to give up?
7. Do you find it difficult to refrain from smoking in places where it is forbidden, *e.g.* in church, at the library, in a no-smoking cinema?
   No   Yes
8. Do you smoke even if you are so ill that you are in bed most of the day?
   No   Yes

Scoring the tolerance questionnaire

Add up your scores as follows:
1. 0–15, *0*; 16–25, *1*; 25+, *2*
2. Low to medium, *0*; Medium, *1*; Medium to high, *2*
3. Never, *0*; sometimes, *1*; always, *2*
4. No, *0*; Yes, *1*
5. Less than 30 minutes, *1*; more than 30 minutes, *0*
6. Score one point if you answered 'The first cigarette of the day'. All others, *0*
7. Yes, *1*; no, *0*
8. Yes, *1*; no, *0*

This questionnaire measures the degree of physical dependence on the nicotine in cigarettes; 0–3, light dependence; 4–7, medium dependence; 8–11, heavy dependence

Use this questionnaire in your selfwatching plan of action to stop smoking. Every point you can knock off your score is a positive step forward. For example, by keeping your cigarette consumption under 26 per day, your score goes down one point. By switching from a brand with a high nicotine content to one with a medium nicotine yield, you can dock another point, and so on. Moreover, regular self-testing with this tolerance questionnaire provides a measure of progress in your stop-smoking programme – a steady fall in your score will boost your morale, while if you find the score creeping up, you can focus on a particular objective to bring it back step by step to your previous best performance.

Addiction to nicotine

More and more evidence has been found regarding the addictive properties of nicotine. When a cigarette is smoked, nicotine is carried to the brain very quickly, within seven seconds approximately. It is similar to injecting a drug. Smokers show all the typical characteristics of drug addiction. They tend to regulate their dosage of nicotine automatically by smoking more when nicotine levels are decreasing and less when they are stable or increasing. Heavy smokers often experience severe withdrawal symptoms when giving up or cutting down drastically. These symptoms range from mild agitation, moodiness, and decreases in blood pressure to marked hostility, irritability, disorientation and an inability to concentrate.

Recently, Dr Karl-Olov Fagerstrom, of the Ulleraker Hospital in Uppsala, Sweden, devised a test to measure the strength of physical dependence on nicotine.[2] This *Tolerance Questionnaire* is presented on the left. Essentially, the test consists of eight items including questions on the quantity of cigarettes consumed, brand smoked, tendency to inhale, and early morning smoking under particular circumstances. Scores from this test are correlated with physiological indicators of addiction. The degree of physical dependence as measured by the Tolerance Questionnaire is positively correlated with decreases in body temperature during withdrawal from cigarettes (one of the physical reactions to nicotine withdrawal) and smaller increases in heart rate after smoking a cigarette (an indication of acquired tolerance to a drug). The questionnaire is useful because when the addiction to cigarettes can be measured, it is possible to monitor progress in a programme to stop smoking and to tailor treatment to allow for individual differences.

Addiction vs. psychological needs

Of all the reasons for smoking, which is most important – physical addiction to nicotine or satisfaction of psychological needs such as relief from tension?

In 1977 Dr Stanley Schachter and his colleagues at Columbia University published a series of studies on the interaction between psychological and pharmacological determinants of smoking.[3] In their initial studies these investigators found proof that heavy smokers regulate smoking rate to keep nicotine at a constant level.

They also found that the proportion of smoked nicotine that stays in the body, as against that eliminated in the urine, is directly related to the acidity of the urine. The more acid in the urine, the greater the excretion of nicotine. Based on this evidence Schachter's research team manipulated urinary pH – the balance of alkali and acid – by giving smokers either acidifying or alkalizing substances to ingest. The subjects smoked significantly more when the urine was acidified, since presumably they were excreting nicotine at a faster rate and trying to compensate by smoking more.

Dr Schachter then wondered whether this urinary pH-excretion phenomenon might be a prime biochemical trigger of excessive smoking. To examine this possibility he chose to study the relationship between stress and smoking. Presumably, people often smoke more under stress in an attempt to alleviate anxiety. Dr Schachter was interested in the possibility that this influence may be physiological rather than psychological.

Thirty-eight smokers were recruited to participate in the study. When they arrived for the experiment half of them were given capsules containing corn starch and the other half provided with capsules containing 3gm of sodium bicarbonate. However, neither the subjects nor the experimenter knew, at that moment, which capsule was being administered to which subject. Bicarbonate of soda tends to raise urinary pH, making the urine more alkaline and less acidic. Corn starch has no effect and was simply given as a placebo. Urinary pH levels were tested to make certain that the sodium bicarbonate was working.

Subjects were then exposed to one of two stressful conditions. In the Low Stress Condition subjects were told that, as part of an experiment on skin sensitivity, they would be asked to experience weak, non-painful electric current applied to their fingers. In the High Stress Condition subjects were asked to experience extremely painful electric shocks. As was expected, the High Stress Condition resulted in significantly more tension and anxiety than the

Low Stress Condition. After the stressful conditions were over, each subject was provided with 12 cigarettes and allowed to smoke. The researchers noted the number of cigarettes smoked by each subject and the number of puffs per cigarette.

The results of the experiment showed an intriguing contrast between the smoking patterns of the two groups. Taking the group which had received the placebo capsule first, we can compare the High Stress and Low Stress subjects. It became clear that the High Stress subjects not only smoked more cigarettes (an average of 2.33 per person as compared to 1.58) but also took about twice as many puffs (23.67 as compared to 11.33) as the subjects who received the minor stress.

However, when urinary pH was made more alkaline (via the bicarbonate of soda capsules), the stress conditions had absolutely no influence on smoking. After taking the sodium bicarbonate, subjects in both the High and Low Stress Conditions smoked just about the same amount. In fact, Low Stress subjects actually took more puffs. Thus, stress affects smoking *only* when urinary pH is more alkaline than acidic.

Another step in Dr Schachter's research occurred when he discovered that urinary acidity has a natural circadian rhythm over a 24-hour period. Urine is acidic in the early morning and becomes more alkaline over the next three to four hours. This indicates that nicotine levels are not only lower in the early morning but also that nicotine is being eliminated more rapidly during this time. Taking this into account, he hypothesized that (1) smokers will smoke more in the morning than at other times in the day and (2) since the nicotine level is low and pH is acidic, the addicted smoker will smoke until he achieves a higher nicotine level in the morning regardless of other factors such as stress. In other words, in the morning, nicotine and pH levels take precedence over any other factors in determining smoking rate.

To put these ideas to the test Dr Schachter ran his original study once again, only this time some subjects were tested in the early morning and some in the afternoon. He found exactly what he had predicted. Morning subjects smoked about 20 per cent more than afternoon subjects. In addition, the High Stress Condition increased the smoking of the afternoon subjects but had no effect on the morning subjects' smoking.

All of this simply indicates that the desire for a cigarette may be caused by a combination of pharmacological and psychological factors with the pharmacological or 'addictive' factors being more important at certain times of the day or when certain biochemical conditions are present.

Deciding to give up

The vast majority of smokers, over 90 per cent, express a desire to give up smoking. Most current smokers have tried at least once and failed. The reasons for deciding to give up are highly personal and not well understood. Some people struggle with the idea for weeks, months or even years. Others seem to make the decision on the spur of the moment. Professor Alan Marlatt of the University of Washington describes one of these sudden decisions which resulted in a very favourable outcome.[4] He reports the case of a 42-year-old radio announcer who stopped smoking overnight. The man was lying in bed one night feeling very pessimistic about his many previous unsuccessful attempts to quit smoking. He felt very helpless and depressed about his inability to change this behaviour. He suddenly realized that he was hopelessly addicted to tobacco, that his addicton was as overwhelming as being addicted to opiates. In the midst of these helpless feelings he began to pray, to ask God for help. After the prayer he felt a great sense of relief. The next morning he awoke free of urges to smoke and has not had a cigarette in three years. Unfortunately such instantaneous 'cures' are rare and most people must struggle over their resolve to give up the habit.

Concerns over health and the medical complications caused by smoking play a very important role in decisions to give up the habit. In this regard physicians can have a considerable impact on their patients' smoking. About 25 per cent of smokers decide to stop smoking solely on account of advice from a doctor. An even higher percentage, 62 per cent, of heart attack victims decide to stop if the physician advises it. Physicians are also beginning to provide better examples to patients. A recent survey of doctors in the United States revealed that only 21 per cent now smoke with 64 per cent having given up over the past few years. Unfortunately, physicians seem to be unaware of their potential influences on patients' habits since most smokers report that they have never been advised by their doctors to stop.

One might ask why only 25 per cent of smokers heed health warnings. Drs J. Richard Eiser, Stephen Sutton, and Mallory Wober of the Institute of Psychiatry in London indicate that the reason may lie in the smoker's basic attitudes towards health.[5] In a survey of 378 people they found that smokers tend to hold less firm beliefs about the damaging consequences of smoking than non-smokers. The vast majority, 89 per cent, of non-smokers believed smoking to be 'really as dangerous as people say' while only 49 per cent of smokers believed in the danger. Smokers and non-smokers were also asked to indicate which of the following two statements was most similar to their own beliefs:

1. If people want to do things which can cause sickness or injury to themselves, they have every right to do so.
2. People have a moral responsibility to avoid doing things which cause sickness or injury to themselves.

Nearly 60 per cent of smokers chose the first statement; arguing that they had every right to put their own health at risk. In fact, even those smokers who felt that smoking is dangerous continued to smoke because of this wider belief in their individual rights. It is interesting to note that smokers are also much less likely than non-smokers to use seat belts while driving.[6] They believe that seat belt use does not make driving safer and even if it did, they still have the right to risk their own health in an automobile accident.

Concern regarding health is certainly not the only reason why people decide to stop smoking. SmokEnders, a commercial programme in the USA designed to help people give up smoking, reports that the major reason for giving up expressed by their members is 'mastery over my own life'. These people feel unhappy about being completely controlled by cigarettes. Secondary reasons included 'disease prevention' and 'setting an example for my children'.

Certainly, children are more likely to smoke if

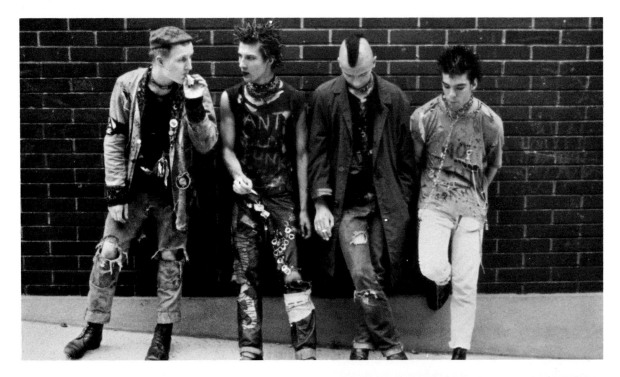

their parents are smokers. In fact, a teenager who has both a parent and an older brother or sister who smoke is four times as likely to take up smoking than a teenager from a non-smoking family. In addition, inhalation of cigarette smoke can be especially harmful to young children and to adults with heart disease or asthma. The cigarette smoke that enters the air around a smoker is much more dangerous than the smoke he inhales. This sidestream smoke is generated by the cigarette while it smoulders, between puffs. It contains greater concentrations of nicotine and carbon monoxide than does exhaled smoke. This is related to the temperature of tobacco combustion when the cigarette is smouldering. Young children growing up with parents who smoke are much more vulnerable to respiratory infections.

Dr Wilbert Aronow, of the Long Beach Veterans Administration Hospital in California, has found that cigarette smoke in the environment can be especially detrimental to men with a history of coronary heart disease. He studied 10 such patients before and after they had been sitting in a room with smokers. After exposure to cigarette smoke the patients experienced notable increases in heart rate and blood pressure. They

Smokers jealously guard their individual rights to smoke: smoking can be part of a confident and respectable image (above) or alternatively signify a socially non-conformist stance (top).

could exercise only about half as long as before the exposure and experienced chest pains after only 2½ minutes of walking on a treadmill.

Stopping smoking

Several issues are involved in giving up cigarettes once the initial decision has been made. How can motivation be sustained over a period of time? Is it better to stop abruptly or gradually? What can be done about cravings to smoke?

Motivation

People who begin any new plan to change their habits radically are usually highly motivated and very enthusiastic during the first few hours or days. When difficulties are encountered or the urge to smoke becomes especially strong, motivation tends to wane. The smoker begins to wonder about the decision to give up, and the reasons for that decision. The 'addicted self' begins to debate with the 'rational self'. 'Is the agony necessary? Why deny the pleasure of smoking? Will just one cigarette make any difference?' There are several effective techniques which can be used to combat flagging motivation.

Public statements about the plan to stop smoking are important. The smoker should tell every family member, friend, and business associate exactly when he or she will have the last cigarette. This places social pressure on the smoker to keep to the plan. Then, if smoking is resumed *after* the final date, the 'ex' smoker has to face not only a sense of personal failure, but also the disapproval of others. Simply realizing this fact helps many people to avoid the temptation.

Bets or a method of imposing fines on oneself can be helpful in ensuring continued motivation. A financial agreement that has been found to be very successful is illustrated by the case of two friends, Hans and Frederick. Hans, a 30-year-old computer programmer, is married with two young children. He had smoked between one and two packets of cigarettes every day from 22 years of age. He had been very athletic, playing soccer and running during his school years. On his thirtieth birthday he decided to get into better shape. One of the first bad habits that had to go was smoking. He was determined to stop not only for his own health and fitness but also so he

Cigarette smoke has three poisonous ingredients – tar, nicotine and carbon monoxide – which effect the health of all who inhale it. Militant campaigns have been launched to stop youngsters from ever lighting up (top) and Punch was stressing the dangers of smoking way back in 1869 (above).

would be a better example for his young daughter.

Frederick is a 39-year-old department store manager who tends to be rather tense and hard-working, an individual oriented to achievement. He began smoking cigarettes at 15 and chain smoked two to three packets per day. His employees rarely saw him without a cigarette in his mouth. After he had suffered from mild but persistent chest pains, his doctor strongly admonished him about his smoking habit. The physician was concerned because Frederick had high blood pressure and a history of early death from heart attacks in his family. Frederick became frightened enough about his prospects to decide to give up smoking.

In fact, Hans and Frederick decided to stop smoking on the very same day and agreed to help one another. They realized that they both needed something that would keep up their willpower when withdrawal symptoms began. Luckily, they had two characteristics in common. Both were thrifty individuals, always careful to use money wisely. In addition, both had very strong political views and were quite active in a local conservative political party. They used these similarities to their advantage. They both wrote 10 personal cheques for $20 each. All the cheques were made out to the local branch of an extremely liberal political party which they both vehemently opposed. Attached to each cheque was a written and signed note which read, 'Your party is doing excellent work. Please add my name to your mailing list. I am enclosing a contribution of $20.' Each cheque was sealed in a stamped envelope and addressed. Hans was given Frederick's cheques to take care of and vice versa. The plan was simple. For each day one of them did not smoke, the other would tear up and destroy one envelope with the cheque inside. However, for each day on which one of them lapsed back into the habit, an envelope would be dropped into the postbox and the contribution sent off. Both men arranged for any family member, friend or co-worker who saw them smoking at any time to report the incident to their partner in this contract.

During the first three days Hans and Frederick had strong cravings. Both admitted to coming very close to lighting up a cigarette. They felt

determined, however, not to disgrace themselves by losing money, especially to their least favourite political organization. Hans expressed it this way – 'I knew that the die was cast. I was trapped by my own arrangement and there was nothing I could do about it.' After both men had successfully abstained for 10 days all the envelopes had been destroyed. Both felt they were over the worst of it and could continue without the financial system, but they admitted afterwards that if it had not been for this rather strong motivation they might have given in to their cravings on the first or second day. In fact, they agreed that should either one start smoking again they would reinstitute the contract.

Another motivation procedure used in self-help groups serves to dramatize and sharpen the emotions associated with personal health implications of smoking. Smokers are asked to read scripts and improvise the roles of patients with an illness, such as emphysema or heart disease, associated with smoking. One smoker might play the part of the doctor breaking the news that cancer has been diagnosed. Another person then responds as if he were actually receiving this dire information. Participants in the role playing are encouraged to become emotionally involved in their parts. This procedure often helps smokers to identify emotionally with their reasons for giving up cigarettes, rather than simply thinking about them in an intellectual way. Periodic role playing over the first two weeks of a stop-smoking programme can help to keep motivation high.

'Cold Turkey' versus gradual withdrawal
The question of whether it is better to stop smoking all at once or to give up gradually has been debated for years. Ex-smokers are usually strong advocates of whichever method was successful for them. Dr Judith Flaxman of the University of North Carolina put this question to the test in 1974.[6] Smokers participating in a non-smoking clinic were assigned to one of three groups each with a different procedure. Group 1 was advised to stop completely on the first day of the treatment programme. Group 2 was instructed to gradually taper off until they felt they could give up smoking completely. Smokers in Group 3 were allowed to smoke during the two weeks of

treatment, but were set a definite target date – the final day of the programme – for stopping altogether.

The most successful procedure was the target date technique used with Group 3. It can be argued that these smokers learned to use and practise the self-management techniques taught in the treatment since they were still dealing with their smoking habit from day to day. Smokers in the 'cold turkey' group had no experience in observing, analysing, and then controlling the factors influencing their smoking behaviour because they had already stopped before learning these methods. They would, therefore, have less understanding of their habit and be less likely to overcome future temptations or cope with temporary lapses of willpower. Smokers who taper off without a target date often reduce smoking to about 5 or 10 cigarettes per day but never quite get past that level. Smokers who reduce smoking but fail to eliminate it altogether are much more likely to relapse.

Most experts on smoking now combine a gradual fading technique, usually over 5, 7, or 10 days, with a target date to stop altogether. This procedure has the advantage of minimizing withdrawal symptoms. Gradual fading is accomplished in one of several ways. Smokers can change brands every day or two, switching each time to a brand that is lower in tar and nicotine content. If the cigarettes smoked are already low in nicotine, the total number smoked can be reduced by 10 to 20 per cent each day until all smoking is finally eliminated. One potential problem with this technique is the fact that, as smoking is reduced, some people unwittingly begin to take more puffs on the cigarette, or to inhale more deeply to compensate for nicotine reductions. Even though they are only smoking half as many cigarettes, this change in smoking style sabotages the fading procedure. Smokers must be made acutely aware of *how* they smoke to ensure that the amount of smoke inhaled remains constant as the number of cigarettes are decreased.

Fading can also be accomplished by gradually eliminating cigarettes smoked under certain circumstances. The first cigarettes to be given up are those that are relatively easy to do without. For example, during Day 2 of the plan the smoker

may eliminate all smoking in automobiles. 'Essential' cigarettes, such as those with the morning coffee, are eliminated only in the final day or two of the fading strategy.

Alternatives to tobacco

In addition to fading, nicotine substitutes are also used to help smokers withdraw gradually. Nicotine chewing gum, developed in Sweden, provides a temporary substitute for tobacco when cravings are experienced. Several studies in England indicate that this reduces tobacco consumption more efficiently than a placebo gum not containing nicotine.

Drs Pekka Puska, Stig Bjorkquist, and Kaj Koskela of the University of Kuopio in Finland recently put this technique to an experimental test.[7] The subjects in their study were 160 people enrolled in a stop-smoking course. Half of the participants were provided with a supply of nicotine chewing gum, each piece containing 4mg of nicotine. The other half were given a placebo gum that was similar in taste but contained no nicotine. For purposes of experimental control neither the subjects nor the experimenters were initially told which type of gum the subjects were receiving. Participants were instructed to chew a piece of gum whenever they

Older and healthier traditions – today snuff is proposed as a less harmful alternative to cigarette smoking.

felt the urge to smoke. On reaching the end of the three-week course 70 per cent of the nicotine chewing gum group had stopped smoking while only 55 per cent of the placebo gum group were wholly abstinent. However, after six months the differential in the success rate diminished with only about 30 per cent of each group remaining non-smokers. It is apparent that nicotine chewing gum is most helpful in the initial physiological withdrawal phases of giving up.

On April 12, 1981, Britain's *Sunday Times* car-ried an article entitled *Killing a Bad Habit: Snuff That Cigarette Out*. In the article Alastair Mac-Donald, a retired accountant, argued the case for using snuff as an alternative to cigarettes. Snuff is a preparation of pulverized tobacco which may be inhaled through the nostrils, chewed, or placed against the gums. Mr MacDonald prefers . . . 'just a good pinch between the finger and thumb, well sniffed up'. Snuff can be quite enjoyable and is available in a variety of scents and flavours. He notes one personal drawback,

Tar and nicotine yields for common US and UK cigarette brands

Tar Yield mg/cig	Brand	Nicotine Yield mg/cig	Tar Yield mg/cig	Brand	Nicotine Yield mg/cig	Tar Yield mg/cig	Brand	Nicotine Yield mg/cig
	LOW TAR			*Low to Middle Tar continued*			*Middle Tar continued*	
Under 4	Embassy Ultra Mild	Under 0.3	15	Benson & Hedges Sovereign Mild	1.2	18	Piccadilly No. 1 (P)	1.4
Under 4	John Player King Size Ultra Mild	Under 0.3	15	Chesterfield King Size Filter	1.1	18	Player's Medium Navy Cut (P)	1.4
6	Silk Cut Extra Mild	0.7	15	Gauloises Caporal Filter	0.7	18	Rothmans King Size	1.4
8	Embassy Premier King Size	0.6	15	Kensitas Club Mild King Size	1.4	18	Slim Kings	1.4
8	John Player King Size with NSM	0.7	15	Kensitas Corsair Mild	1.1	18	Three Fives Filter Kings	1.5
8	Piccadilly Mild	0.5	15	L & M Filter	1.1	18	Weights Plain (P)	1.2
9	Consulate Menthol	0.6	15	Merit	1.2	18	Winston King Size	1.4
9	Craven A King Size Special Mild	0.7	15	More	1.5	18	Woodbine Plain (P)	1.5
9	Dunhill International Superior Mild	0.8	15	More Menthol	1.5	19	Benson & Hedges Sovereign	1.4
9	Dunhill King Size Superior Mild	0.7	15	Pall Mall Filter	1.4	19	Capstan Medium (P)	1.3
9	Embassy No. 5 Extra Mild	0.7	15	Three Fives Medium Mild King Size	1.3	19	Embassy No. 1 King Size	1.4
9	John Player King Size Extra Mild	0.7	15	Three Castles Filter	1.0	19	Embassy Plain	1.3
9	Lambert & Butler King Size Mild	0.7	16	Cadets	1.2	19	Gallaher's De Luxe Green (P)	1.5
9	Peer Special Extra Mild King Size (with Cytrel)	0.7	16	Camel Filter Tip	1.1	19	Gold Flake (P)	1.3
9	Silk Cut	0.8	16	Carroll's No. 1	1.2	19	John Player King Size	1.5
9	Silk Cut International	0.9	16	Carroll's No. 1 King Size	1.3	19	Kensitas Club	1.5
9	Silk Cut No. 5	0.7	16	Dunhill International	1.4	19	Lambert & Butler International Size	1.5
10	Belair Menthol Kings	0.6	16	Dunhill King Size	1.3	19	Lambert & Butler King Size	1.5
10	Consulate No. 2	0.6	16	Guards	1.1	19	Major Extra Size	1.3
10	Embassy Extra Mild	0.8	16	Kensitas Club Mild	1.3	19	Park Drive Plain (P)	1.5
10	Embassy No. 1 Extra Mild	0.8	16	Marlboro	1.3	19	Park Drive Tipped	1.5
10	Peter Stuyvesant Extra Mild King Size	0.8	16	Phillip Morris International	1.4	19	Player's Filter Virginia	1.4
10	Player's No. 10 with NSM	0.7	16	Piccadilly Filter De Luxe	1.4	19	Player's Gold Leaf	1.5
10	Player's No. 6 Extra Mild	0.7	16	Piccadilly King Size	1.3	19	Player's No. 6 Filter	1.3
10	Silk Cut King Size	0.9	16	Rothmans International	1.5	19	Player's No. 6 King Size	1.6
10	Silk Cut No. 3	0.8				19	Player's No. 6 Plain (P)	1.2
				MIDDLE TAR		19	Player's No. 10	1.3
	LOW TO MIDDLE TAR		17	Craven 'A' Cork Tipped (P)	1.3	19	Regal King Size	1.4
11	Gauloises Longues	0.6	17	Craven 'A' King Size	1.3	19	Senior Service Plain (P)	1.6
12	Gauloises Filter Mild	0.6	17	Kent De Luxe Length	1.2	19	Sterling	1.6
12	Gitanes International	0.9	17	Lucky Strike King Size Filter	1.4	19	Woodbine Filter	1.3
12	Rothmans King Size Mild	0.9	17	MS Filter	1.3	20	Kensitas Plain (P)	1.6
12	St. Moritz	0.9	17	Rothmans Royals	1.5	20	Nerit	1.5
13	Gitanes Caporal Filter	0.7	17	Silva Thins	1.5	20	Three Fives International	1.7
13	John Player Carlton King Size	1.5	17	Sobranie Virginia International	1.5	20	Three Fives Selected Virginia (P)	1.4
13	John Player Carlton Long Size	1.4	18	Benson & Hedges Gold Bond	1.5	22	Sweet Afton Bank Size Plain (P)	1.9
13	John Player Carlton Premium	1.2	18	Benson & Hedges Gold Bond King Size	1.5			
13	Player's No. 10 Extra Mild	0.8	18	Benson & Hedges King Size	1.6		**MIDDLE TO HIGH TAR**	
14	Black Cat No. 9	1.0	18	Benson & Hedges Supreme	1.7	24	Lucky Strike Plain (P)	1.8
14	Dunhill International Menthol	1.0	18	Du Maurier	1.5	25	Gallaher's De Luxe Blue (P)	2.1
14	Gauloises Disque Bleu	0.6	18	Embassy Envoy	1.2	25	Gauloises Caporal Plain (P)	1.2
14	Kensitas Mild King Size	1.4	18	Embassy Filter	1.4	25	Gitanes Caporal Plain (P)	1.4
14	Kent	1.0	18	Embassy Gold	1.3	26	Capstan Full Strength (P)	2.7
14	Lark Filter Tip	1.1	18	Embassy King Size	1.4	27	Pall Mall King Size (P)	2.2
14	Peer Special Mild King Size (with Cytrel)	1.2	18	Embassy No. 3 Standard Size	1.4			
14	Peter Stuyvesant King Size	1.2	18	Embassy Regal	1.4	New Brands introduced during Nov. 79 to Apr. 80 not yet analysed by the Government Chemist for a period of 6 months.		
14	Piccadilly No. 7	1.1	18	Emperor King Size	1.4			
			18	Fribourg & Treyer No. 1 Filter De Luxe	1.5	14	Du Maurier King Size	1.2
			18	Imperial International	1.6	15	Benson & Hedges Sovereign King Size	1.3
			18	John Player Special	1.5	18	Benson & Hedges Academy	1.8
			18	Kensitas Club King Size	1.5	19	John Player Special King Size	1.4
			18	Kensitas Corsair	1.3			
			18	Kensitas Tipped King Size	1.5			

Becoming aware of when, where and why we smoke is essential to unlearning the habit – here a woman seeks professional help to stop smoking.

however, and warns, 'you may have to dye your handkerchiefs brown'!

Today there are an estimated 500,000 regular snuff users in Britain. Scientists at the Addiction Research Unit in London feel that a resurgence of snuff taking could provide a boon to health. Since there is no tar or carbon monoxide in tobacco without combustion, snuff contains no cancer-producing agents. Because it is not inhaled into the lungs, there is no risk of lung cancer. In addition, snuffing increases the blood nicotine level within less than five minutes. A cigarette smoker does not reach a peak nicotine level until after about 10 minutes or more of smoking. Snuff, then, can be used to lessen withdrawal symptoms while giving up smoking, or as a permanent substitute for cigarettes.

Rapid smoking

Dr Edward Lichtenstein of the University of Oregon has pioneered a special strategy to help smokers to give up. During this procedure several smokers are seated in a circle in a small room. Each participant is instructed to light a cigarette and smoke very rapidly – taking a puff every six seconds. Smoke is inhaled and puffing continues until smoking is no longer bearable. The smokers are told to pay attention to the negative aspects of this rapid smoking. Most people cannot tolerate more than two or three cigarettes smoked in this manner. Participants experience burning sensations of the nose, throat, and eyes, watering of the eyes, dizziness, and nausea. Treatment usually consists of six to eight sessions with two to three such procedures per

session. Lichtenstein has reported excellent results using this method, with abstinence rates of 50 per cent or better, even six months after treatment.

A major drawback of the rapid-smoking procedure is that it temporarily intensifies the harmful physiological effects of smoking. The heart rate and blood pressure are increased and added stress is put on the cardiovascular system. Due to this fact, the technique cannot be used with people over 40, diabetics, pregnant women or those with a history of high blood pressure, heart or lung disease. Unfortunately, these are just the people who most need to stop smoking.

As a safer substitute, a technique known as *focused smoking* has been developed. During these conditioning sessions smokers are instructed to smoke the way they usually do, but to concentrate on the negative aspects of smoking. For example, holding the smoke in the mouth for a longer time before inhaling increases the burning sensation in the mouth. Focused smoking is not as potent as rapid smoking but it is also not as harmful.

A selfwatching plan of action

Because of its repetitive nature, cigarette smoking becomes a strong, learned habit that is triggered by various circumstances, thoughts and feelings. The goal of selfwatching is to help the smoker unlearn the habit by breaking conditioned associations and developing methods of coping with cravings.

A selfwatching plan of action involves the following elements: (1) self-evaluation, (2) a tapering-off procedure, (3) self-management techniques, (4) craving-control techniques, (5) thought-control techniques, and (6) relapse prevention.

1 Self-evaluation

The smoker must first keep a behavioural diary as detailed in Chapter 2. In this way he can become more aware not only of the number of cigarettes he is smoking but also of the times, situations, thoughts, emotions, and physical sensations that trigger smoking. A smoking diary should be kept for at least one or two days before the smoker even tries to give up cigarettes. Self-evaluation should continue until the smoker has completely stopped.

2 Tapering-off procedure

Once a base rate of the number of cigarettes smoked each day has been established, a procedure for gradually tapering off must be established. Cigarettes should be reduced in number by 25 per cent each day until abstinence is attained. If someone were smoking 30 cigarettes a day he would be allowed the following number of cigarettes as time progressed:

Day 1	*Day 2*	*Day 3*	*Day 4 (Stop Day)*
22	15	7	0

Those cigarettes that are the easiest to do without should be eliminated first. Cigarette brand should be changed each day so that the smoker is switching to cigarettes with lower and lower nicotine content. An attempt should be made to inhale less deeply and take fewer puffs per cigarette as time progresses.

3 Self-management

During the gradual quitting procedure and for several days afterward, the smoker should use the self-management techniques described in Chapter 3. In particular he should break patterns of behaviour associated with smoking. The coffee-cigarette connection can be broken by substituting tea or soft drinks for coffee for the first few days. All reminders of smoking including ashtrays, cigarette packages, and matches should be removed. All clothing should be laundered or dry cleaned to remove the residual smell of tobacco smoke.

Routines of living must also be modified. Times of day when smoking is most likely to occur should be scheduled with alternative activities. Exercise, hobbies, new interests can be substituted for smoking. Smokers are especially vulnerable after meals and should plan structured activities at those times – anything that will change the old pattern.

Behavioural contracts, mentioned earlier in the chapter, can help motivate the smoker. The contract should be a written agreement with another person (preferably someone else who is trying to stop smoking) specifying the consequences for failing to reach the non-smoking goal. Such consequences are usually monetary.

4 Craving-control techniques

Cravings must be reduced and overcome as soon as possible. One method of reducing physical cravings for nicotine is through the rapid smoking technique described in this chapter. Another useful method is *cue exposure* as described in Chapter 4. This technique allows a smoker to feel more at ease among situations that normally trigger cravings.

Emotions, especially tension, depression and anger, are danger signals for the person trying to stop smoking. They often cause cravings to become quite strong. Methods of relaxation and emotional control described in Chapters 5 and 6 must be practised and used frequently.

5 Thought control

Self-control through thought control is extremely important to keep the smoker on the right track. The *ultimate consequences technique* as described in Chapter 3 is especially useful. This forces the individual to keep the reasons for stopping smoking in the forefront of the mind.

6 Relapse prevention

Relapse prevention techniques as described in Chapter 17 are essential for long-term success. New pleasures and rewards must be found to take the place of the satisfactions from smoking. Exercise in the form of daily walking or physical fitness workouts help to lessen the chance of weight gain experienced by some ex-smokers. Friends and relatives can also offer helpful encouragement and support.

OVEREATING

Obesity is a major health problem that has devastating personal, social and medical consequences. Current estimates in the United States indicate that there are between 40 and 80 million overweight Americans and that obesity is on the increase. Men are likely to show a tendency to overweight in their early thirties while women show this pattern later in life – during the late forties and early fifties. Between the ages of 40 and 49 years, 30 per cent of men are overweight, compared with 40 per cent of women.

Obesity is also related to social status and cultural factors. It is six times more common in lower socio-economic groups than higher ones. It is also more prevalent in Italy and Greece than it is in Britain. This is most probably due to differences in eating patterns, lifestyles and food preferences.

Consequences of overweight

The damaging effects of being overweight are well documented. Obesity is associated with high incidences of heart disease, high blood pressure, stroke, kidney ailments, gallstones and diabetes. Let's suppose there are two friends, Howard and Jack, each of whom is 40 years old and 6 feet (1.9m) tall. Jack weighs 170lb (76.5kg), an ideal weight for his size. Howard has gained weight over the past few years and now weighs 205lb (93kg). At that weight, Howard runs a 40 per cent greater risk of death than his friend Jack. If his weight were as high as 235lb (106.5kg), his risk of death would be 80 per cent greater than Jack's.

In a study of an extreme example of obesity, the gargantuan Sumo wrestlers of Japan were compared to a group of men of normal weight in

Revealing the size of the problem – two friends at the beach (left). Japanese Sumo wrestlers (above) although well exercised are still at risk.

a number of health factors. The wrestlers ate an average of 5000 calories per day, more than twice as much as their normal weight counterparts. In spite of strenuous daily sports training, the wrestlers were quite unhealthy. The incidence of diabetes, gout and high blood pressure was significantly higher among the wrestlers than among the men of normal weight.

Obesity can also lead to surgical complications and breathing difficulties. Some overweight individuals suffer from a breathing disorder known as the Pickwickian Syndrome. This problem takes its name from Charles Dickens' famous book *Pickwick Papers*, in which he described a fat boy who had difficulty staying awake.

'Damn that boy,' said the old gentleman, 'he's gone to sleep again.'

'Very extraordinary boy, that,' said Mr Pickwick. 'Does he always sleep in this way?'

'Sleep!' said the old gentleman, 'he's always asleep. Goes on errands fast asleep, and snores as he waits at table.'

.   .   .   .   .

The fat boy rose, opened his eyes, swallowed the huge piece of pie he had been in the act of masticating when he last fell asleep, and slowly obeyed his master's orders – gloating languidly over the remains of the feast as he removed the plates and deposited them in the hamper.

Accumulated fat around the chest and lungs can result in laboured breathing, drowsiness and frequent episodes of falling asleep during the daytime. Peter Miller treated a very obese schoolteacher with this syndrome. She weighed 400lb (181kg) and kept falling asleep in the middle of her classroom lectures, much to the chagrin of the headmaster and the delight of her students.

In addition to physical problems, obesity has severe psychological consequences. Depression, loss of self-esteem, even self-hatred, social embarrassment and discrimination in employment are among the problems of chronically overweight individuals. Overweight children and adolescents are particularly susceptible. Such children are often emotionally sensitive, passive and socially withdrawn.

Several studies have indicated that obese children and adults are subject to social discrimination and negative stereotypes that are similar to those experienced by minority groups. For example, overweight children are viewed by their slim friends as being ugly, sloppy, nasty, stupid, lazy and dishonest. Even health professionals view fat children in an unfavourable light. In a recent study, physicians and nurses were generally found to view children with physical disfigurements and deformities as more likeable than overweight children. These prejudiced attitudes have led to the development of a 'fat liberation' movement in the United States, which maintains that people have a right to be fat and a right to choose to remain fat. One assumption made by this group is that the frustrations of unsuccessful dieting are more detrimental than staying overweight. Widespread acceptance for

The fat boy awake on this occasion only.

this new notion may be difficult to gain, since our ideas of beauty and health tend to be based on a slim body. However, this definition of beauty is not universal. For example, the first explorer to discover the East African kingdom of Karagive gave an account of the excessive obesity of the king's young harem girls. Obesity and sex appeal were one and the same in this society. Apparently, the girls were fed a continuous supply of milk and were force-fed if their appetites waned. Some of the girls were reported to be so 'beautifully' obese that they could not stand upright.

Shakespeare's Julius Caesar not only expressed a positive attitude towards the obese, but distrusted those who were not plump:

Let me have men about me that are fat;
Sleek-headed men and such as sleep o'nights;
Yond Cassius has a lean and hungry look;

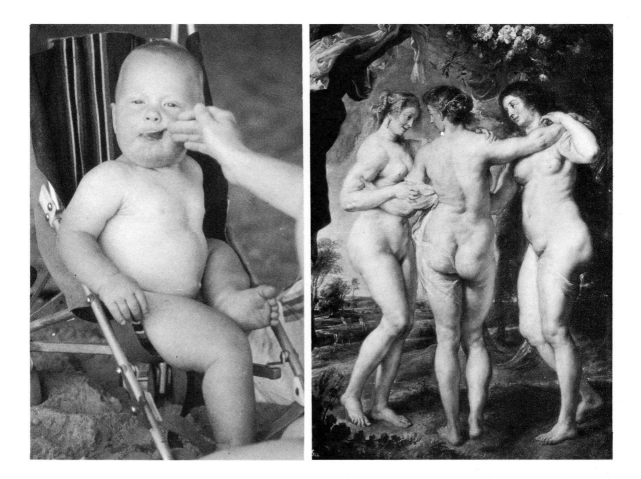

He thinks too much: Such men are dangerous. . . .
Would he were fatter! (Act I, Scene 2)

What is obesity?

Body weight
An adult is considered overweight if the total
body weight exceeds the ideal healthy weight by
20 per cent or more. Ideal body weights for
height, gender and body frame have been calculated by insurance companies on the basis of
mortality risk factors and represent the optimum
healthy weight for a long life. These standard
weight tables are helpful in determining ideal
weight but are sometimes open to distortion. For
example, when different weights are listed for
different body frames, people may have difficulty determining which category they belong
to. Many people use the classic excuse, 'I'm not
fat, I just have big bones.'

*Fat has had a bad press for much of history. The Fat Boy in
Dickens'* Pickwick Papers *(far left) was not a lovable
figure. On the other hand, it is generally assumed that fat
babies (above left) are healthy babies, which seems to be true
of the specimen here, but is often false. The Three Graces
(above) painted by Rubens were glamour girls in their time,
but they are rather beefy for the modern taste, and would
have been susceptible to heart disease.*

Body weight

Guidelines for body weight. Adapted from the recommendations of the Fogarty Center Conference 1973 (Bray, 1975)

METRIC

Height* (m)	MEN Weight (kg)* Average	Acceptable weight		WOMEN Weight (kg)* Average	Acceptable weight	
1.45				46.0	42	53
1.48				46.5	42	54
1.50				47.0	43	55
1.52				48.5	44	57
1.54				49.5	44	58
1.56				50.4	45	58
1.58	55.8	51	64	51.3	46	59
1.60	57.6	52	65	52.6	48	61
1.62	58.6	53	66	54.0	49	62
1.64	59.6	54	67	55.4	50	64
1.66	60.6	55	69	56.8	51	65
1.68	61.7	56	71	58.1	52	66
1.70	63.5	58	73	60.0	53	67
1.72	65.0	59	74	61.3	55	69
1.74	66.5	60	75	62.6	56	70
1.76	68.0	62	77	64.0	58	72
1.78	69.4	64	79	65.3	59	74
1.80	71.0	65	80			
1.82	72.6	66	82			
1.84	74.2	67	84			
1.86	75.8	69	86			
1.88	77.6	71	88			
1.90	79.3	73	90			
1.92	81.0	75	93			

IMPERIAL

Height* Ft in	MEN Weight (lb)* Average	Acceptable weight		WOMEN Weight (lb)* Average	Acceptable weight	
4 10				102	92	119
4 11				104	94	122
5 0				107	96	125
5 1				110	99	128
5 2	123	112	141	113	102	131
5 3	127	115	144	116	105	134
5 4	130	118	148	120	108	138
5 5	133	121	152	123	111	142
5 6	136	124	156	128	114	146
5 7	140	128	161	132	118	150
5 8	145	132	166	136	122	154
5 9	149	136	170	140	126	158
5 10	153	140	174	144	130	163
5 11	158	144	179	148	134	168
6 0	162	148	184	152	138	173
6 1	166	152	189			
6 2	171	156	194			
6 3	176	160	199			
6 4	181	164	204			

* Height without shoes, weight without clothes

The most up-to-date and accurate guidelines for body weight, developed by Dr George Bray and colleagues at the University of California, are here presented in table form in both pounds and kilograms.

Suppose Sylvia is 5ft 6in (1.62m) tall. Her average healthy weight would be 128lb (54kg). But it could vary between 114lb (49.5kg) and 146lb (63.5kg) and still be acceptable. Of course, the closer to the average, the better. However, Sylvia should also take into account how she feels at varying ideal weights. For example, she may feel physically and psychologically uncomfortable at 128lb. She may find that she has to keep very strict control over her appetite at that weight, whereas at 135lb (59.5kg) she feels fine and can control her weight much more easily. In that case, 135lb would be a more rational choice of ideal weight. Some possible reasons for differences in how one feels at different acceptable weights will become apparent as this chapter progresses.

Body fat

Many experts argue that obesity is more properly defined as excess fat rather than excess weight. One reason is that body weight as measured by scales is a very crude index. The scale weighs everything – muscle, skin, fat, water and bone. To see how an index of weight can be misleading, take the case of an American professional football player. 'Mean' Joe Greene, a defensive lineman for the Pittsburgh Steelers, is 6ft 4in (1.92m) tall and weighs 280lb (127kg). By football standards his size is ideal. Looking up his weight and height on Table 1, however, we find that he should weigh approximately 181lb (81kg). Thus, on the basis of body weight alone, he is 55 per cent overweight and should be considered obese. However, his body is mostly muscle with very little fat, but the scales, of course, cannot tell the difference. Measuring body fat would be much more appropriate in this case.

Body fat measurements are also a better indication of progress during dieting because of water retention. Judy may stick very closely to a 1000-calorie diet from Monday to Saturday. On Friday evening she and her husband go out to a restaurant where, even though her calorie intake is low, she eats a meal that has been heavily salted by

Obesity – a result of overeating – is on the increase in the West. It has been estimated that in Britain and America nearly half the population is carrying too much fat.

the chef. Excessive salt intake can result in increased water retention in the body. When Judy weighs herself on Saturday morning she finds she has lost no weight. This is extremely discouraging because she has not exceeded her 1000-calorie a day limit all week. Actually, Judy *has* lost 2½ pounds of fat. But she has retained 2½ pounds of fluid, so that her overall weight remains the same. The fluid, of course, will be gone in a day or two. But, since Judy has no way to measure fat separately from total body weight, the result in terms of the diet targets are discouraging.

When exercise is combined with dieting, the measurement of body fat is even more important. Exercise tends to build and firm muscle tissue. Since muscle weighs more than fat, muscle weight may replace fat weight and the total weight lost may be small, though the person will actually be slimmer than before. Let's suppose that June, a 50-year-old secretary, signs up for a physical fitness programme. She is 5ft 5in tall, weighs 140lb and wears a size 14 dress. While she is not obese, she looks a bit plump and flabby. Her fitness programme includes a high-protein, low-fat diet and a strenuous exercise routine. She walks three to five miles per day, plays tennis three times a week, and goes to an exercise class on Monday, Wednesday and Friday. At least three days a week she adds a jog of one mile to her walking routine. After four weeks, June is disappointed to discover that she has lost only

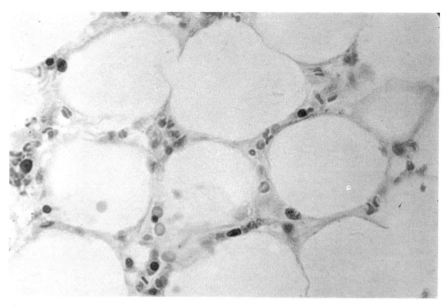

Adipose tissue (right) is constituted almost entirely of fat cells – this shows one of the several varieties. The interstices between are filled with collagen and fibroblast which produces the elastic fibres.

eight pounds. Actually, she has done quite well. She looks slim and trim even though she is not that much lighter than when she began. Her dress size has gone from 14 to 10, and she has lost a total of 12 inches from her arms, waist, hips and legs. In evaluating her progress, weight loss alone would be very misleading.

Body fat can be measured by several scientific methods. However, they require special equipment which is not available to the average individual. For example, one method involves submerging a person completely in a tank of water. Known as hydrostatic weighing, this method determines body fat by equations taking into account the average density of water being displaced. Results can be compared to the ideal content of body fat, which is approximately 15–18 per cent for men and 20–25 per cent for women.

Probably the best way to measure body fat is to use a tape measure. Subtract the waist dimension in inches from the height in inches. If the remainder is less than 36, the person is obese.

Why are some people fat?

The reasons why some people are fat and others are not are complex and not completely understood. However, the major factors involved in obesity appear to be (1) heredity, (2) metabolism, (3) the 'energy equation', and (4) learning.

Heredity

Is obesity inherited? The most accurate answer based on present knowledge is – perhaps. Certainly, overweight runs in families. A child with one overweight parent has a 40 per cent chance of being overweight. If both parents are overweight, their child has an 80 per cent chance of being overweight. It is still not known, however, whether this indicates a genetic pattern or whether children of obese parents simply learn to overeat by example. Some experts feel that many people are born with a predisposition to gain weight easily but they won't be overweight unless they overeat and are inactive. Obviously, some people seem to eat whatever they want and never gain weight. Others can gain several pounds during a weekend holiday.

Two theories have been proposed to account for these differences, particularly as they relate to a genetic predisposition.

The set-point theory

Our bodies appear to function in many ways in order to maintain homeostasis, the body's status quo. This may be especially true of weight. Each individual may have a set weight that has been biologically programmed. If the weight changes, the body will have a tendency to revert to this biological weight, whether it be higher or lower. In other words, this biological weight is the most physiologically suitable for that individual. It is probably determined by several factors, including genetic inheritance, prenatal conditions, infant nutritional patterns, and even the way in which certain parts of the brain develop (most notably the hypothalamus, which controls hunger and satiety).

If a person's biological weight and ideal, healthy weight are similar, then obesity is less likely. However, if the biologically programmed weight is much higher than the ideal weight, the individual faces a constant battle for control. Such people often find that when they are eating freely and not dieting their weight increases, but only to a certain point. They may gain 40 pounds but then stay at that weight. In fact, they may discover that they can maintain this weight, without gaining more, with relative ease. The catch is that health and appearance suffer at this level.

Unfortunately, there is no way as yet to measure this biological weight, if it really does exist. The theory, though, implies that some people may always have to keep a close watch on what they eat.

The fat-cell theory

When a person gains weight the fat cells become larger. That is, fat cells do not increase in number but in size. However, some people have more fat cells than others. If they have more cells that can increase in size, they may therefore have a greater tendency to gain weight. The number of fat cells is determined genetically and possibly also by feeding patterns. Fat cells are formed during infancy and again in adolescence, so that eating patterns at these times may be critical.

People with more fat cells may not only gain weight easily but also have more difficulty losing weight. This may depend upon an interaction between the fat-cell theory and the set-point theory: the number of fat cells may be a factor determining the biological ideal weight. Once the technique of counting fat cells has been refined, we may be able to predict, at infancy, who is most likely to be fat. Then, parents can restrict calories and encourage exercise throughout childhood.

Metabolism

When one is looking for an answer to why people are obese, the subject of metabolism comes to mind. In fact, many overweight individuals believe that their problem is simply due to a sluggish metabolism.

Before we analyse this possible cause, it is necessary to define exactly what is meant by the term metabolism. Simply put, basal metabolism is the amount of energy required to maintain life at rest. Specifically, it represents the amount of energy used by the body when lying quietly in a comfortable, relaxed environment. Thus, your body burns calories in order to keep itself going, whether you are physically active or not. The basal metabolism of adults ranges between 1200 and 1800 calories per day. Unfortunately, basal metabolism alone does not explain obesity. There are no differences between the absolute values of the metabolism of individuals who are overweight and those who are not. However, there may be differences in the *efficiency* of their metabolisms.

A prime example of this efficiency is the phenomenon known as the 'thermic effect'. The term refers to the increase in metabolic rate and heat loss that occurs immediately following a meal. It's a bit like turning up a furnace to burn excess fuel. Everyone has this reaction whether they are fat or slim. However, obese individuals show much less of this metabolic increase than slim ones. One recent study indicated that the metabolic increase for slim people one to two hours after a meal ranged from 19 per cent to 25 per cent. Overweight individuals showed an increase of only 3 per cent to 9 per cent. The lean person burns more calories after each meal without even trying.

This inefficiency of metabolism seems to be the result of the obesity itself. The process of being overweight, dieting, losing weight, then regaining that weight has devastating effects on metabolism. Since this is so often the pattern with the obese, their metabolism gradually becomes very sluggish and ineffective. The absolute level of their metabolism remains the same but they no longer achieve the boosts in metabolic rate they need. Slowly their bodies become very adept at storing fat. As the fat content increases, weight loss becomes more difficult. By constantly overeating and under-exercising, the overweight person is telling his body to store fat. His body does exactly that and more. It becomes expert at fat storage. Once this occurs it becomes quite difficult to reverse the process.

Three other factors that influence basal metabolism deserve mention. The first is gender. Here women are at a distinct disadvantage. The rate of basal metabolism is considerably higher in men than in women even when they are the same size. Basal metabolism in healthy men requires about 1600 to 1800 calories a day while women burn only about 1200 to 1450 calories daily. This metabolic difference alone could account for a weight difference of up to 20 or 30 pounds in a year.

The second factor affecting metabolism is body size. Generally, the larger someone is, the higher is his metabolic rate. A person who is 6ft 2in (1.88m) tall and weighs 200lb (90.6kg) would have a substantially higher basal metabolism than someone 5ft 4in (1.58m) tall weighing 120lb. It simply takes more energy to run a large body than a small one.

The final influence on metabolism is age. Yes, it is true that metabolic rate decreases with age. No one can eat the same amount of food at the age of 50 as at 20, and anyone attempting to do so is sure to gain weight. Because of the low metabolic rate in women, given the same relative body size, the metabolism of a 35-year-old woman is equivalent to that of a 65-year-old man!

Looking at factors of gender, body size and age, it is obvious that metabolism varies considerably from one person to another. Generally speaking, small, old women will have the slowest metabolic rate, while large, young men will have the fastest. Unfortunately, there is very little one can do to change most of the factors influencing these differences.

Finally, there are a small number of people who have thyroid problems resulting in metabolic disturbances. However, they are a small percentage of the overweight and this is a specialized problem that need not be discussed here.

The energy equation

Dr Jean Mayer, a noted expert on nutrition and the president of Tufts University in Massa-chusetts, has long stressed the importance of the energy equation in explaining weight control. This illustrates the rather simple but important relationship between caloric input and output. When calories consumed equal the number of calories burned through metabolism and exercise, weight is maintained. As long as the energy equation balances out, weight will not be gained or lost. Overweight people generally have both sides of the equation out of balance. That is, they eat too much and exercise too little. Someone may eat a moderate amount of food but because of age or size does not burn off enough calories for the equation to balance. Either less food or more exercise could balance the equation. In fact, some people stay physically active mainly so that they can eat more.

The energy equation

INPUT	=	OUTPUT
(calories eaten)		(1. Basal Metabolism
		2. Physical Activity)

Even a slight imbalance in the energy equation can have drastic effects on weight over a period of time. Let's suppose that someone eats 2500 calories of food per day and burns only 2000 calories. This would result in an excess of 500 calories per day that are taken in but not burned off. Since there are 3500 calories in one pound of body fat, this person would gain one pound every seven days. That's at least four pounds a month and over 48 pounds a year.

Learning when to be hungry

Learning plays a large role in how, when, what, how much and why we eat. Contrary to popular belief, hunger is only related in a small way to eating, particularly in the overweight. In fact, people who are overweight have a very difficult time determining when they are really hungry. They are less responsive to internal hunger cues than are slim people.

Several years ago Dr Albert Stunkard, a leading authority on weight control, conducted an experiment to demonstrate this lack of internal responsiveness among the overweight. He asked volunteer subjects – some fat, some thin –

People respond to external stimuli – like this attractive spread – and have an appetite for food irrespective of whether they are hungry or not.

to swallow a gastric balloon attached to a tube which in turn was fitted to a measuring device. When the balloon reached the stomach it was inflated with water. Whenever stomach contractions occurred, indicating physical hunger, the measuring device was activated. All volunteers had been without food for approximately 15 hours. Subjects were asked to let the experimenter know when they felt hungry.

Dr Stunkard found that when the subjects of normal weight reported feeling hungry, their stomachs were usually contracting. However, with the overweight subjects, there was no relationship between stomach contractions and the subjective experience of hunger. Perhaps this indicates that physical hunger cues are not as strong among the obese or that the obese are simply not paying attention to these cues. Apparently, what happens is that fat people lose touch with real hunger sensations after years of inappropriate eating. They eat in so many different situations and in response to so many different external signals that hunger cues become secondary in determining eating behaviour.

Not only are overweight people unresponsive to internal hunger sensations, they are also over-sensitive to external ones. The time of day, the taste of food, and its visibility are extremely important cues for the overweight, who are more likely to crave food and experience hunger merely from seeing food. Whether the stomach is full or empty is irrelevant.

External cues affect both the behaviour and the physical responses of the overweight. Dr Judith Rodin of Yale University recently conducted a study of the bodily reactions to food of overweight and normal weight people. She found that an individual who is overweight, whether or not he or she has just eaten, experiences strong reactions at the mere sight of appetizing food. The pancreas begins to secrete insulin. The body becomes aroused and, because of past conditioning, anticipates consumption of the food. One effect of increased insulin output is a decrease in the blood sugar level, which is associated in turn with feelings of hunger, particularly a craving for sweets. The psychological temptation triggers a bodily reaction which brings about a real physiological craving for food. This reaction seems to be more prevalent in overweight people, especially those who have been overweight since childhood.

External conditioning also leads to a general misinterpretation of internal sensations and feelings. In particular, obese people have trouble differentiating hunger from other emotional states. Feelings of fatigue, boredom, restlessness and tension are frequently interpreted as hunger. In a recent study of this problem obese men and others of normal weight were fitted with earphones which supposedly allowed them to hear their own heart rates. Subjects were divided into three groups. Group 1 subjects were led to believe that their heart rates would increase during the experiment, while Group 2 subjects were led to believe that their heart rates would decrease. Group 3 subjects were not given any particular instructions.

Subjects' eating behaviour was measured unobtrusively and their true heart rate recorded. When the obese subjects were calm, they ate very little, regardless of the expectations they were given. When they were aroused (their heart rate was high), they ate more when they had not expected that arousal. That is, when they thought the increase in heart rate was due to internal factors, rather than factors inherent in the experiment, they were more likely to label the increased arousal 'hunger'. If they were given an explicit reason for the increased arousal, such as unusual noise or commotion during the experiment, they did not experience 'hunger' and did not eat more.

From day to day an obese person must work out reasons for feelings without help, and the potential for mislabelling is great. Mislabelling feelings is most likely to occur when the reasons for emotional sensations are unclear. Thus, when one feels general excitement, depression or restlessness without a specific precipitating event, these feelings may be misinterpreted as hunger. Training in the appropriate identification of hunger is a necessary element of permanent appetite control.

External triggers to eating

Situations: the force of habit

Since overweight people have difficulty in 'reading' hunger ones, factors other than appetite become influential in triggering eating. Often eating is triggered by external, rather than internal, factors. Any external circumstance that has been associated with eating can trigger feelings of hunger. The more an individual eats at different times of the day, in different rooms of the house, or while engaged in different activities, the more factors will trigger eating.

Other people

What other people say and do can also trigger overeating. Sometimes social pressures are very direct. The case of the overzealous hostess is a good example. At a dinner party a dieter may be confronted with the following remark, 'Oh, Joan, please have some of this chocolate layer cake for dessert. I know it's always been one of your favourites and I made it especially for you.' These social pressures to eat begin very early in life. A child learns what to eat and how much to eat through parental teaching. A classic example of such pressure has been repeated in household after household. Parents chide, 'Eat up everything on your plate. You don't know how lucky you are. Food was rationed during the war, so don't you waste it now.' Eating becomes associated with pleasing someone else or preventing world-wide hunger rather than with physical appetite. Dieters must develop methods of coping with this social pressure and tactfully refusing food that is not wanted or needed. Some people are experts at pushing food and making others feel guilty if they do not eat it.

Other social influences are more complex. Some friends or relatives appoint themselves as dietary guardians. They feel that it is their job to advise you, to supervise you and to remind you about your diet. Unfortunately, these people are usually close relatives and friends who are well meaning. This makes the situation even more difficult to deal with.

In earlier chapters we discussed the importance of using social skills to be direct and assertive with others. Social support *is* important but it must be the appropriate kind of support. It is essential to identify who your 'friendly enemies' are and exactly what they say and do to trigger your eating.

Learning to identify when we are actually hungry, and distinguishing our desire for food from other emotional needs and feelings, are crucial to changing our eating habits.

Negative thinking

In some cases the enemy is within. That is, *you* are your own worst enemy. It is easy to become discouraged when dieting, since the effort expended is often greater than the results achieved. There are 'plateau' weeks when a dieter can eat the correct number of calories, exercise diligently, and still not lose any weight. This is just a fact of life for dieters. But thoughts such as 'I'm not losing fast enough. This diet isn't working' can lower motivation and put a quick end to a diet.

Dieters also suffer from feelings of self-pity and personal deprivation. A dieter might think, 'It's not fair. Why should I have to diet? Terry is as skinny as a rail and can eat anything he wants,' or 'I always have to deprive myself of something. Just for once I'd like to do exactly as I please.' This 'poor-me' syndrome can lead to anger, depression *and* overeating. Dieters must

learn to identify these thought patterns and modify them using cognitive self-management techniques as described in Chapters 3, 6 and 8.

Another obstacle to successful weight control is rationalization or excuses. We all provide ourselves with apparently rational reasons for our behaviour, especially our unhealthy behaviour. The following are some typical reasons given for overeating: 'I'll start my diet on Monday. It's impossible to diet with weekend guests arriving today'; 'I'll faint if I don't have something to eat'; 'I have too many problems in my life. If other people would just understand me I could control my eating with no trouble.' People use the same arguments on themselves time after time and often refuse to realize how nonsensical their excuses are. These thought patterns can be recognized and changed.

Many dieters develop a pattern of what is

called dichotomous reasoning. That is, they view their food world in very concrete, all-or-nothing terms. In fact, they often divide people into two categories – dieters and non-dieters. A dieter's own self-concept revolves around this dichotomy. As long as he is sticking strictly to a diet, he considers himself to be a good, 'legal' dieter. One deviation from the old diet, just one biscuit or piece of cake, turns him into a 'cheat', no longer a dieter. Such comments as 'I'm off my diet again' illustrate the idea that there is 'good' eating and 'bad' eating but nothing in between. Overweight people perceive dieters as controlled, strong-willed, determined and successful. Non-dieters are perceived as weak-willed failures. Such value judgements only serve to excuse a person from developing a normal, balanced nutritional programme.

When a slim person eats too much, this is simply perceived as having eaten more food than usual. There is no basic change in self-concept. It is quickly forgotten and a normal eating schedule is resumed. The overweight person cannot do this. He or she fails to see that eating patterns vary along a continuum. This is why overeating while on a diet leads to frustration, guilt and self-criticism. The guilt in turn triggers off more eating and more guilt. It never dawns on the fat person that this cycle can be stopped and eating appropriately taken up once again. He or she has lost what Dr Albert Bandura calls the feeling of self-efficacy, or the feeling that there is the capacity to cope. The lapse is perceived as a complete loss of control. An overweight person rarely stops to realize that self-control is never lost but merely becomes dormant.

Along with this dichotomous pattern exists a tendency to look at one's failures rather than successes and to reproach oneself for these deviations. In the overweight person's mind, one slip can erase ten successes. No credit is given for avoiding temptation. Rarely does an overweight person say, 'Well, I ate too much last night but I've avoided so many other temptations this week, I'm not going to let it bother me. All of my successes prove that I have willpower.' Instead, the more likely reaction is: 'Well, I really messed up my diet last night. That just proves that I don't have any willpower. I'll just never be able to lose weight.'

The pull of emotions

Emotions can exert a strong influence on eating. Anger, boredom, loneliness and tension can trigger frustration and overeating. Several studies indicate that many overweight individuals eat in response to emotional arousal while slim people typically eat because of hunger and for enjoyment. Food can be used both as a tranquillizer and as a mood elevator. The use of food to make oneself feel better emotionally is even seen in very young children. Dr Miller and a colleague recently studied food concepts in four- and five-year-old children. The children were asked to choose between chocolate, a kitten, puppets, flowers, fudge and a toy telephone under various social-emotional conditions. Anger proved to be the emotion most significantly related to food. When angry nearly half the children chose a food item (either chocolate or fudge) to make themselves 'feel better'. This is really not surprising when one considers how many ice cream cones are dispensed to crying children to soothe their feelings.

Suppressed anger can result in overeating in an attempt to obtain emotional relief or to retaliate against the target of one's anger. Eating helps some people release pent-up emotions. Some people also find themselves eating out of spite. This is particularly true when 'friendly enemies' offer unwanted advice or supervision. The dieter may be sufficiently irritated to break the diet, seeing this as a chance to demonstrate the freedom to choose in personal behaviour.

Depression, boredom and loneliness are also closely related to excessive eating. While loss of appetite is usually considered one of the classic symptoms of depression, many overweight individuals react to depression in just the opposite way. They automatically overeat when depressed, often to the point of bingeing. While overeating provides short-term relief, it eventually leads to more depression and guilt. These negative feelings precipitate further eating in a futile attempt to obtain emotional relief.

Physical sensations

Sometimes eating is triggered by physical sensations. While these are often related to hunger, sometimes they are simply a function of physical discomfort. Eating can be used as a method to

Monitoring our eating habits helps us understand when and why we eat the food that we do – sampling the pleasures of 'junk food' (above), or letting the snack at the pub replace dinner (right). Learning to eat regular nourishing meals is part of taking responsibility for our own well-being.

obtain relief from headaches, backaches, fatigue and dizziness, for example.

The physical sensations of hunger are not as straightforward as one might assume. While we know little about physical hunger sensations in individuals of normal weight, even less is known about the day-to-day hunger cravings of the overweight. Dr Jean Mayer and Lenore Monello conducted a study of hunger sensations at the Harvard School of Public Health. The subjects were over 600 adults and children of both sexes ranging in age from 9 to 61. When hungry, most subjects experienced specific gastric sensations (a rumbling stomach, for instance), restlessness and excitability. Unexpectedly, the investigators found a difference in the way men and women sense hunger. Men experience hunger in a more specifically physical way than women. That is, they report specific sensations in the stomach, mouth, throat and head. Emptiness in the stomach, salivation, and an unpleasant sensation in the throat were common. Women, on the other hand, experience hunger in a more diffuse, cerebral way. More females than males reported feelings of irritability and tension. They also had stronger urges to eat and more thoughts about food when hungry.

It is extremely important to pinpoint the specific sensations of hunger so as to differentiate it from other physical experiences.

Where to begin
The process of changing eating habits must begin in a very systematic manner. Initially, the overweight individual must examine the motivation to change. Recently, *Slimming Magazine* conducted a survey in England to study motivation to lose weight. A total of 82 per cent of the respondents cited personal appearance as the major reason for wanting to diet. Only 18 per cent reported that they were losing weight for health reasons. Health seems to be more important to men and to older people, but there is some evidence that the health motive can be enhanced by personalized discussions on health education conducted by a professional. The survey also found that the obese felt they could be helped most by structured, controlled discussions, overt praise for weight loss, and a firm attitude on the part of others.

This desire for firmness and structure is important. While obese people can be very structured and controlled in many aspects of their lives, this structure escapes them when it comes to food and exercise. When an overweight individual is asked to keep a record of eating patterns from day to day, it becomes obvious that the pattern is highly inconsistent. Eating times are haphazard and meal planning is poor. Usually, an obese person skips breakfast and eats snacks during the late morning. There is then the temptation to grab a quick lunch or even miss lunch in an attempt to cut down on calories. By late afternoon hunger again asserts itself and a snack is needed once again, usually followed by a heavy evening meal. The appetite is often strongest in the late evening, between 9 pm and bedtime. Some people, known as night eaters, do most of their eating after midnight.

The picture is one of inconsistency, lack of planning, missing meals and then becoming ravenous during the late afternoon and evening. People who are slim may have a more consistent pattern to their eating, taking three meals a day and eating mainly in response to hunger rather than the time of day or emotional factors.

When an obese person overeats, a typical response is to compensate for the 'crime' by missing a meal or even by fasting for a day. This inconsistency is rarely effective. In fact, skipping meals simply triggers hunger later in the day and the whole process backfires. An extra half-hour walk would be a much better way to undo gastronomic wrongdoing than missing a scheduled meal. Correct nutritional patterns must become an important priority in one's life.

After these factors have been considered, the triggers for overeating must be analysed. The exact combinations of situational, social, cognitive, emotional and physical factors related to eating must be determined. This can best be accomplished by a process of self-monitoring. Self-monitoring consists of keeping a daily diary of foods eaten and the times, situations, circumstances, feelings and thoughts associated with overeating and snacking. This selfwatching is also very helpful while one is on a diet or trying to maintain an ideal weight.

Actually, it is relatively easy to establish a pattern of eating about 1000 calories a day and

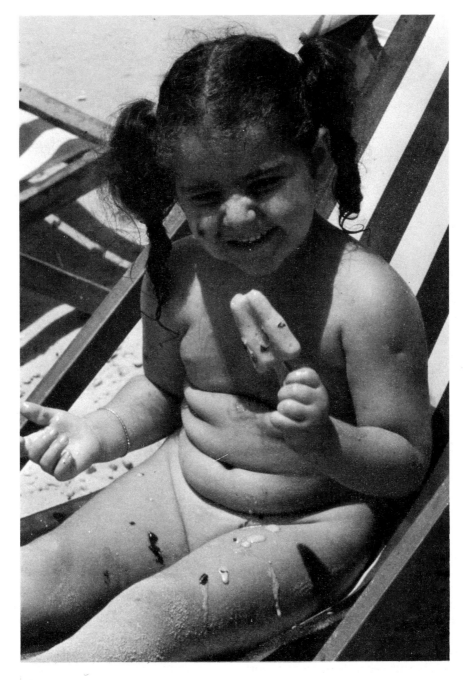

taking regular walks. The difficult part is keeping up the programme and maintaining motivation from day to day. The secret of motivation is staying in control of the antecedents that trigger eating. The selfwatching strategies discussed in earlier chapters are designed to teach the discipline necessary to attain permanent control over eating patterns.

Bribing children to behave well by giving them rewards of food establishes unhealthy eating habits from an early age. Fat children do tend to grow into fat adults.

10
WORKAHOLISM

According to the Protestant work ethic, work is good for you. It is considered indispensable for a happy, healthy and productive life. Without work we are lazy good-for-nothings of dubious character and morality. With it we are pillars of the community, pure in mind, body and soul. Achievement, productivity and accomplishment are, the ethic persuades us, worthy ambitions. Work is a virtue, as truth and honesty are virtues.

So if some work is good, more work must be even better. Society rewards the diligent worker with status, money and praise. There are some individuals, however, who live out the work ethic to its extreme: they become addicted to work and achievement to the detriment of their health and happiness – they become, to use a current term, 'workaholics'.

As the word implies, a workaholic is addicted to work in the same way that an alcoholic is addicted to alcohol. Work comes first, before family, friends or personal enjoyment. Although achievement may have been the initial goal the workaholic gradually comes to crave work itself rather than the results of it and works for the sake of working.

Portrait of a workaholic

The workaholic typically spends long hours at his job. Whether self-employed or working for someone else he shows up early and works late, frequently works over weekends and holidays, and seldom takes a vacation. Everyone, except perhaps his family, looks up to him, thus providing reinforcement for his efforts.

Any time spent not working – however actively employed – gives rise to vague feelings of guilt and unease. Lengthy vacations are not welcome because they result in 'withdrawal' symptoms: most of the time is spent in anxiety about the job and the desire to be back at work; the workaholic makes daily telephone calls to his place of business and tells his secretary and business associates exactly where to reach him at all times.

Dr Charles Garfield of the University of California in San Francisco, who recently completed a 14-year study of workaholics, found that while work fanatics appear extremely busy, they are often not as productive as other people. Nevertheless they see themselves as making a major impact on the efficiency of their company

or business. Dr Garfield also found that work-aholics' career patterns were very predictable. The typical workaholic tends to be the 'whizz kid' type, identified early in his career as 'up-and-coming'. He rises quickly in the company but levels off in his mid-40s. He still puts in the hours, but his addiction begins to take its toll. He suffers from chronic stress disorders, takes to drink or drugs as antidotes, rows with his wife, alienates his friends – all of which undermine his performance at work. So he puts in more and more hours in a desperate effort to stay efficient, which only makes the problem worse.

The compulsion that kills
In the late 1950s and early 1960s two physicians, Drs Meyer Friedman and Ray Rosenman of the Harold Brunn Institute for Cardiovascular Research, began a series of studies which have had far-reaching effects on health research in general. They found that workaholics show a number of specific and easily identifiable com-mon traits, but more importantly the studies proved that workaholism is a compulsion that can kill.

The change from a feudal to a capitalist economy brought new work routines and a stress on the evils of idleness (above). Would you want to work for a hostile and harassing boss? (below).

This questionnaire is designed to assess Type A behaviour. It is based on the work of Friedman and Rosenman and was developed by Dr James Nora, Professor of Preventive Medicine at the University of Colorado School of Medicine.

Type A personality questionnaire

PLEASE TAKE YOUR TIME ANSWERING THESE QUESTIONS. It is important to give as frank an answer as possible. Feel free to ask your spouse or friends how you should answer the question. Some of these items, such as the way you talk, may not be apparent to you, but would be to those who know you well.

1 Do you feel there are not enough hours in the day to do all the things you must do?
(   ) yes   (   ) no

2 Do you always move, walk, and eat rapidly?
(   ) yes   (   ) no

3 Do you feel an impatience with the rate at which most events take place?
(   ) yes   (   ) no

4 Do you say. 'Uh-huh, uh-huh,' or 'yes, yes, yes, yes,' to someone who is talking, unconsciously urging him to 'get on with it' or hasten his rate of speaking? Do you have a tendency to finish the sentences of others for them?
(   ) yes   (   ) no

5 Do you become unduly irritated or even enraged when a car ahead of you in your lane runs at a pace you consider too slow? Do you find it anguishing to wait in line or to wait your turn to be seated in a restaurant?
(   ) yes   (   ) no

6 Do you find it intolerable to watch others perform tasks you know you can do faster?
(   ) yes   (   ) no

7 Do you become impatient with yourself as you are obliged to perform repetitive duties (making out bank deposit slips, writing cheques, washing and cleaning dishes, and so on), which are necessary but take you away from doing things you really have an interest in doing?
(   ) yes   (   ) no

8 Do you find yourself hurrying your own reading or always attempting to obtain condensations or summaries of truly interesting and worthwhile literature?
(   ) yes   (   ) no

9 Do you strive to think of or do two or more things simultaneously? For example, while trying to listen to another person's speech, do you persist in continuing to think about an irrelevant subject?
(   ) yes   (   ) no

10 While engaged in recreation, do you continue to ponder your business, home, or professional problems?
(   ) yes   (   ) no

11 Do you have (a) a habit of explosively accentuating various key words in your ordinary speech even when there is no real need for such accentuation, and (b) a tendency to utter the last few words of your sentences far more rapidly than the opening words?
(   ) yes   (   ) no

12 Do you find it difficult to refrain from talking about or bringing the theme of any conversation around to those subjects that especially interest and intrigue you, and when unable to accomplish this manoeuvre, do you pretend to listen but really remain preoccupied with your own thoughts?
(   ) yes   (   ) no

13 Do you almost always feel vaguely guilty when you relax and do absolutely nothing for several hours to several days?
(   ) yes   (   ) no

14 Do you attempt to schedule more and more in less and less time, and in doing so make fewer and fewer allowances for unforeseen contingencies?
(   ) yes   (   ) no

15 In conversation, do you frequently clench your fist or bang your hand upon a table or pound one fist into the palm of your hand in order to emphasize a conversational point?
(   ) yes   (   ) no

16 If employed, does your job include frequent deadlines that are difficult to meet?
(   ) yes   (   ) no

17 Do you frequently clench your jaw, or even grind your teeth?
(   ) yes   (   ) no

18 Do you frequently bring your work or study material (related to your job, not to school) home with you at night?
(   ) yes   (   ) no

19 Do you find yourself evaluating not only your own but also the activities of others in terms of numbers?
(   ) yes   (   ) no

20 Are you dissatisfied with your present work?
(   ) yes   (   ) no

Every *Yes* answer scores 1 point and every *No* answer 0. Total scores are broken down into the following categories: 4+ (14 or more points), 3+ (9–13 points), 2+ (4–8 points) and 1+ (3 or fewer points). Categories 2+ and 3+ are considered to be relatively neutral. A person who scores 4+ can consider himself significantly more at risk of a heart attack than 2+ or 3+ people; a 1+ person is least likely of all to have a heart attack.

In 1964 Friedman, Rosenman and their colleagues began publishing the results of a very important study, the Western Collaborative Group Study. Preliminary results in 1959 had convinced them that it was possible to identify workaholics clearly, and that workaholic behaviour patterns might actually contribute to cardiovascular disease. For the purpose of the Western Study they recruited over 3500 men from all levels and activities in industry and commerce, from automobile mechanics to presidents of major corporations. They collected information on dietary habits, exercise, smoking habits, weight, and family history of coronary heart disease. They also assessed each recruit for workaholic behaviour on the basis of what they were later to label as the Type A Behaviour Pattern. They then followed up this large sample for the next ten years. By 1972 well over 250 of the original group had suffered from an episode of coronary heart disease.

Which elements of all the information obtained at the start of the Western Study were the clearest predictors of heart disease? Cholesterol, or a fatty diet? Exercise history? No. These factors were certainly relevant, but the most

Agitated and abusive – he is a danger to himself as well as to others on the road (above). Unpleasant to live with – workaholics can be irritable and withdrawn, and seldom do their share of the domestic tasks.

important was the Type A Behaviour Pattern, workaholism. Did the compulsion to work simply precede heart problems, or was the connection closer? Could workaholism be responsible for heart problems?

Type A behaviour

To quote Drs Friedman and Rosenman, the workaholic is 'aggressively involved in a chronic, incessant struggle to achieve more and more in less and less time, and if required to do so, against the opposing efforts of other things or other people'. The four most important ingredients of Type A behaviour are: feeling that one is under terrible time pressures; being intensely involved with one's job; driving oneself and others hard and competitively; and being unreasonably impatient and hostile.[1]

The first of these, being under pressure of time, is usually the most obvious trait of the workaholic. Life is run strictly by the clock, with business and personal activities ordered in terms of deadlines, serried ranks of them. In an effort to achieve, the workaholic takes on more and more work, setting tighter and tighter deadlines. The more formidable the workload the greater the feeling of stress. Eventually, becoming so bogged down with details, schedules and deadlines, the individual reaches a point where very little is actually achieved. Creativity is stifled and efficiency drops. More and more effort accomplishes less and less.

The workaholic's sense of urgency is especially pronounced in private and family life. The following is a description by Sidney, a 56-year-old chemical sales manager, of a typical Saturday at home with his family:

I woke up about 6:30 am, fixed some tea and read the newspaper. Since nobody else was up yet I took the opportunity to catch up on my reading of recent issues of financial newsletters and chemical journals. At 8:30 I woke up Marge and the children. We ate breakfast and I suggested that we all coordinate our schedules for the day. I had a list of chores – mowing the lawn, repairing little Georgie's bicycle and putting up some new shelves in the storage room. I had made a list of which chores I would do first and about

how long each would take. The children wanted to go for a bike ride in the afternoon so I scheduled an hour from 3:00 to 4:00 o'clock. I wanted to go into work for a little while after lunch to catch up on a report that was due next week. The children didn't seem to want to wait until 3:00. Those kids have no patience. They want to do everything *now*; they have no appreciation for the importance of time. Marge wanted to visit her mother and wanted me to go with her. She didn't understand when I told her that I just could not possibly go with her. I wish she would let me know these things in advance. I must have time to plan my schedule.

To someone who is not a Type A person, a tight schedule for a family day off is unthinkable. To Sidney, spontaneity in daily activities is unthinkable. It makes him very anxious. The worst thing one can do to a workaholic is take away his wristwatch and remove all the clocks from his house. If his sense of time is frustrated he quickly becomes anxious, agitated, angry and disorganized.

The second ingredient of Type A behaviour, job involvement, is not difficult to picture either. Seven or eight hours' work a day is never enough; the job in hand always requires overtime; the number of jobs done becomes extremely important.

A workaholic college professor might derive more satisfaction from publishing 100 run-of-the-mill research papers than from producing 10 outstanding ones. He may feel that his colleagues are judging him on the number of papers he produces. In fact, after a certain number, his colleagues probably care less about the quantity than the quality of his work.

Given a choice, the workaholic tends to prefer promotion to a pay rise. Status is extremely important and job titles and prestige become the *raison d'être*.

A person who cannot work or play without feeling the need to prove superior strength and intelligence is also displaying a Type A behaviour trait. Whether going after a rival's business account or playing tennis, this person is out to win. Competition is a serious matter. There can be no funny side to it and jokes or teasing about, for example, fluffing a match point, are completely unacceptable. Even at leisure, the workaholic simply cannot stop striving.

The fourth Type A trait, impatience and hostility, is often discernible at an early age. Many potential workaholics are described by family and friends as having a quick temper. As fully fledged workaholics they get irritated very easily, especially by other people and by upsets to their schedules. Irresponsibility, sloppiness and vagueness drive them 'up the wall', which is why they find it particularly difficult to get on with their children, especially teenagers who are developing independent lifestyles.

The workaholic does everything – eat, talk, walk, even play – in a hurry. As the years go by, he or she tries to hurry everyone else, becoming extremely impatient with the 'dawdling' pace of others. Workaholics loathe waiting in queues or waiting in traffic. They even try to hurry people during conversation, repeatedly asking 'Yes? Yes? Yes?', interjecting 'Uh-huh, uh-huh, uh-huh', or finishing off phrases and sentences for them. All of which can result in a very frustrating and tedious conversation for all concerned.

Workaholics and stress

Because of the nature of their compulsion and the behaviour patterns associated with it, workaholics live under a great deal of stress. Over a period of time day-to-day stress can have devastating physical and psychological consequences. Often it leads to secondary compulsions and addictions, such as smoking, overeating, excessive drinking or drug use. The sufferer ends up with two or three problems instead of one.

In addition, chronic stress triggers off increases in blood pressure, heart rate, breathing

---

The case of Clyde:
One addiction causes another

The term *burn-out* has often been used to refer to the fatigue, irritability, and listlessness resulting from workaholics being under too much stress for too long. In his book *Burnout: The High Cost of High Achievement*, Dr Herbert Freudenberger describes the case of Clyde, a classic example of how workaholism not only strains the emotions but also leads to other addictions.

Clyde grew up in Texas, living with his mother, two older brothers and a younger sister. His father died suddenly when Clyde was a teenager. Because the family had little money Clyde, now at high school, spent his evenings working in a local restaurant. After graduation he took a full-time job as a waiter. He felt a responsibility to help support his family. His older brothers had gone off on their own leaving him to support his mother and sister.

He threw himself into his work. After a few years Clyde went into partnership with his employer to open a new restaurant. He worked even harder, determined to make the new venture a success. He spent almost all of his time at the restaurant, building the business and worrying about the future. He had little time for recreation. The restaurant became a huge success and he worked even more hours.

When Clyde's mother remarried he was free to slow down a bit, to start a life on his own. Unfortunately, he had become trapped in a pattern of work addiction that was difficult to stop. He decided to go on to bigger and better things. He sold his share of the restaurant for a substantial profit and headed for New York. He was determined to open an elegant restaurant and make it the best in the city. He found the New York business world a lot more difficult than he had expected. He spent weeks trying to establish contacts. Neither his money nor his Texas reputation seemed to impress anybody.

He worked and planned even more diligently, more compulsively. He became more and more frustrated. One evening he met some people at a bar who introduced him to cocaine. The cocaine made him feel alive and supercharged. It gave him the same feeling of exhilaration that he experienced when working. Since his compulsion to work was not giving him the same satisfaction as it once did, he found cocaine to be an effective substitute.

He began spending more and more money on drugs. Although he still tried in vain to get his restaurant started, he met with failure at every turn. He became extremely dependent on cocaine, needing it every day. He gradually developed a chronic runny nose and nose bleeds from snorting cocaine. When he was not working compulsively he was using cocaine compulsively. He finally ended up with little money working as a waiter. His double addiction had cost him his career and his dream.

rate, metabolism, and blood flow to the muscles – the 'fight or flight' response. For our remote ancestors, of course, this response was adaptive, in the sense that it enabled them to survive. Nowadays most of us are seldom faced with physical danger which threatens our lives. We have evolved into more cerebral creatures, solving our problems through reasoning and talking rather than fighting or running. But there is a catch to this new situation: our bodies still react to real or perceived threats as they always did. The stress felt by a workaholic on a more or less daily basis triggers off an emergency response over and over again. The irony is that the stress is largely self-induced. Not meeting every goal, not being promoted at every opportunity, having to suppress anger towards an obnoxious client, having to wait for answers and decisions from others – these are inevitable in the business world. Because of intolerance and impatience, the workaholic is a prime candidate for chronic stress reactions. Dr Herbert Benson, Professor of Medicine at Harvard Medical School and Director of the Hypertension Section of Boston's Beth Israel Hospital, has demonstrated that frequent triggering of the 'fight or flight' response can lead to a *permanent* state of arousal and hypertension. The workaholic can only reduce stress by changing the behaviour pattern. Breaking the Type A pattern could mean a happier life and very possibly a healthier one and a longer one.

Once a workaholic, always a workaholic? Unfortunately most workaholics do not begin to even try to change their behaviour until a crisis occurs. This is equally true of other compulsions and addictions. The necessity of weaning the workaholic away from the addiction to work may only become apparent when a heart attack, a stroke or a broken marriage has already occurred. As more and more information appears in the popular press on stress, overwork, and the need for health and fitness, more and more workaholics are recognizing their problem and seeking help.

Workaholic, Type A behaviour *can* be changed. One method of modifying it is the Cardiac Stress Management Program developed by Drs Richard Suinn and Larry Bloom of Colorado State University. To put the programme to the

Do we live solely to work? Today leisure and exercise are increasingly emphasized. Taking pleasure in movement (left) by participating in organized sport, and (above) the contrast between a work-day and a day spent relaxing and playing with the children at the beach.

test they recruited 14 men aged between 38 and 55, all of whom were in professional or managerial jobs and showed evidence of Type A behaviour and excessive stress related to work. Half their number were given Cardiac Stress Management Training, while the others served as a control group.

Three months of training were given. First, subjects were taught a technique of deep muscle relaxation. Then they were asked to imagine stressful situations (missing an important appointment with their boss, for example) and trained to identify the specific physical sensations associated with stress. Then they practised recognizing stress cues early enough to be able to use deep muscle relaxation to counteract them. Just as important, they were encouraged to think of, and to rehearse in their imagination, alternatives to Type A behaviours. For example, they were asked to imagine being caught in rush-hour traffic and that, instead of becoming upset, they were concentrating on something else – a song on the radio, the trees beside the road, or the sky in the distance. The next step was to put these imagined alternatives into practice.

This training had a marked effect. The total Type A score of those who were given the training (as measured by the Jenkins Activity Survey) decreased from 11.1 to 6.8. The group which did not receive the training showed little change in their scores. The blood pressure of the training group also decreased (from 130/80 to 116/77mmHg) but not markedly enough to be of real statistical significance. In other studies with workaholics recently hit by heart attacks, the training programme outlined above resulted not only in Type A behaviour changes but in a marked drop in cholesterol and triglyceride (blood fat) levels.

Putting the fun back into life

According to Dr George Sheehan, physician, philosopher and guru of many world-class athletes, the ability to enjoy life is becoming a lost art. For too many of us the joy of living, the joy of playing as we did when we were children, has gone. Dr Sheehan is talking, not simply about happiness, but about physical and psychological self-fulfilment. Unless one makes a conscious decision to improve the texture and quality of life, he argues, living can become a dull, energy-sapping routine of schedules, work and responsibilities.

Of no one is this more true than the workaholic, to whom even pleasures represent 'achievements', assessable in terms of 'spin-offs' and 'fringe benefits'. One successful approach to the problem of workaholism tackles this aspect of behaviour head-on, by asking the workaholic to take positive steps to put fun into everyday life.

Andrew is a 51-year-old executive working for a large advertising agency. He is married and has one child, now grown up. His wife writes children's books and is moderately well known. Andrew is totally dedicated to his job and works 10 to 12 hours a day six days a week. His wife has learned to live with his workaholism: her main sources of satisfaction and self-esteem are her writing and her social activities. Andrew knew that his work patterns were threatening his marriage and social relationships, but was afraid of what might happen to his career if he devoted less time to business affairs.

The technique used with Andrew, called lifestyle balancing, is based on Dr Alan Marlatt's work at the University of Washington. As a first step Andrew was asked to imagine his life as a series of balloons of different sizes, the size of each balloon to correspond to the amount of his time and energy invested in each area of his life. The drawing shows Andrew's own assessment: quite clearly the Self balloon, representing the things that a person really *wants* to do for sheer enjoyment, had suffered most. Andrew was asked to divert some 'air' from his Work balloon to inflate the Self balloon. To help him do this, Andrew was encouraged to draw up two activity lists: the first, his *Should* List, consisted of all the activities he regarded as responsibilities; the second, his Want List, was made up of all the things he really wanted to do. His Want List, he was told, should include small sources of pleasure such as reading a bestseller or playing squash more often as well as larger fantasies about what he would 'ideally' like to do. He was encouraged to be as creative as possible. Initially, Andrew had rather a long Should List and only two items on his Want List. He admitted to considering other Wants but said he ruled them out as being impractical or too time consuming. Here is his first list:

Shoulds

1. Work
2. Get promotion in my company
3. Make a good living for my family
4. Be a good father
5. Join civic organizations
6. Do volunteer work
7. Get to appointments on time
8. Socialize with business associates
9. Save money for the future

Wants

1. More spare time
2. Read more often

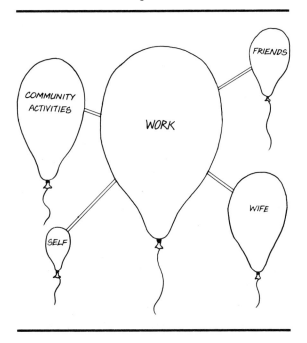

Impracticality was just what Andrew needed. To help him overcome his loathing of impracticality he was encouraged to imagine that he was being transported to a fantasy island where he would have no commitments to anybody or anything, and unlimited time and resources. With this mental set he began to list many more Wants.

Part of the workaholic's problem is a very narrow view of individual existence. Such a person never stops to think 'Why am I doing this? Is this really necessary? Is this really important to my life?'

Allowing for time to fulfil old dreams . . .

Here is a partial list of Andrew's Shoulds and Wants once he had adopted the 'fantasy island' way of thinking.

Shoulds

1. Work
2. Get promotion in my company
3. Make a good living for my family
4. Be a good father
5. Join civic organizations
6. Do volunteer work
7. Get to appointments on time
8. Socialize with business associates
9. Save money for the future

Wants

1. Play squash more often
2. Read more science fiction
3. Travel
4. Woodworking
5. Learn to fly an airplane
6. Garden
7. Take golf lessons
8. Buy an English bulldog
9. Buy a house in the country
10. Become an actor
11. Get deeper into photography as a hobby
12. Go whitewater rafting
13. Entertain friends more often and business associates less often
14. Watercolour painting

To start making his Wants a reality he was instructed to try out one Want each week to see whether he would enjoy it. It was stressed that enjoyment and pleasure were what mattered and that achievement and accomplishments were irrelevant. For example, if he really enjoyed painting in watercolour he should keep painting regardless of the results. It simply did not matter whether he painted like J. M. W. Turner or a chimpanzee.

Wants which involved major change and commitment, such as buying a house in the country, were to be approached in stages. He was simply to take a ride in the country or read the Houses for Sale columns in the newspaper – moving in the general direction of a Want can provide some pleasure even if the Want is never accomplished. Andrew's wish to become an actor was partially fulfilled through a local community theatre. Although he only played small parts and helped to build scenery he enjoyed himself immensely. He also met a wide circle of new friends.

As Andrew developed new interests he found himself becoming more effective and efficient at work. He accomplished more and in less time. His marriage improved because his new interests were those his wife could share with him.

Another method of breaking up Type A behaviour is to turn one of the workaholics' favourite stratagems against him: scheduling. First, all non-work activities are arranged according to a daily or weekly schedule; these activities take priority over work. Any necessary work is scheduled around non-work. The workaholic cannot then use the 'Sorry, no time' or 'Can't fit it in' excuse for not enjoying himself. Of course, this approach must be tempered by practicality. In Andrew's case, the following activities were scheduled into his weekly routine.

1. Thirty minutes of exercise four times a week.
2. Two full hours of uninterrupted concentra-

tion every day for drafting reports, answering letters, etc. (during this time he was to close his office door and instruct his secretary to hold all calls and tell visitors he was unavailable).

3. Thirty minutes a week considering how and to whom he might delegate some of his minor responsibilities at work.

4. Three relaxing meals every day.

5. One full hour of recreation every day, to be devoted to an activity on the Want List.

Specific times were set aside for each of these activities, and all of them were to be regarded as unbreakable 'appointments'. Unless new schedules are rigidly adhered to, new priorities will progressively fade and the old work-oriented activities crowd back in. For example, Andrew scheduled a 30-minute physical fitness routine for himself each day at 7:00 am. One day a client telephoned suggesting an appointment for that same early hour. The 'old' Andrew would have said yes without a moment's hesitation. The half reformed Andrew might have said yes and felt frustrated about missing his exercise session, or even decided 'Exercise is simply impossible with a schedule like mine.' But the 'new' Andrew simply informed his client that he was unavailable at 7:00 am but that any other time would be fine. His non-workaholic self considered exercise or body time to be as important as his most important client. It was simply a matter of re-arranging priorities.

There are other methods of tackling particular facets of workaholic behaviour. To reduce the effects of 'hurry sickness', for example, Friedman and Rosenman advise three or four planned 'breaks' in the day. This allows the workaholic to pace himself. During these breaks, spaced throughout the day, he stops whatever he is doing, takes two or three deep breaths and relaxes. The relevant relaxation techniques are described in Chapter 5. These moments of relaxation are for taking stock, for ruminating on the fundamental value and purpose of life. By pondering questions such as 'Will what I am doing now be of any importance 10 years from now?' the Type A person puts his life into a broader, longer perspective.

The study of workaholics and their problems is a relatively new field for doctors and psychologists, and one in which we can reasonably expect significant therapeutic advances in the next few years. The questionnaire on page 128 should enable readers to spot dangerous tendencies in themselves or others before their health or personal relationships are threatened. The cure for work sickness is fairly obvious: lead a more balanced life, re-arrange priorities, learn to relax, and refuse to rise to provocation.

A new social agenda might emphasize time with friends and family – a day out fishing, or being a different kind of 'workhorse' for the kids!

11
COMPULSIVE GAMBLING

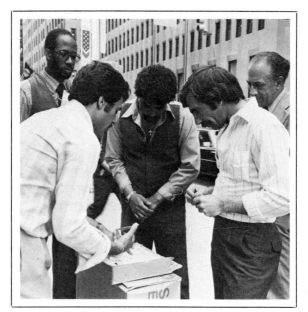

A recent study by the United Kingdom Royal Commission on Gambling reported that 94 per cent of adult Britons gambled occasionally and that 39 per cent did so regularly. Activities on which bets are made vary throughout the world. Yet whether you are betting on mah-jong in China, three card monte in South America, two-up in Australia, fan-tan in Korea, football in the United States, roulette in Monte Carlo, the tiercet in France, or the lottery in Ireland, the basic attractions are the same: excitement, and getting something (sometimes a lot) for nothing (or very little).

A tremendous amount of money is lost through gambling – an estimated £8000 million in the United Kingdom in 1977. But Lady Luck can always bring losers back for more. Theodore Roosevelt is said to have borrowed $10 for one spin of the roulette wheel in Monte Carlo, and quickly ran up winnings of $25,000. In February, 1980, a British man won a record £953,874 ($1.8 million) on the football pools.

While some people gamble for fun and some gamble for a living, others gamble because of a compulsion. Compulsive gambling is a progressively abnormal behaviour. Eventually the person has an uncontrollable urge to gamble and a preoccupation with gambling, and continues to bet even when losing heavily. The consequences – financial, occupational and marital – are often serious. Compulsive gambling is not a minor problem; in the USA alone it is estimated that there are over one million compulsive gamblers.[1]

Though gambling is not the vice of any one class or calling, it is far more frequent among men than women. Almost always the compulsive gambler is of above average intelligence, but there the similarities end. Three notorious Roman emperors, Nero, Claudius and Caligula, were compulsive gamblers and so was the Russian novelist Dostoevsky; he spent every rouble his publishers paid him on roulette.

The annals of gambling are probably richer in anecdote than those of any other compulsion. Parysatis, Queen of Persia, played craps with a slave – for his life or his freedom. The dice worked for her, but not for him, and he was tortured to death. Doubtless if the stakes were always as grim as this there would be few compulsive gamblers. An aficionado of Russian roulette would probably blow his brains out long before he developed a behaviour problem!

Triumph (right) and hopeless despair (left): the twin aspects of the compulsive gambler. It is the risk and excitement that are alluring.

Are you a compulsive gambler?

Take the following test to see if your gambling is just an innocent hobby or a serious compulsion for which you need help. Answer 'Yes' or 'No' to each question:

1. Has your family or marriage ever been disrupted due to gambling?   _____Yes _____No

2. Have you ever defaulted on a debt or other financial obligation as a result of gambling?
   _____Yes _____No

3. Have you ever lost time at work to pursue gambling activities?   _____Yes _____No

4. Have you ever borrowed money for gambling or to pay gambling debts? _____Yes _____No

5. Have you ever committed crimes to obtain money for gambling? _____Yes _____No

6. Have you ever been unable to account for losses of money?   _____Yes _____No

7. Have you ever been 'bailed out' by another person to repay gambling debts?
   _____Yes _____No

If you answered 'Yes' to any *3* of these questions you are a problem gambler and need to institute Selfwatching techniques.

The consequences of compulsive gambling are less dramatically fatal, but slowly and surely the gambler gets heavily into debt, and his compulsion comes to affect his family, friends and job. His only way out, as he sees it, may be to embezzle money and he will bet with money needed for food, rent and other necessities. The next bet is always going to be the big one, the jackpot. One big win will enable him to recoup his losses and pay back his creditors. Only seldom, very seldom, does this happen.

Luck versus skill

If you ask an inveterate gambler what makes him win, his answer will probably include the word 'luck' or 'lucky'. Winning is attributed to 'beginner's luck', lucky numbers, 'hot dice', the day of the week, and so on. Is this belief in luck well founded?

Newcomers to any form of gambling are said to have beginner's luck – it is assumed that the odds are slightly in their favour. But the beginner's luck argument is illogical and circular. If you ask someone: 'How do you know so-and-so has beginner's luck?' he will answer 'Because he won.' When you asked him 'Why did so-and-so win?' he will reply 'Beginner's luck, probably!' Behaviour is inferred from the luck and luck is inferred from the behaviour. If beginner's luck were a valid phenomenon, first-time gamblers would tend to win more than experienced gamblers, but this is simply not true.

That is not to say that *belief* in beginner's luck does not have a powerful influence over a person's gambling behaviour. In one particular study undergraduates were given money to gamble with, and it was found that those who won near the beginning of the gambling session (during the first 22 bets) continued gambling longer, even when they were losing, than those who won at a later stage. In other words, beginner's luck resulted in greater persistence and perhaps greater compulsiveness. This effect was investigated further by telling some of the students that they had beginner's luck, that they were doing better than the others, even though they kept on losing. This information made them more persistent. So believing in luck, despite financial evidence to the contrary, will keep you gambling long after your 'unlucky' friends have given up.

Aptly named the 'one armed bandit', this machine will empty your purse with your complete co-operation.

Probability versus skill

In some ways the compulsive gambler's belief in luck is easier to understand than his belief in skill. If gambling were taken at face value, as a game of chance rather than a game of skill, perhaps fewer people would gamble. Of course, different forms of gambling involve different ratios of luck and skill. Flipping a coin or playing a slot machine are matters purely of luck and probability. Blackjack, or 21, and perhaps betting on horse-racing, involve a combination of luck, skill and judgement.

Most dedicated gamblers have their own 'system' for winning. They believe that the odds can be beaten, or at least reduced, by applying skill. Now the odds that a coin will come up heads are even; no matter how many times the coin is flipped (assuming the coin is not 'fixed') the odds are the same each time. Despite this incontrovertible fact people persist in believing in 'the Monte Carlo fallacy': if a coin comes down heads three times in a row it *must* be more likely to come down tails the next time.

Put ten gambling experts together and the odds against their agreeing on the best method of beating the odds are very long indeed! One popular gambling book suggests that in 21 a gambler should bet in a progressive fashion based on winnings. If he wins back his original £2 bet he should then bet £4; if he wins that he should bet £6, then £10. As soon as he loses he is advised to return to his original £2 bet. The author of that book is assuming that luck runs in patterns, but this is not necessarily true. In contrast, other experts advise that bets should be doubled after several losses 'because your time is coming'. Others advise you to quit while you are winning, others that the sensible time to stop is when you are losing. Casinos would probably prefer their clients to quit while winning in order

to entice other clients to the 'lucky' table. If everyone gave up when they first started to lose, there would be no such thing as compulsive gambling.

Superstitions

Addicted gamblers become very superstitious about their gambling. This is not surprising, as studies of learning patterns have shown. Any behaviour which occurs more or less simultaneously with a reinforcement (some kind of reward) is strengthened, whether or not the behaviour actually produced the reinforcement. In a gambling context this means that every time you cross your fingers for luck and win, the more likely you are to cross your fingers the next time. Superstitions like this can grow into strong habits. Some gamblers go through quite elaborate superstitious rituals. Crap shooters, for example, are notorious for stacking chips in a precise and personal way, rubbing the felt on the table before throwing the dice, repeating nonsense catch-phrases like 'Baby needs a new pair of shoes', or asking a glamorous woman to touch or blow on the dice for luck. None of these behaviours can possibly influence the outcome of the bet. The gambler knows this is so, but still goes through the ritual – just in case.

Probably the prize for the most bizarre gambling ritual should be awarded to a gambler named Mr Blanchard. As he walked into the casino at Monte Carlo one day a pigeon flying overhead soiled his hat. That day he won $15,000. On all his subsequent visits, he would walk around in circles outside the casino before going in, hoping for another lucky charm from the heavens.

The gambling bug and how it bites

There is a serious shortage of reliable research into the development of gambling behaviour. The most puzzling thing about compulsive gamblers is this: why do they continue gambling in the face of repeated losses? Part of the explanation seems to lie in what the noted psychologist B. F. Skinner calls 'schedules of reinforcement'.

Reinforcement, or reward, for a given behaviour may occur every time the behaviour occurs, or only occasionally. As we all know, most of life's rewards and pleasures come intermittently rather than continuously. The psychological consequence of intermittent reinforcement is that it creates behaviours which are very difficult to break, 'very resistant to extinction' as psychologists would say. Extinction should occur when the reward is no longer provided. If a fisherman who catches a fish every time he casts his rod suddenly stops catching fish, he might give up and go home after just a few casts. But if he catches a fish only once in

Whether it's cock fighting (far left), the betting shop (centre) or the horse races (right), for the gambler the ratio of expectation to fulfilment is high. There is excitement, true, but also stress and misery.

every 15 casts, and then catches nothing for a long time he will not give up so easily. He will not even suspect that his luck has changed until he has cast at least 15 times. The first fisherman becomes suspicious after the first unlucky cast.

Gambling machines and games reinforce betting very intermittently. Therefore risk-taking persists even though there is often no pay off. In one of the earliest experiments on gambling Drs D. J. Lewis and C. P. Duncan investigated the effect which frequency of winning has on gambling behaviour.[2] Students were given money to use in a gambling device similar to a fruit machine. The machine was fixed so that it paid some students every time they pulled the lever and others only about half the time. After a while the machine was re-fixed so that it would not pay out to anyone. Under these conditions the students who had been winning only half the time continued to gamble much longer than those who had been winning all the time. Another interesting thing about this experiment was that it showed the irrationality of the greater persistence encouraged by intermittent reinforcement. Under 'no pay off' conditions the ex-winners stopped gambling when their losses were still small, but not so the others. It was as if they believed that the more money they lost the better chances they had of winning.

One of the first researchers to study real-life

Punters anxiously watch and wait as the bookie chalks up the new odds.

gambling situations was the British psychologist Mark Dickerson. Having discovered that 90 per cent of the members of Gamblers Anonymous (a self-help group for compulsive gamblers) were formerly addicted to off-course race betting, he wondered whether there was something about betting offices which made them 'training grounds' for compulsive gamblers (betting shops were legalized in the United Kingdom by the Betting and Gaming Act of 1960). For anyone who has never seen the inside of a betting shop, Dickerson gives the following description:

> Such offices often have a shop front like other high street shops. A view into the shop is often obscured by a display of racing pictures. Inside, the shop floor area (20 to 30sq. yd) is usually bare. A large display board shows runners and riders of the day's meetings. Form sheets are pinned around the walls. There are betting slip dispensers and ledges on which to lean. The place-take counter is usually placed across the far wall with security glass to the ceiling. There is always a clock and a loudspeaker (blower) to which is piped a live commentary from the race courses.[3]

On any weekday afternoon there may be between 24 and 32 dog and horse races taking place. Approximately four minutes before the start of a dog race and 15 minutes before the start of a horse race a sequence of information about the race begins. This sequence includes such comments as 'They're parading', 'They're at the start', 'They're in the stalls.' These announcements continue until the cry 'They're off!', which is followed by a running commentary on the race. Betting continues until the moment of the 'off', at which time no further bets can be placed on that particular race.

Dr Dickerson and his colleagues closely observed customers in two betting shops in Birmingham, England. The number of bets placed by each customer and the times they were made were carefully recorded. For the purpose of this study each customer was identified as a high-frequency gambler (bets placed on eight or more races on three or more days in any one week) or a low-frequency gambler (bets placed on three or fewer races in any one day).

Dickerson found that the high-frequency group tended to place their bets just before the 'off', whereas the low-frequency group placed their bets well before the 'off' as shown below. Some high-frequency gamblers were even seen to hold their betting slip at the betting window ready to pass it under the grill at the very last moment. As you can see, the high-frequency group tended to bet more money than the low-frequency group, placing more bets of over £1 and fewer of less than 50p. Approximately 60 per cent of the bets placed by the low-frequency gamblers were for 50p ($1 approx.).

Dickerson's study clearly showed that the betting behaviour of high-frequency gamblers, those most likely to be compulsive, is markedly different from that of the occasional gambler. The characteristic behaviour of the high-frequency gambler is a relatively high stake and betting at the last possible moment. Several cus-

tomers were asked about this last-minute behaviour and most agreed that late betting increased the element of skill; the more information punters have about changes in odds, which reflect increasing or decreasing interest in a particular horse, the better equipped they are to exercise their judgement. Unfortunately, the statistics explode this plausible theory: 80 per cent of all wagers made in betting shops are lost regardless of the time they are placed.

Dickerson and his colleagues concluded that there are two distinct reinforcers at work when a compulsive gambler walks into a betting shop. The first and most obvious is money, either cash paid out after a win or the expectation of cash to come. The second and possibly the more important, is the subjective experience of gambling, what it feels like to gamble. The excitement starts with the pre-race commentary, and the fluctuation of the odds, and builds to tremendous intensity towards the closing moments of the race itself. It is this high emotional charge which seems to be the primary craving of the inveterate gambler. The act of gambling is its own reward regardless of the financial outcome, which brings us to another possible explanation of how gambling behaviour develops.

The arousal theory

Several psychologists, including Drs David McClelland and P. T. Young, have put forward theories about human motivation based on 'arousal', our level of emotional and physiological excitement. These theories suggest that we all behave in ways designed to maintain our arousal at an optimum level. We are happiest at this level.

Professor Hans J. Eysenck of the University of London has taken this concept a step further. His studies indicate that extraversion and introversion may be linked to levels of arousal in the cortex, the outer rind, of the brain. Extraverts have low arousal levels and so tend to be sensation-seekers. The reverse is true of introverts. Extraverts behave in ways designed to increase stimulation, and are naturally attracted by excitement, noisy social gatherings and risky situations. They are also more likely to become addicted to coffee and cigarettes than introverts, because both contain substances which increase

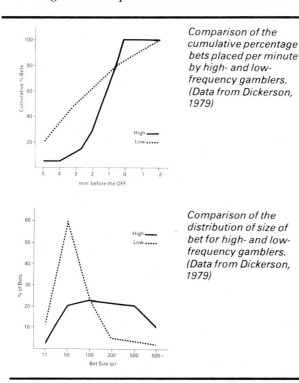

Comparison of the cumulative percentage bets placed per minute by high- and low-frequency gamblers. (Data from Dickerson, 1979)

Comparison of the distribution of size of bet for high- and low-frequency gamblers. (Data from Dickerson, 1979)

arousal. This consumption of caffeine and nicotine constitutes a form of self-medication.

From the admittedly scanty information we have about gamblers, it appears that most compulsive gamblers are more extraverted than introverted. Gambling provides risk and excitement and is reinforced by subsequent increases in arousal level. Gambling, particularly high-risk gambling, continues in spite of losses because it helps the gambler to achieve an optimum arousal level. He gets accustomed to associating arousal with gambling. And every time he gambles the link between arousal and gambling gets stronger. He is conditioning himself. Eventually, he has only to anticipate gambling and he feels aroused. The reinforcement, then, is gambling itself, the thrill of risk. Winning or losing becomes irrelevant.

The case of William illustrates this point. William is a 32-year-old loan officer for a large bank in Atlanta, Georgia. He is married with two small children, and describes himself as a fun-loving sort, but also hard working, achievement-oriented and competitive. His life was of only average complexity until, in May of 1980, his gambling caught up with him. People began to notice how much time he was taking off work, and it was discovered that he had excessive gambling debts.

William had begun to gamble at the age of 15, innocently enough at first, betting on sporting events with friends. As a boy he had always been a sensation-seeker. He enjoyed taking part in all forms of sport, especially football. As a university student he took up skydiving, hang-gliding and downhill skiing. He seemed to thrive on the thrill of taking chances. The risks he took skiing resulted at different times in a fractured ankle, a broken arm and a dislocated shoulder.

His betting increased in frequency while he was at college, with the willing co-operation of a local bookie who ran bets on professional football, basketball and baseball games. Twice weekly he played poker for money with friends. This pattern continued when he left college. He noticed, however, even at this stage, that he became very uneasy and tense whenever he missed a poker game or did not place a bet on a sporting event. Gambling was slowly assuming greater importance in his life.

The glamour of Las Vegas. But how many lives are mortgaged to its casinos? Fun all too easily becomes addiction, followed by an uneasy lurching between frenzy and despair.

When he was 27 he attended a banking convention in Las Vegas. The excitement of the casinos had a tremendous impact on him. This first visit to Vegas was a major turning point in his life, like 'finding religion' as he put it. He had never experienced such emotional excitement before. He played 21 and craps for three days and ended up winning $1200.

Soon after that he met a girl named Gloria and six months later married her. Over the next few years he put all his energy and enthusiasm into his banking career, his status and salary increased rapidly, and the couple had two children, a boy and a girl. William still gambled – poker once a week and the occasional bet on a sporting event – but not with the frequency of his bachelor days. A few years passed and he began to feel hemmed in by the routines of work and family. He became mildly depressed, lost his energy and enthusiasm, and had difficulty concentrating on his work. This was the time when he began placing more bets with his bookie and joined a second poker group during the week. Betting provided the excitement he needed. Then he and some friends made a three-day trip to Las Vegas, an elixir as far as he was concerned:

> I feel more in touch with the world in the casino. I guess this sounds funny but I feel more normal when I'm gambling. The noise around me, the excitement at the craps table is mesmerising. I lose track of time. Since I'm playing with chips I lose track of money. Money becomes meaningless. Everything else in my life becomes meaningless when I'm gambling.

When the three days in Las Vegas ended, William's friends went home but he stayed, unable to tear himself away. In two more days he lost $3500. This was vastly more than he could afford and when he returned home he and his wife quarrelled badly.

Guilty though he felt about his losses, his trip to Las Vegas only seemed to intensify his desire to gamble. After two weeks at home even the poker games and sports betting did not seem to satisfy his urge to gamble. One day he borrowed $1000 from his brother, took all of his own savings (about $5000) out of the bank, and told his wife that he was going on a business trip for a week. Instead, he bought a one-way ticket to Las Vegas. After 24 hours of 21, poker and craps he had lost everything. He became panicky. Just one more big bet, he told himself, and I'll be able to win it all back. He was given $2000 credit at Caesar's Palace and made wins bringing it to $6000 at the craps table. He placed another bet and lost and still another lost again. When he was back down to $2000 he repaid the debt to the casino and left. He paid his flight home with a credit card. His reappearance was greeted with chagrin and concern by his wife and brother. Filled with remorse he promised never to gamble again. Within two days he was again placing bets with his bookie and within a week he had lost money that he did not have. He took out a second mortgage on his house and borrowed

$10,000 from his bank. He paid his bookie $1500 that he owed him and left on the next plane for Las Vegas.

This was a pattern which continued with increasingly sinister variations over the next few weeks. The financial and marital problems worsened. Job, marriage and financial stability were all called into question. In spite of all this, William felt compelled to continue gambling. Caught between his compulsion and its effect on those nearest to him, he became extremely depressed and required short-term hospitalization.

What can be done
To put an end to compulsive gambling we first need to identify the problem gambler. The criteria listed earlier in this chapter help to define whether a person is at risk or not. Generally, a problem exists when gambling consistently produces family, legal, employment or financial problems. Is gambling an essential part of the person's life or can he take it or leave it? Compulsive gamblers must be confronted with their behaviour as soon as possible by friends and relatives – it is no kindness to them to keep silent. Helping the compulsive gambler by lending him more money only reinforces his behaviour and keeps him trapped in the vicious spiral of more gambling, more borrowing, more gambling, more borrowing. . . .

Like alcoholics, compulsive gamblers usually deny the extent of their problem. They repeat the worn out phrase 'I can stop any time I want to.' But that actions speak louder than words is especially true with compulsions and addictions. A strict promise to refrain from gambling for 30 days usually demonstrates to the gambler and to those around him that he is unable to stop even for a few days. Unfortunately, the compulsive gambler usually seeks treatment only after his life is in a crisis state.

Gamblers Anonymous is a self-help organization modelled on Alcoholics Anonymous. It holds informal meetings which allow compulsive gamblers to share their problems with others in the same predicament. Key steps in the recovery process involve admitting the problem, being willing to accept help from others, looking realistically at one's own strengths and weaknesses and helping others with similar problems.

Gamblers Anonymous is also a support group for the spouses of compulsive gamblers. The relatives of compulsive gamblers are often under a great deal of stress and do need help, if only to see their difficulties in a more objective light.

Imposing legal sanctions is one way of trying to prevent compulsive gambling. Ideally, sanctions ought to control those methods of gambling most likely to lead to compulsive behaviour. Many countries have gambling commissions or similar bodies, but their primary function is to see that gambling establishments pay the proper amount of tax and that standards of honesty are maintained. The UK Royal Commission on Gambling publicly claims to be concerned about pathological gambling but does not regard itself as obliged to do anything about it. On the other hand it does recommend that bettors be provided with as much information on odds and chances of winning as possible. If anything this recommendation probably encourages more rather than less compulsive gambling. As Dickerson convincingly showed, commentaries and updates on odds and other race details actually heighten the excitement and the appeal of gambling. Social policy on gambling remains fragmentary and currently does little to prevent or cure the problems gambling can cause.

The self-watching techniques described earlier in this book offer a highly constructive approach to the problem. The most practical of these are (1) development of self-control skills, (2) development of alternative behaviours which offer the same excitement as gambling, (3) understanding the conditioning processes which reinforce the compulsion to gamble, (4) learning and practising the problem-solving skills needed to sort out marital, financial and legal difficulties and (5) keeping a selfwatching diary as a running check on behaviour changes.

Mrs Anne R: A success case

Although compulsive gambling is more common among men than women the case of Anne illustrates how devastating this problem can be for a young housewife. At 26 years of age Anne is married to an electrician and has two young children. Her husband makes a moderate salary, but with the current inflationary economy, the couple has trouble making ends meet.

Anne started gambling only about a year before she came for professional help. At her first treatment session she described her frustration and turmoil:

'I'm so depressed and guilty I don't know what to do. I can't stop myself from gambling. I was so desperate last week that I gambled away the grocery money. The week before I used the money we were saving for the children's new winter coats to pay off my gambling debts. What kind of a mother am I? I must be a monster! I've never been so miserable in my life.'

Anne was extremely depressed, tearful and humiliated. Her husband was understandably upset and angry. This was not the first time that their hard-earned money had disappeared.

Anne started gambling as a teenager when she accompanied her uncle to the track to watch horse racing. He was an inveterate gambler. She immediately fell in love with the excitement. Eventually, she would gamble on anything – cards, horses, sporting events. She had always been an insecure person and as she put it, 'I feel important when I'm gambling. It really doesn't matter if I win or lose. When I'm making a bet, especially if it's larger than someone else's, I feel like I'm the most important person in the world. People respect me. And, the excitement I feel! I can't really describe it but it's exhilarating!'

Anne's compulsion to gamble was so strong that she was afraid she would never be able to quit. Her love for her husband and children provided the motivation. She learned and applied Selfwatching techniques quickly. She particularly used the relaxation and cue exposure procedures described in Chapters 4 and 5. Social skills training enabled her to be more open and assertive in her relationships with others and to become a more confident person. To provide an alternative to the 'excitement' of gambling, Anne took a part-time real estate job. She had worked in real estate once before and had found it extremely challenging. The excitement of closing a large deal and the personal challenge of having her own career proved to be invaluable in her treatment. In addition, she began bringing in extra money for the family.

Anne managed to stop gambling completely and has not had a single bet for over a year. Her own comments tell her success story best:

'I feel like a different person. Gambling no longer rules my life. I have confidence and I take charge of things. When I was gambling, I felt like a pinball machine. It was as though someone else was controlling me. Well, that's all in the past. I now have a happy family life.'

12
ALCOHOLISM

In terms of disease and in its wider social costs, alcohol is arguably the most dangerous drug available. It can cause death directly through such diseases as cirrhosis of the liver and as a contributory factor in acts of violent aggression and road accidents. It has been claimed that alcoholism in industry in the United States costs $10 billion a year: the comparable figure in the United Kingdom is £40 million, of which £20 million is paid out in sickness benefit. On the one hand alcohol is associated with fun, relaxation, entertainment and good fellowship. On the other it is the 'demon drink', responsible for the huddled, ragged figures to be seen on city streets all over the world. Yet individuals need not conform to the stereotype of the Skid Row alcoholic to experience severe personal and social problems as a result of drinking. In this chapter we present a summary of what is known about alcohol, its effects on human beings, the kinds of problems it can cause and how alcohol dependence can come about. In the process, we shall examine some selfwatching strategies for fighting alcohol dependence.

What is alcohol?
The drug ethyl alcohol is the effective ingredient of all alcoholic drinks. It is naturally produced by the fermenting action of yeast on some kinds of sugars. It can be produced artificially, and in a more concentrated form, by distilling – essentially, boiling off the water content in naturally fermented alcohol. The box overleaf shows the alcohol content by glass of popular drinks.

What does it do?
Alcohol acts to depress the activity of the nervous system. In small doses this results in a lessening of tension and a feeling of relaxation and lack of inhibition. Increased dosage, however, leads to a progressive loss of control over judgement, skills and emotions, often accompanied by violence and aggression. In large doses alcohol poisons the whole system and may result in coma followed by death. Alcohol also has a long history of inducing a dependence which is notoriously difficult to break. Finally, alcohol can cause irreversible damage to tissue in organs such as the brain and the liver.

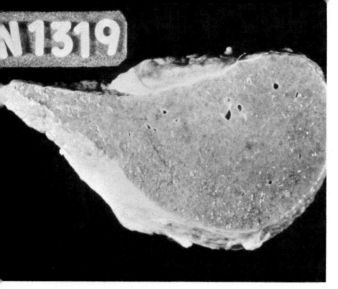

N1319

The poisoned liver of an alcoholic who died of cirrhosis. In a healthy person damage to the liver is quickly repaired.

What is an alcoholic?

Most of us have experienced the pleasurable and relaxing effects of alcohol at some time or another. It is these effects that reinforce regular use and dependence. But when does habitual use become alcoholism? Although many books have been written on the subject, the exact definition of alcoholism is still a matter of debate. There is no absolute point, for example, at which a heavy drinker suddenly becomes an alcoholic. It is much more useful to say that alcohol dependence is not an all-or-nothing phenomenon but, like deafness or obesity, it is present in degrees. When do we say that a person is deaf rather than hard of hearing? At what point do we say that a

Alcohol Questionnaire

1 Do you occasionally drink heavily after a disappointment, a quarrel, or when the boss gives you a hard time?

2 When you have trouble or feel under pressure, do you always drink more heavily than usual?

3 Have you noticed that you are able to handle more liquor than you did when you were first drinking?

4 Did you ever wake up on the morning after and discover that you could not remember part of the evening before, even though your friends tell you that you did not 'pass out'?

5 When drinking with other people, do you try to have a few extra drinks when others will not know it?

6 Are there certain occasions when you feel uncomfortable if alcohol is not available?

7 Have you recently noticed that when you begin drinking you are in more of a hurry to get the first drink than you used to be?

8 Do you sometimes feel a little guilty about your drinking?

9 Are you secretly irritated when your family or friends discuss your drinking?

10 Have you recently noticed an increase in the frequency of your memory blackouts?

11 Do you often find that you wish to continue drinking after your friends say they have had enough?

12 Do you usually have a reason for the occasions when you drink heavily?

13 When you are sober, do you often regret things you have done or said while drinking?

14 Have you tried switching brands or following different plans for controlling your drinking?

15 Have you often failed to keep the promises you have made to yourself about controlling or cutting down on your drinking?

16 Have you ever tried to control your drinking by making a change in jobs, or moving to a new location?

17 Do you try to avoid family or close friends while you are drinking?

18 Are you having an increasing number of financial and work problems?

19 Do more people seem to be treating you unfairly without good reason?

20 Do you eat very little or irregularly when you are drinking?

21 Do you sometimes have the shakes in the morning and find it helps to have a little drink?

22 Have you recently noticed that you cannot drink as much as you once did?

23 Do you sometimes stay drunk for several days at a time?

24 Do you sometimes feel very depressed and wonder whether life is worth living?

25 Sometimes after periods of drinking, do you see or hear things that aren't there?

26 Do you get terribly frightened after you have been drinking heavily?

If you have answered 'yes' to any of the questions, you have some of the symptoms that may indicate problem drinking. 'Yes' answers to several of the questions indicate the following stages:

Questions 1–8 – Entering the risk area
Questions 9–21 – Middle stage
Questions 22–26 – Beginning of final stage

Alcohol content per glass of various drinks

| ½ pint beer | 1 glass of table wine | 1 glass of sherry | 1 single whisky | 1 unit of alcohol | 15mg/100ml |

person is obese rather than fat? Alcohol dependence is a continuum ranging from slight to severe, and there is nothing to be gained from agreeing to a cut-off point above which the heavy drinker is an alcoholic and below which he or she is just a problem drinker. Anybody who wants to drink less, but has difficulty doing so, is to some extent alcohol-dependent.

What are the signs of severe alcohol dependence?

The concepts of tolerance and physical dependence are important in understanding how people come to be addicted to any drug. Tolerance refers to the tendency of the central nervous system to adapt to the intoxicating effects of a drug so that a larger dose is needed to produce the same effect. Tolerance of alcohol is displayed not only by the heavy social drinker who boasts that he can drink his friends under the table, or by the severely dependent alcoholic who can consume half a bottle of whisky without appearing to be intoxicated, but also, in experimental conditions, by rats given daily doses of 6gm per kg of body weight over a two week period.

Physical dependence has been defined by the World Health Organization as 'an adaptive state that manifests itself by intense physical disturbance when the administration of the drug is suspended'. The parallel development of tolerance and physical dependence lead to an increased level of consumption, since a large dose of alcohol is needed to produce the same effect. To add to the problem, drinking is likely to be continued in order to avoid actual or expected withdrawal symptoms. So the person who is severely dependent on alcohol is both psychologically and physiologically dependent, and is suffering from the alcohol dependence syndrome. This syndrome can be described in the following way. First, there is a subjective awareness of a compulsion to drink so that drinking takes priority over other activities. Drink becomes more important than one's family, job, friends and health. There is a narrowing of the drinking repertoire so that the more dependent a person becomes, the more stereotyped his or her drinking behaviour.

Tolerance to alcohol increases and withdrawal symptoms such as shakiness, sweats and de-

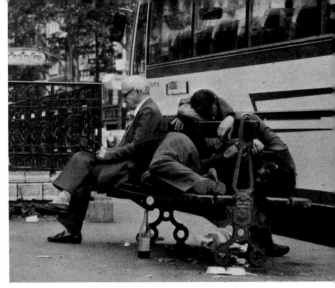

This is the public stereotype of the alcoholic, but the range of alcohol dependency is much wider.

pression tend to occur, especially on the 'morning after', when the level of alcohol in the bloodstream is much lower. If the sufferer drinks in order to avoid withdrawal symptoms, these symptoms typically disappear very rapidly after only a few drinks. With bottles hidden away at home or at work, the alcoholic is always prepared for the sudden onset of withdrawal symptoms. Finally, even if the severely dependent alcoholic is able to remain abstinent, there is still great risk. If drinking is resumed, there is a strong possibility that old habits will reappear as strongly as ever within a few days.

Alcohol and society

The decision to drink is the result of a complex interaction between the drinker and his social environment. Many investigations have clearly demonstrated that heavy drinking is strongly influenced by one's sex, ethnic group, occupation and country, as well as price and availability. One survey confirmed that drinking problems differ with ethno-religious groupings: most Jewish men drink, but few of them drink heavily or get into trouble because of their drinking; most Catholics and liberal Protestants drink, and an above average proportion have drinking problems – whereas conservative, or 'puritan', Protestants (from denominations favouring total abstinence) show a high proportion of abstainers, although the heavy drinkers among them frequently have problems.

Economic costs of alcohol misuse and alcoholism in the United States, 1975

Item	Cost (Billion $)
Lost Production	$19.64
Health and Medical	12.74
Motor Vehicle Accidents	5.14
Violent Crime	2.86
Social Responses	1.94
Fire Losses	0.43
Total	**$42.75**

Source: Third Special Report to the U.S. Congress on Alcohol and Health.

The wine-producing countries contain a disproportionately large number of heavy drinkers probably because drink is freely available and drinking is an incidental part of everyday living. The generally permissive attitude towards drinking influences not only the drinking habits of individuals but also the social policies of governments.[1] With regard to laws about licensing hours for bars and cafés, for instance, France and Italy are notably more liberal than the United Kingdom.

Occupations, too, play a part in the tendency to drink heavily; company directors, publicans and inn-keepers, stage managers, actors, entertainers, musicians, cooks and seamen have a high death rate from alcohol, including cirrhosis of the liver. We do not fully understand why some of these groups should tend to drink to excess, but it has been suggested that relevant factors include the availability of drink, social pressure to drink – or, looking at it from the other side, the fact that people who are already heavy drinkers may select occupations in which drink is readily available and acceptable.[2]

IN A TEST WITH PROFESSIONAL DRIVERS THE MORE THEY HAD TO DRINK THE MORE CERTAIN THEY WERE THAT THEY COULD...

DAMN AND BLAST!

HE'S KNOCKED OVER HALF OF THEM!

..DRIVE BETWEEN THESE MOVEABLE POSTS... AND THE LESS ABLE THEY WERE TO DO IT.

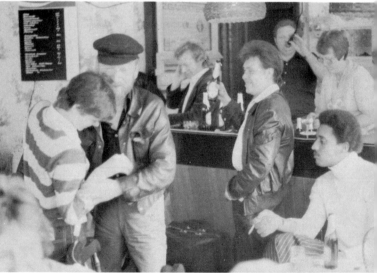

Leaving, well, before you go why not let me buy you 'one for the roa

Social problems

Public drunkenness is a punishable offence mainly because the disinhibited drunk is frequently a public nuisance and is likely to be overtly aggressive. There are now over 100,000 convictions for drunkenness in England and Wales every year – resulting in about 3000 prison sentences. While many of these are petty offences, alcohol has been implicated in a high proportion of distressing crimes of violence.

The impact on national economies in terms of absenteeism and inefficiency at work has already been described. Apart from the excessive cost of alcoholism to society and to the health of the drinker as an individual, an alcoholic may subject other people in the immediate environment to almost intolerable experiences.

Alcohol and accidents

Alcohol intoxication can lead to the type of fearless and foolhardy behaviour which makes a party swing, but at the same time may incur tragic consequences, especially as a result of traffic, domestic or industrial accidents.

Impaired performance is detectable in drivers at alcohol levels as low as 30mg/100ml, and is clearly evident at a level of 80mg/100ml (the legal limit in Britain). The average deterioration in performance is about 12 per cent. The risk of a driver being involved in an accident is about 10 times higher than normal at 150mg/100ml and 20 times higher at 200mg/100ml.

The World Health Organization estimates that in Australia, for example, at least 50 per cent of the deaths resulting from traffic accidents are associated with alcohol consumption. This type of alcohol-related accident kills more people than all the infectious diseases put together. The percentage of traffic accidents which can be attributed to alcohol varies from country to country and appears to be as low as 3 to 10 per cent in some; but even these low figures should exert some influence upon social policy and our attitude towards the drunken driver.

Alcohol is also implicated in a significant proportion of domestic and industrial accidents. One study of accidents at work in a region of Paris found that 10 to 15 per cent were probably

Cirrhosis and alcohol consumption

Cirrhosis Mortality per 100,000 Population 25 Years of Age and Older and Alcohol Consumption Per Capita. Death rates for the USA and Belgium are 1971, all other death rates are for 1972 (World Health Statistics Annual, 1973). Consumption figures are the 1968–70 average (Sulkunan, 1975).

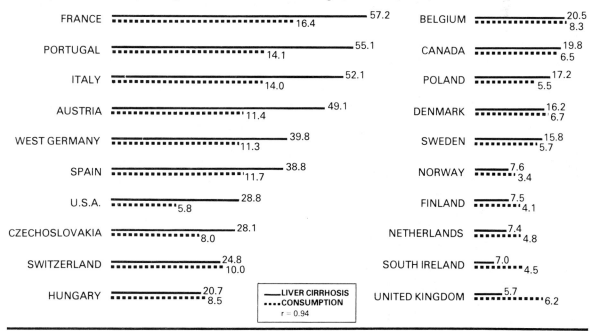

	LIVER CIRRHOSIS	CONSUMPTION
FRANCE	57.2	16.4
PORTUGAL	55.1	14.1
ITALY	52.1	14.0
AUSTRIA	49.1	11.4
WEST GERMANY	39.8	11.3
SPAIN	38.8	11.7
U.S.A.	28.8	5.8
CZECHOSLOVAKIA	28.1	8.0
SWITZERLAND	24.8	10.0
HUNGARY	20.7	8.5
BELGIUM	20.5	8.3
CANADA	19.8	6.5
POLAND	17.2	5.5
DENMARK	16.2	6.7
SWEDEN	15.8	5.7
NORWAY	7.6	3.4
FINLAND	7.5	4.1
NETHERLANDS	7.4	4.8
SOUTH IRELAND	7.0	4.5
UNITED KINGDOM	5.7	6.2

LIVER CIRRHOSIS
....CONSUMPTION
r = 0.94

Drunk, disorderly and destitute in the antique manner (above). Alcohol is addictive, behaviour cues can be established early in life (below).

due to alcoholic intoxication. Another study of non-traffic accident victims in Switzerland between 1964 and 1970 showed that 24 per cent of them were under the influence of alcohol when they were brought into hospital. It is clear that alcohol adds considerably to the risks of any occupation in which accidents are avoided only by vigilance and a clear head.

Alcohol and the body

Liver cirrhosis is such a common consequence of prolonged heavy drinking that cirrhosis rates are often used as an index of a country's drinking problem. There is enough evidence to suggest that drinking between 5 and 10 pints of beer or more each day, or an equivalent amount of wine and spirits, directly increases the risk of cirrhosis. Some research reports have suggested that more than 80 per cent of people who drink ten pints per day or more are likely to suffer from liver damage. Stomach and duodenal ulcers are also linked to alcohol consumption, and more than 20 per cent of people with alcoholism have some kind of ulceration.

The severely dependent alcoholic risks brain damage and intellectual impairment, chiefly of learning ability and memory. Extreme befuddlement, called Korsakoff's syndrome, is usually the result of years of excessive drinking.

The foetal alcohol syndrome is now being intensively studied in the United States. There is evidence to suggest that a pregnant woman who drinks heavily is causing physical harm to her unborn child. Such a baby might suffer from mild or moderate mental retardation, with an abnormally small head, congenital heart disease and other congenital deformities.

So alcohol, like any other drug, can cause enormous mental and physical damage if taken in excess. Add together the increased risks of developing liver cirrhosis, ulcers, cancer and brain damage, as well as the increased risk of accidents, self-poisoning and violence, and it would appear that the life expectancy of a heavy drinker is likely to be drastically reduced. In one British study, a group of 935 patients were followed up 10 to 15 years after admission to a hospital with the diagnosis of alcoholism. It was found that the mortality rate for this group was about 300 per cent above that expected for the general population.

There is no doubt, then, that alcohol taken to excess can cause untold harm. In addition to self-inflicted physical damage, families have been ruined, children have been harmed by their drinking parents and alcoholics have destroyed their own self-esteem and their standing in both social and business communities. Because alcohol is addictive, and because heavy drinking leads on to psychological, social and physical harm, we must all be concerned by the recent world increase in alcohol consumption.

Drink watching

Looking at drinking in terms of learned behaviour, influenced by antecedent cues and reinforcing consequences is a far cry from the traditional methods of viewing alcoholism in terms of a disease or a mental illness. If the alcoholic or heavy drinker can identify the antecedent cues that result in a desire for drink then he or she is in a position to try out ways of coping with these cues by desensitizing them or simply avoiding them by changing their life style (see Chapters 2–4).

The causes of alcohol dependence

The emergence of physical dependence is important in the development of alcoholism, but does not fully explain it. The process begins, not with physical dependence but psychological dependence. Typically the problem drinker regards alcohol as a reliever of tension, especially social tensions. Consider the case of this musician, who suffered badly from stage-fright: on one occasion his 'nerves' were so bad that he literally could not face his audience. With the best of intentions a colleague offered him a tumbler of whisky:

> The effect was instantaneous ... and it worked. From that moment on, I was never to be without a bottle on any engagement I undertook, and this state lasted for the next 20 years ... I made a pact with the stuff: 'I'll drink you and you'll take my nerves away.'

As we have already stated, we choose to regard habits, addictions and compulsions as learned behaviour. With alcohol the user initially learns about the effect of alcohol on his or her psychological state; that boredom and tension

---

Selected indications of problem drinking

Adult

Becoming belligerent (getting into fights) after having a few drinks

Impaired work performance related to drinking

Experiencing illness or accident related to drinking

Arrested for driving while intoxicated, or other drinking-related offence

Developing tolerance (need for increased amounts to achieve desired effect or experiencing diminished effect with same amount)

Taking a drink in the morning (to relieve a hangover)

Impaired control – cannot stop drinking before becoming intoxicated

Experiencing 'blackouts' (memory losses) of events during drinking episodes

Youth

Frequent episodes of intoxication

Negative consequences from drinking (e.g., difficulties with school, civil authorities, or family because of drinking; driving while intoxicated)

---

can be relieved, that withdrawal symptoms can be avoided by topping up. Unfortunately the lesson which follows these is that giving up is difficult. Subsequently the alcoholic also learns that alcohol leads to inter-personal problems, accidents, illnesses and bad moods, but these long-term negative consequences cannot counteract the more immediate feeling of freedom or relief that alcohol can engender.

Treating alcohol dependence as learned behaviour does not ignore the biological basis, especially the development of tolerance and withdrawal symptoms. The emphasis, however, is upon learning experiences which shape drinking behaviour before and after the development of physical dependence. A clear understanding of the use and abuse of alcohol must consider reasons, antecedent cues and short-term effects. Once identified, these can act as the basis for effective counter-strategies.

Why do people drink?

One way of answering this is to ask the individuals concerned. The reasons given by alcoholics and problem drinkers to explain their drinking behaviour may not, of course, reflect the real causes. But we cannot simply ignore their opinions. Griffith Edwards and his colleagues made a study of this subject in a London suburb.[3] They asked a large number of men why they drank and among the replies identified the following cluster of answers:

> 'I drink because it helps me to relax.'
> 'I drink sometimes when I am restless and tense.'
> 'I drink because it helps me to forget my worries.'
> 'I drink when things get me down.'

A high proportion of those who replied in these terms tended in fact to be problem drinkers. In another study Gloria Litman of the London Institute of Psychiatry asked over 100 alcoholics about their reasons for relapsing after a period of abstinence and found that the following clusters emerged:[4]

– negative emotional states such as anxiety and depression
– anxiety about facing or dealing with other people
– sudden cravings in situations in which finding drink was easy
– taking risks or reducing vigilance. A common reason is 'I felt confident that I could take just one drink.'

An American survey by Dr Alan Marlatt of the University of Washington identified anxiety and depression, frustration, anger and social pressure as prime reasons for relapse.

It is reasonable to assume that at least some of these answers are realistic assessments of cues which precipitate heavy drinking. One approach to testing them is to set up psychological experiments to see if drinking increases immediately a particular cue is brought into play.

The power of antecedent cues

John is a 36-year-old television writer and producer who is moderately dependent on alcohol. Whisky on the rocks has, for many years, been his comfort, his medicine and his tranquillizer, but recently this happy relationship with alcohol has begun to deteriorate. During the last five years, the amount of alcohol consumed has increased from an average of a quarter of a bottle a day (8 drinks) up to about three quarters of a bottle. Now he wants to get his drinking under control because, in his view, alcohol contributed to the break-up of his marriage as well as his reduced efficiency and creativity at work. Furthermore, his family doctor has recently noted that John's liver is not functioning normally.

After keeping a behavioural diary in which he recorded not only his drinking, but also his urges to drink, it soon became apparent that his greatest difficulty in resisting the temptation to get drunk was linked to definite events or psychological states. The following simple profile of his drinking cues helped him to understand the way in which his drink was linked to these antecedents, and also how to go about planning a self-help programme.

a) When my work is criticized, I feel like an inadequate schoolboy and the urge to drink appears to emerge instantaneously.

b) I have tried to be totally abstinent and failed. Nowadays, if ever I pledge myself to abstinence *for life*, I immediately start to crave.

c) I've always had difficulty chatting up women and now, as a fat middle-aged drunkard, I just don't have the skill. Any situation which involves a woman, whether it involves just social or sexual intercourse, sets up an urge to drink heavily until my drunken self takes over.

d) I have to attend numerous social gatherings where temperance is the exception rather than the rule. I find it almost impossible to stick to non-alcoholic drinks on these occasions.

e) Frequently, I experience 'writer's block', especially in the afternoons. This is usually accompanied by a craving for drink.

f) If I'm busy and tense whilst producing a programme, I can go for days without a drink. For me, the celebration when it is all over and the feeling of 'letting go' are very strong cues for drinking.

These major antecedent cues give us a clear understanding of the particular person's unique pattern of dependence. It is essential to identify such cues before a treatment programme can be individually tailored to suit a particular person's needs. The way in which these cues become linked to the compulsive urge to drink is of crucial importance from a theoretical point of view, but it is not essential if we are to help a person cope with his problem in the here and now.

Psychological experiments on antecedent cues

A number of experiments have shown the degree to which situations involving threat, criticism or social pressure will drive heavy drinkers and alcoholics to drink more. In one study Alan Marlatt and his colleagues investigated the effects of social anxiety on the amount of alcohol consumed in a wine-tasting test.[5] The participants were asked to rate a number of wines on a scale of 1 to 10. In numerous experiments Marlatt has shown that this is a good test of desire to drink, since those people with a strong urge to drink will surreptitiously consume more than they actually need to form a judgement on the wine. In this particular study, volunteer subjects in a 'high-threat' group were told that, after the wine tasting task, they would be asked to participate in a discussion of personal attractiveness with a group of young women and that the women would be told to rate the men's attractiveness. Men in the 'low-threat' group did not have to face this threatening and potentially embarrassing social interaction. There was a very clear effect of this kind of threat on drinking with high-threat subjects drinking twice as much wine during the test as the low-threat subjects. This experiment confirms the notion that certain types of stresses can increase alcohol consumption and also suggests that hypotheses about 'real-life' drinking can be tested in a psychological laboratory.

A study by Peter Miller and his colleagues at the University of Mississippi found that criticism increases alcohol consumption among heavy drinkers.[6] Eight alcoholic and eight social drinking volunteers were asked to participate in an assertive training session, during which they would have to practise being assertive in a simulated inter-personal encounter. At the end of the session, some subjects were told that they had actually performed very badly and that it was very clear that they were the type of person who would let other people boss them around. Afterwards, they were allowed to obtain drink by repeatedly pressing the button of an alcohol dispenser. In this experiment, the hypothesis that criticism would increase desire for alcohol was confirmed, but only for the alcoholics. Of course, at the end of all these experiments on criticism and aggression, subjects were told the

This 'macho' biker with his insignia and confident swagger displays the behaviour expected of his sub-culture, but he may be shunned and rejected by the rest of society.

real purpose of the experiment.

These psychological experiments, and others, confirm the popular view that drinking is sometimes related to threat and criticism. Yet another method of studying drinking behaviour is to observe the *effects* of alcohol instead of manipulating *antecedent* cues.

The psychological effects of alcohol

A number of experiments have shown that alcohol reduces anxiety. But, of vital importance both to the problem drinker and to society is the effect of alcohol in relieving inhibitions on *aggression*. Alcohol has often been implicated in anti-social behaviours ranging from homicide to football hooliganism. One study of homicides committed in Philadelphia between 1948 and 1952 showed that alcohol was involved in about 70 per cent of the 356 murders by physical assault, including stabbing, kicking and beating, and in about 50 per cent of 232 shootings and other types of murder.

Richard Boyatzis of Boston, Massachusetts, reported a well-designed investigation into the effect of alcohol on aggression under conditions which were very close to a real-life situation.[7] Male volunteers, who were told that leisure activities were being studied, participated in a series of four-hour sessions during which they played bar games, starting with darts, cards and dice, and then moving on to more competitive games as the evening progressed. A group leader made sure that the men competed fully. Interactions were videotaped at three points throughout the evening and these tapes were then rated for aggressive behaviour. A total of 163 men participated in these sessions. They were divided into three groups: one group drank spirits throughout the four-hour session, one group was given only beer and the third group drank soft drinks only.

The object of the experiment was to see if the men consuming alcohol would display more aggressive behaviour than those consuming soft drink and whether this difference would be most apparent later on in the evening as more competition and stress was provoked. The results showed that this clearly happened. Three features of this experiment strengthen the author's conclusion that alcohol does increase aggressive

behaviour. First, the videotapes were independently rated for aggression by two teams of scorers and there was a very strong agreement between them showing that consistent measures of aggression can be obtained in this way. Secondly, subjects were asked to fill in a questionnaire about their general activities, in which some of the questions related to aggressive behaviour. It turned out that those men who were rated as aggressive during the videotaped sessions were usually the ones who tended to get into fights and reported trouble due to their drinking, a finding which adds to the validity of the videotape ratings of aggression. As a final check on validity, a question about smoking behaviour was compared with actual smoking behaviour during the experimental session, the number of cigarettes smoked being unobtrusively recorded. There was a good match between smoking behaviour as reported by the subjects and as observed during the experiment.

This study, then, not only shows that drinking alcohol can release aggressive behaviour, but also suggests that some people are more susceptible than others. It also gives the layman some idea of the ways in which psychologists check the reliability and validity of the information they collect. Since we wish to link the reasons why people drink with the effects of drinking, we must consider the possibility that some people drink in order to be more aggressive or, at least, more assertive.

Alcohol and sexual performance

The notion that alcohol releases inhibitions has been applied equally to sexually aggressive behaviour. For example, it is usually reported that about 50 per cent of convicted rapists and paedophiles were drinking at the time of the offence and it is argued that this relationship between sexual crimes and alcohol consumption is a direct result of intoxication. Another common assumption, implicit in both our folk-lore and professional opinion, predicts that a large dose of alcohol can have a detrimental effect on sexual performance. For instance, Masters and Johnson conclude, on the basis of their clinical experience, that:

> Secondary impotence developing in the
> male in the late forties or early fifties has a

higher incidence of direct association with excessive alcohol consumption than with any other single factor. When a man is traumatized by the inability to achieve or to maintain an erection while under the influence of alcohol he frequently develops major concerns for sexual performance and rarely associates his initial disability with its direct cause.

Shakespeare's MacDuff is given a clear description of this effect by a porter working in Macbeth's castle (Act II, Scene 3).

MACDUFF
Was it so late, friend, ere you went to bed,
That you do lie so late?

PORTER
Faith, sir, we were carousing till the second cock: and drink, sir, is a great provoker of three things.

MACDUFF
What three things does drink especially provoke?

PORTER
Marry, sir, nose-painting, sleep and urine. Lechery, sir, it provokes, and unprovokes; it provokes the desire, but it takes away the performance: therefore, much drink may be said to be an equivocator with lechery: it makes him and it mars him; it sets him on and it takes him off; it persuades him and it disheartens him: makes him stand to, and not stand to, in conclusion, equivocates him to sleep, and, giving him the lie, leaves him.

Although alcohol can have an unfortunate effect on sexual performance, a majority of drinkers appear to believe that alcohol is a sexual stimulant. In one study of 6000 male business executives, 61 per cent of those who consumed 4 drinks or more per day believed it to be so. Luckily for this group of businessmen, the effect of alcohol on sexual arousal is strongly influenced by beliefs. For example, Terry Wilson of Rutgers University has shown that beliefs about the effects of alcohol as well as beliefs about the alcoholic content of a drink can have a stronger effect than the actual amount of alcohol, at least at moderate doses.[8]

The evidence presented so far shows that alcohol can reduce anxiety, increase aggression or assertiveness and increase or decrease sexual

Expectations and the effects of alcohol

The available evidence now clearly shows that there is no simple direct relationship between the pharmacological effects of alcohol and its behavioural consequences. What a person expects to happen can be as influential as the drug effect. This is demonstrated in the following study carried out by Terry Wilson and his colleagues at the Rutgers Alcohol Behavior Research Laboratory.

Male social drinkers volunteered to take part in a study of the influence of erotic films on sexual arousal. Before watching the films, half were given vodka and tonic and half were given just tonic, but some of the subjects were misinformed about the contents of the drink. Half of the men consuming the vodka were told that the drink was just tonic and half of those consuming tonic were told that the drink contained some vodka. In other words, subjects were put into one of the following four groups:

Group A (given vodka, told vodka). Subjects were told that they had consumed vodka and, indeed, they had consumed vodka.

Group B (given vodka, told tonic). Subjects in this group were told that they had consumed pure tonic containing no alcohol whatsoever.

Group C (given tonic, told tonic). Subjects were correctly informed that they had consumed tonic.

Group D (given tonic, told vodka). Subjects consumed tonic, but were actually told that the drink contained vodka.

Only subjects in the first two groups were *given* vodka. The dose being equivalent to 4 drinks, which produced a blood alcohol level of about 40mg per cent.

After the experiment, subjects were interviewed to assess the credibility of the information that they were given. None of them doubted its authenticity. In this experimental design, Groups B and D were misinformed about the alcohol content of the drinks, allowing Wilson and his colleagues to assess whether the *drug* or the *belief* is the more powerful influence on sexual arousal. In order to avoid the need to rely on subjective reports of sexual arousal, penile tumescence was continuously recorded throughout the experiment, using a penile plethysmograph. The results were very clear. At the relatively low dose used in this experiment, alcohol *per se* had no effect on sexual arousal, but subjects who believed that they had consumed vodka manifested greater sexual arousal than those who believed that they had consumed tonic, irrespective of the *actual* content of the drinks.

Alcohol and anxiety reduction

A dramatic illustration of the effect of alcohol on anxiety was shown by a lady being treated at the Maudsley Hospital, London, for both a phobia of insects and a drinking problem. As part of an initial assessment, she was asked to walk into a room in which there was a live spider resting quietly at the bottom of an open jam jar. When sober, she could just about get into the room, and there was no doubt that she was very anxious. Half an hour after taking a quarter of a bottle of vodka, she appeared to be a different woman. Boldly she walked straight up to the the jam jar and put her finger in it, to within half an inch of the spider. There were no signs of fear and she reported that she felt totally relaxed. A few hours later, when her blood alcohol level had dropped to zero, she was re-tested and again her sober self would not let her get very far into the room.

The effect of alcohol is not always as dramatic as this. As with other drugs, it depends to some extent upon the expectations of the drug user (set) and the situation (setting), as well as the dose.

arousal depending upon the dose. Some of these effects are mediated by the pharmacological action of ethyl alcohol but some effects are also influenced by beliefs and expectations. The evidence demonstrates that heavy drinkers and alcoholics will increase their drinking if they are angry or frustrated, anxious or depressed, or when exposed to tempting situations or to social pressures. Every time a heavy drinker gets relief in these situations his dependence is increased. A vicious circle of increased consumption leading to physical dependence is set in train.

The most successful methods of helping people to stop

Broadly speaking, there are two ways of helping problem drinkers to regain control. One is to make sobriety more interesting and rewarding so that there isn't the need to drink as much. If craving is experienced against a background of boredom and loneliness, then resisting drink is very difficult. A second approach is to rehearse different ways of coping with craving just as an airline pilot has to practise dealing with a variety of emergencies before he is allowed to fly. These two approaches have proved to be effective in the treatment of problem drinkers, whereas most other forms of help, including drug therapy and psychoanalysis, have simply not worked.

Making sobriety more rewarding

Nathan Azrin and his colleagues, working at the Anna State Hospital, Illinois, have demonstrated that alcoholics are much more likely to remain abstinent if they are helped in very systematic and practical ways, to develop better work, social and marital relationships. This, of course, is easier said than done, but the research evidence does suggest that it is possible. Unemployed alcoholics who wanted a job were first of all persuaded that, to some extent, *job-finding* is a skill requiring an overall plan and a great deal of persistence. The plan involved contacting friends and relatives to ask them to look out for job leads, contacting the major factories and plants in the area, placing adverts in the local papers and rehearsing job interviews. A job-finding club was formed to facilitate this process. *Social counselling* procedures involved the systematic planning of contacts with non-drinking acquaintances, in order to increase the probability that relationships could develop. A former tavern was converted into a self-supporting social club providing a band, juke box, card games, dances, picnics and other social activities. *Marital counselling* involved discovering what behaviour from the husband would increase the wife's happiness and vice versa. The changes requested had to be reasonable and negotiable. For example, the wife might ask the husband to pick up the children from school, chat to her every evening about nothing in particular and plan an evening out once a week. In return, the wife would also promise to change her behaviour towards her husband in small and very specific ways. Making such changes in behaviour may appear to be trivial, but they can, in time, lead to larger changes especially in attitudes and feelings.

Azrin and his colleagues have demonstrated that this overall plan, involving gradual changes in vocational, social and marital behaviour, does help to increase the pleasures of sobriety and gives the alcoholic a strong reason to resist drink when experiencing craving.

Seeking the counsel of those with experience. Alcoholics Anonymous began as a self-help group in 1935, and today has over one million members.

Rehearsing coping skills

Edmund Chaney, Michael O'Leary and Alan Marlatt, working at the Veterans Hospital and University of Washington in Seattle, have shown that mentally practising coping strategies for a range of high-risk situations has a beneficial effect on problem drinking, even one year after treatment. The practice was carried out in groups and involved first of all identifying high-risk situations or cues and then thinking of as many ways of coping with them as possible. For example, one very common high-risk situation involves a social event such as a wedding, an office party or a celebration where lots of drink is available. There is social pressure to drink and some degree of social anxiety is involved. The aim of coping-skills training is to mentally rehearse a variety of different ways of coping in order to be prepared when a similar situation is experienced in real life. For example, the following list of coping strategies was used by one female problem drinker.

1. Stay for half an hour and then leave.
2. Get over my anxiety by just listening to people. Forget about trying to impress.
3. Drink tonic, because people might think it is vodka and tonic. They will then be less likely to pressure me into drinking.
4. If I feel a craving coming on, then I'll walk around the block until it disappears, that is the craving not the block.
5. I must remember how good I felt at Charlie's party two months ago when I successfully resisted the pressure to drink.
6. Be assertive. Tell all and sundry that I am not drinking and I will be very angry if they offer me a drink.

This type of mental practice is not only designed to produce specific strategies that can be used in specific situations, but also to learn a general approach to high-risk situations, that is to quickly think of a number of alternative ways of coping and then select one or two of them.

This approach is discussed elsewhere in this book. It is a very reasonable common-sense approach, and furthermore, there is research evidence to support its use.

13
DRUG DEPENDENCE

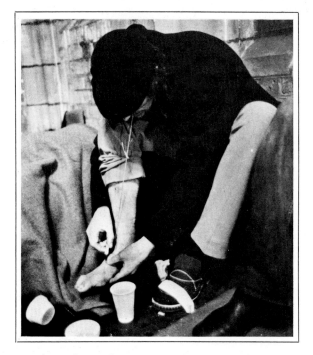

For many people, the terms 'drug dependence' or 'drug addiction' evoke the image of a junkie in a big city hustling for the next fix and injecting heroin through a dirty syringe until he or she succumbs to a fatal mixture of alcohol and opiates. This image is partly to do with society's attitude. Heroin use is illegal, it is connected with crime and the underworld, and the conventional view is that drug addicts are bound to be strange people.

An alternative, more useful and realistic, image of drug dependence is described in a 1965 World Health Organization report:[1]

> A state, psychic and sometimes also physical, resulting from the interaction between a living organism and a drug, characterised by behavioural and other responses that always include a compulsion to take the drug on a continuous or periodic basis in order to experience its psychic effects, and sometimes to avoid the discomfort of its absence. Tolerance may or may not be present. A person may be dependent on more than one drug.

The frequent or excessive use of licit drugs such as alcohol and tobacco clearly have to be included under this definition.

The WHO committee attempted to categorize all the drugs which can lead to dependence on the basis of similarities in effects and similarities in the behavioural patterns which develop with excessive use. The following 9 categories or classes of dependence-producing substances were proposed:

The alcohol-barbiturate group
Amphetamine-like substances
Cannabis (marijuana, hashish)
Cocaine
Hallucinogens (LSD and related drugs)
Khat (a stimulant used in Yemen and Ethiopia)
Opioids (the term used to include opium and its derivatives, as well as certain synthetic substances, such as morphine, which bring about opiate-like effects)
Volatile solvents (glue, acetone, etc.)
Tobacco

It is necessary to separate in our minds the state of being dependent upon a drug from the

An increasingly common phenomenon today – this youngster is sniffing glue (above). Heating heroin before using it (right).

harm which the drug may cause and the prevailing social attitudes towards addicts. Dependence means only the compulsion to use the drug; the term does not describe the consequent effects or the surrounding cultural values. A highly respectable, apparently healthy grandfather, who has smoked a pipe for years and failed in numerous efforts to give up, is a drug addict. So is a doctor who has access to a synthetic opioid which he comes to rely on in daily use to alleviate severe headaches and reduce the stress he feels in his job. Anyone who regularly consumes a quantity of alcohol to gain relaxation in the evening is drug dependent if the habit becomes impossible to break, even though it is socially acceptable and causes no embarrassment to family or friends. The characteristic common to all types of drug dependence is a compulsion to go on using the drug.

How does the compulsion develop?

It was formerly believed that severe drug dependence was just a function of *physical dependence*, that is biological changes in the body occurring through prolonged use of a drug, which result in withdrawal symptoms when the drug is withheld. If this were true then the strength of the habit would be strongly related to the intensity of the withdrawal syndrome. In fact, although tobacco, amphetamines and cocaine are at the bottom of the list in terms of the physical distress experienced during withdrawal, they can all lead to severe drug dependence which is very difficult to break. Millions of smokers can attest to the fact that cigarettes are difficult to give up and heroin addicts often comment that stopping smoking is even more difficult than giving up heroin. Escaping from and avoiding withdrawal symptoms is certainly one important factor involved in the excessive use of drugs, but a dependence can develop simply because of the positive, reinforcing effect of the drug. The desire for immediate pleasurable effects can strengthen the drug-taking habit until it becomes compulsive and difficult to give up.

Drugs and reinforcers

Laboratory animals with a catheter implanted in a vein will press a lever to obtain a shot of opioid drugs, alcohol or a barbiturate. They will get into the habit of doing this even when trials are so far apart that physical dependence does not develop. In both monkeys and rats the habit is reinforced even though withdrawal symptoms do not occur when drug consumption is stopped. Animals develop a drug-taking habit with most of the drugs that lead to dependence in man, especially opioids, amphetamines, cocaine, alcohol and barbiturates.[2] They will also press a lever to obtain nicotine and caffeine but compared to cocaine these commonly used drugs are very weak reinforcers indeed. On the other hand, LSD, cannabis, and chlorpromazine (a tranquilliser), do not have the allure for rats and monkeys that they appear to have for human users.

The very fact that most of the addictive drugs will lead to a drug-taking habit in rats and monkeys without the development of physical dependence indicates that the immediate rewarding effects of drugs are crucial determinants of addiction. With human beings, personality and social factors must be taken into consideration if we are to explain the whole process of initial experimentation leading to casual or recreational use

and then on to excessive use or dependence. But the immediate pleasures derived from taking a drug are of paramount importance. We cannot argue for monkeys as some have done for humans that:

> The mis-use of drugs by monkeys is the manifestation of dissatisfaction and loss of faith in the prevailing social system.

> Drug use in monkeys is part of the search for different perceptions and ideas.

> Monkeys start and continue to use drugs because they decide that they want to do so, not because of the intrinsic nature of the drug.

Psychological and social factors

Initial experimentation with drugs and the recreational use which follows is clearly influenced by the availability of the drug, cultural attitudes and peer group norms. Many French people

Enjoying a candle-lit joint. Cannabis is the least harmful of all the proscribed drugs and results in the least dependence.

think nothing of drinking wine with every meal and when at a loose end throughout the day. This is the result of both cultural attitudes and availability. Although such a pattern of drinking may appear to be civilized, since public drunkenness is avoided, it actually leads to higher levels of liver cirrhosis (see page 151). The use of cannabis, cocaine and heroin is similarly influenced by availability and the degree of social acceptance. The majority of drug addicts first learn how to use drugs from a member of their own subculture.

Environmental influences are still important when dependence is more advanced. For example, during the Vietnamese War thousands of American soldiers used pure heroin for many months. Almost 50 per cent of the regular users became physically dependent. Despite this, when they returned home, over 90 per cent were able to discontinue heroin use unaided. This finding came as a surprise to many people who believe that withdrawal symptoms and craving are wholly determined by the amount of drug consumed, which produces biological changes in the brain. In fact, environmental and social factors are also of crucial importance. Back in the United States, when heroin was no longer cheaply available and social attitudes towards it were largely negative, relapse was the exception rather than the rule.

Viewing drug use in terms of antecedent cues and reinforcing consequences highlights the importance of psychological factors. In Chapter 1 we described the development of Tom's drinking habit, noting that for him social situations were minefields because he had frequently used alcohol to reduce his social anxieties. In one study it was shown that university students find alcohol more reinforcing when imbibed in a social setting than when taken alone. Clearly psychological and social factors have a considerable influence on the patterns of drug taking among humans.

Since drug dependence is a complex relationship between personality, the effect of the drug and social situation it is not surprising that no single entity called 'the addictive personality' has been identified and described. There are many reasons for taking drugs and many types of people will succumb.

Opium and heroin

During the major part of the 19th century opiates in the form of patent medicines were as freely accessible as aspirin is today. In grocery and general stores these products were not called smack or dope, but were sold as Mrs Winslow's Soothing Syrup, Godfrey's Cordial and McMunn's Elixir of Opium. They were widely advertised as pain killers, cough mixtures, women's friends, teething and soothing syrups for children and cures for consumption. Laudanum, a mixture of alcohol and morphine, was the choice of a majority of opium users, including Thomas De Quincey, the author of *Confessions of an English Opium Eater*. Morphine is the pure drug that gives opium its characteristic effects and an early derivative of morphine was introduced into medicine as a cough suppressant towards the end of the 19th century. Its name was heroin.

Opium and its derivatives produce euphoria, drowsiness and reverie. Heroin has, in addition, a powerful initial effect usually called 'the rush'. This is a feeling of ecstasy which immediately follows an injection of the drug. Within just a few weeks of regular use, the duration of euphoria

---

Caffeine

Caffeine, found in coffee and tea, is probably the world's most popular drug. An average cup of coffee in Britain and North America contains about 70mg of caffeine, but, of course, a strong brew might contain twice this amount. In the U.S.A. and Canada, a cup of tea contains about 30mg but the British prefer a stronger brew with a caffeine concentration approaching that of coffee. Caffeine is a stimulant. It postpones fatigue and it has been reported to increase endurance in trained cyclists. Taken at bedtime, it delays the onset of sleep and reduces the depth of sleep. Recent research has suggested the possibility that regular use of more than 600mg per day is associated with cancer of the bladder, as well as heart disease, but the evidence here is not clear-cut. Nevertheless, it has been noted that if caffeine were a newly discovered drug about to be introduced, then it would be available on prescription only. It is often very difficult for heavy users to cut down if, for example, they are advised to do so by their doctor. To this extent, it is a dependence-producing drug.

becomes quite short and overall mood slightly depressed. This rapid development of tolerance means that higher and more frequent doses have to be taken to get the same effect.

After a period of habitual use, heroin users begin to experience cravings for the drug which are accompanied by certain physical symptoms, the so-called 'withdrawal symptoms'. These are quite severe but it has been noted that they are no worse than the symptoms of a severe attack of influenza. Within the first twelve hours there will be muscle pain, sneezing, sweating, crying and yawning. Within about 36 hours the withdrawal symptoms will increase in intensity. Chills alternate with excessive flushing and sweating, there will probably be an increase in heart rate and blood pressure as well as diarrhoea and sleeplessness. These symptoms gradually subside over a five to ten day period.[3]

Today, in most countries of the world, opioids are not available for recreational use. Those who want to achieve the opioid high must buy the drug (usually heroin) from an illicit source at a high price. Naturally many people are deterred from using heroin under these conditions and those who habitually use it are likely to come from a delinquent background or at least be relatively unconcerned about social sanctions. In the United States more than half of those who are identified as heroin addicts have a history of delinquent behaviour or a criminal conviction before their first experience of heroin. But there are also many people who use opiates infrequently or even regularly and never come in contact with medical or law enforcement agencies of any kind.

Many addicts do give up but they run considerable risks until that time. Follow-up studies of heroin addicts registered at London clinics found that about one-third were functioning well without the drug a few years after treatment. About half were still using opioids obtained from clinics, others were in prison, while the death rate was about 1.5 per cent each year, many times greater than the expected rate in non-addicted people of the same age. Those addicts who are able to give up usually attribute their success to some change in their social situation. Gaining the love and trust of a specific person, moving out of their drug subculture or some comparable change in lifestyle are the most frequently cited reasons. This evidence supports the selfwatching philosophy which is the foundation of this book – that environment, attitude and motivation are the key factors in long-term behavioural change.

The opium poppy (top left) is the source of opium, morphine and heroin. It is grown largely in the Golden Triangle of South East Asia – Burma, Thailand, Cambodia and Laos – but this harvest (above right) is from Turkey. Ensuring a constant supply on the streets is a highly organized business; a Chinese courier from Hong Kong passes on a consignment of heroin to a merchant in Europe (above centre). 'The only hope is dope' cry of the sixties and slogan of the counter-culture (below).

Uppers and downers

Within the brain there is a mechanism which increases or decreases electrical activity, rather like the volume control on an amplifier. Roughly speaking, the stimulants turn this control up and the sedatives turn it down.

The *amphetamines* are a family of drugs that produce an elevation of mood, a decrease in fatigue and a lowering of appetite.[4] The need for sleep is reduced. For some people a typical dose leads to hyperactivity and irritability. Amphetamines are often therefore called *uppers*.

The class of drugs derived from barbituric acid and called *barbiturates* have roughly the opposite effect and are called *downers*.[5] Depending on the dose, this large family of drugs produce sedation and relaxation, decreased anxiety, and the ability to sleep.

Amphetamines

During the Second World War, amphetamines were often given to pilots and soldiers to reduce the need for sleep. In Japan, at the end of the war, tons of stockpiled amphetamines were released for general sale and this increased availability led to an 'epidemic' of amphetamine use.

The availability of amphetamines is generally carefully controlled, but they are still sometimes prescribed by physicians to alleviate fatigue. A report in the *New York Times* in 1972, 'Amphetamines used by a Physician to Lift Moods of his Famous Patients', described how a Dr Jacobson had accompanied President John F. Kennedy on his trip to Vienna to meet with the Russian premier Krushchev, and had given the President injections of amphetamines to help him cope with the demanding nature of this visit. As the article stated, this was 'far from the typical picture of rag-tag youths dosing themselves with illegally obtained drugs . . .' In addition to this example, amphetamines were used quite legally and carefully when they were given to American astronauts, to help them conquer fatigue and rise to the demands of space flight.

Amphetamines were first introduced commercially in nasal inhalers because they produce constriction of the blood vessels and relieve a stuffy nose. But the public soon discovered their stimulating effects.

Several patterns of amphetamine use have been described. In one, relatively small amounts are used to lift mood and reduce fatigue. This pattern is characteristic of college students burning the midnight oil, long-distance lorry drivers, women who discover the stimulating effect of their diet pills, and busy executives who want to keep going without sleep. The main danger of this pattern is that there might be a tendency to keep using the drug in order to avoid the low feeling when the effect wears off. In the United States, in 1977, 10 per cent of adolescents and 21 per cent of young adults in the 18–25 age group reported having used stimulants at some time, but only a very small percentage used these drugs regularly.

A second, more dangerous pattern, is typical of the 'speed freak' who injects large amounts of amphetamine intravenously for several days. A severely dependent amphetamine addict will remain awake for up to six days and sometimes longer, becoming more and more tense, tremulous and paranoid. After the end of a 'run' the addict 'crashes' into a deep sleep lasting as long as 48 hours and then repeats the cycle. When laboratory animals are given access to amphetamines they, too, behave like 'speed freaks'. They will repeatedly press a lever to obtain the drug, appear to be hallucinating, chew their own limbs and stop eating. Somehow they manage to continue pressing the lever until death supervenes after a few weeks. In humans, injecting amphetamine causes massive increase in blood pressure which may result in heart failure or brain haemorrhage. Strong evidence suggests that long-term use leads to brain damage.

Cocaine

Unlike amphetamines, *cocaine* is a naturally occurring stimulant. In 1860 it was extracted from the leaves of the South American coca shrub by Albert Nieman and was very quickly taken up by the medical profession and purveyors of patent medicines. It was added to many tonic wines and for about 10 years (until 1903) it was an ingredient of a new and little known American soft drink called Coca Cola.

In its refined form, cocaine is a white powder. Users either 'snort' it – inhaling it into the nose, often through a tube of tightly rolled paper – or inject it directly into the bloodstream. Use of the

These goofballs – barbiturates and amphetamines – were found in your car, mister. How do you plead?

Freud and cocaine: a case-history

Sigmund Freud, when working as a young neurologist, experimented with cocaine on himself and his patients. He was inspired to try it after reading glowing accounts in the medical literature of its stimulating effects. In his article *On coca*, he noted its properties as a stimulant and also advocated the use of cocaine to treat digestive disorders, asthma, wasting diseases such as cancer and as an effective local anaesthetic. A few years later it became apparent that cocaine was not as harmless as Freud believed. His colleague, Ernst von Fleischl, had developed a morphine dependence as a result of medical treatment and Freud advised the substitution of cocaine. Unfortunately, von Fleischl found himself taking larger and larger doses and eventually he developed an acute mental illness, probably a cocaine psychosis. He experienced hallucinatory experiences in which worms and snakes were burrowing beneath his skin; his thinking became very paranoid and he remained seriously disturbed until his death.

drug rapidly leads to dependence, higher tolerance of the effects, and thus the need to increase the amount and frequency of the dose. The effects are to produce a feeling of intense elation, together with a sense of great physical strength and energy. At the physiological level cocaine causes the pupils to dilate and an increase in blood pressure and heart rate. In its natural form the Indian peoples of the Andes chew coca leaves as a protection against fatigue and hunger, enabling them to perform tiring work for long periods at altitude on very little food.

In the early years of the 20th century, cocaine use spread to the poor classes of America's countryside and cities. It relieved hunger and gave the brief illusion of well-being.

During the last decade the use of cocaine has increased significantly, especially among young people. In the United States a national survey showed that 20 per cent of 18 to 25 year olds had tried cocaine, although for most of them the use was experimental and not habitual. Many users regard the drug as harmless, but this is to ignore strong evidence for the dangers of long-term use. These include damage to the mucous membranes lining the nose, and disturbing feelings of restlessness, overexcitability, irritability and intense fear. Heavy daily use of cocaine can result in users experiencing itchy skin reactions and an uncomfortably sharp awareness of sounds and smells, real and imagined. At worst these symptoms may develop into a condition called cocaine psychosis, in which users fall victim to delusions of persecution and threat. In some reported cases, sufferers have come to believe that the agonising skin reactions they experience are caused by burrowing parasites and have literally torn their skin in a desperate attempt to root out the imaginary culprits.

Barbiturates

There is no doubt that *barbiturates*, or 'downers', can also lead to severe dependence. These are sedative-hypnotic drugs based on barbituric acid derivatives which first became available at the end of the 19th century. They were originally prescribed to calm anxiety and restlessness, promote relaxation and induce sleep. Soon after they appeared came the first reports of people using barbiturates to get the same intoxicating effects as alcohol. Their habit-forming potential has been known since 1927, but it is only during the last 20 years that physicians have started to prescribe them less frequently. In the United States they are manufactured in vast quantities to this day, enough to provide every man, woman and child with 30 pills a year.

Dependence on barbiturates can occur in a number of ways. Some people take a large daily dose and, although seemingly unaffected, simply cannot function without them. Others mix barbiturates and alcohol to produce an intoxicated high. Heroin addicts often use barbiturates when heroin is unavailable, or mix both drugs in order to eke out their supply. In some respects severe barbiturate dependence is an even more serious problem than heroin dependence. Abrupt withdrawal of the drug can produce a very unpleasant syndrome with anxiety, shakiness, insomnia and sometimes delirium tremors and convulsions. Another problem occurs when the excessive use of downers leads to an accidental overdose, especially if the user takes a heavy dose to get to sleep at night, perhaps after consuming a fair amount of alcohol at a party. Barbiturates are the drugs most commonly used to commit suicide. In 1977 nearly 20 per cent of adults in the United States reported using them in a medical context and 18 per cent of 18 to 25 year olds had used them in a non-medical context. Clearly these drugs are still easily obtained.

Minor tranquillizers

The *benzodiazepine* family of drugs (e.g. Librium, Valium and Dalmane) are usually called minor tranquillizers and are very frequently prescribed for anxiety and insomnia. They have now displaced the barbiturates in medical practice because they are safer, they produce less euphoria, and an overdose is less likely to be fatal. Nevertheless these drugs can be habit-forming and recent evidence of physical dependence has been reported. In one study carried out by Malcolm Lader and his colleagues, working at the London Institute of Psychiatry, the benzodiazepine withdrawal syndrome was investigated in 24 patients who had been taking a normal therapeutic dose for long periods varying from 1 to 16 years. All experienced a withdrawal

reaction which was characterized by anxiety, sensitivity to bright lights and noise, unsteadiness, and changes in the electrical activity of the brain. This syndrome was at its peak 4 to 6 days after stopping the drug, and subsided after 8 to 10 days.

The published evidence leaves us in no doubt that dependence on the benzodiazepines does exist, although the available information does not permit a clear estimate of the extent of the problem. In the UK, it has been estimated that from 1960, when the drug was first introduced, up to the middle of 1977, these drugs have been used for 150 million patient-months. Since so many people are using these drugs, it is very likely that, in years to come, dependence on them will become a substantial problem.

Psychedelic drugs

The term psychedelic was coined by Dr Humphrey Osmond to refer to those drugs that induce in the mind (the psyche) ecstatic and mystical experiences, dreamy detached feelings and sometimes hallucinatory episodes. Such experiences are reported by the users of *d-lysergic acid diethylamide* (LSD), *mescalin* and *psilocybin*. The last two substances are found in nature but LSD is a

Left: An open market in Coca leaves, source of the drug cocaine; right: Cannabis Sativa, the Hemp plant, better known as marijuana.

Reactions

Pupillary dilation: increased blood pressure; increased body temperature; occasional nausea; subjective reports of weakness and giddiness.

Changes in body image: strange and distorted feelings about body and limbs.

Dreamy, detached feelings: light-headedness and detachment from reality; unusually rapid flow of ideas.

Reduced intellectual proficiency: impaired performance on tests measuring memory, mathematical skills, and ability to accomplish other tasks requiring focused attention.

Changes in time perception: marked slowing of the passage of time.

Changes in sensory experience: increased richness of colours; heightened sensitivity to touch and smell; changes in depth and size perception; occasional synesthesias, for example, 'smelling a sound' or 'feeling a colour'.

Changes in moods and emotions: highly variable, ranging from ecstasy and transcendental experience to great anxiety, depression, and despair.

After-effects

Chromosomal damage: reported in some early studies, but not replicated and currently believed not to be a danger.

Positive psychological effects: self-reports of improved functioning, but little adequately controlled documentation.

Negative psychological effects: rare instances of psychotic-like reactions, most often in people with a past history of psychopathology; occasional 'flash-backs' (vivid re-experiencing of some portion of an earlier drug experience).

synthetic compound developed by a Swiss chemist, Albert Hoffman, in 1953.

In 1896 mescalin was first extracted from the peyote cactus, which is native to certain areas in Mexico and Central America. Peyote has been used for centuries in the religious rites of the Mexican Indians. Psilocybin is the active ingredient of the mushroom *Psilocybe mexicana*. Both substances have similar effects to LSD but they are not nearly so potent: only 0.0001 grams of LSD is needed to match the effect of 0.5 grams of mescalin, and a 3lb bag of LSD would be enough to give a psychedelic experience to the combined populations of New York and London. The effects of LSD have been more closely studied than those of any other mind-altering drug. A summary of the effects, based on more than 2000 research investigations, is shown on the right.

As with other mind-altering drugs, the effects of LSD are dependent upon expectations (set) and circumstances (setting). A 'bad trip' can occur if the user is unprepared for the experience or psychologically disturbed.

Rats and monkeys put LSD towards the bottom of their list of preferred drugs: they do not get into the habit of pressing a lever to obtain it. This is consistent with most of the evidence on human consumption which indicates that the compulsive use of LSD is very rare.

In recent years a relatively new substance has made an impact on the drug scene in the United States. *Phencyclidine* or PCP was developed in 1959 as a new anaesthetic agent but has now been abandoned by physicians. Known in the street as 'angel dust', 'crystal', 'horse tranquillizer' and 'rocket fuel', its use almost doubled in the year 1976 to 1977 amongst 18 to 25 year olds. Users of this drug nearly always experience some negative effects and actually experience positive reactions on only 60 per cent of occasions. This is an example of intermittent reinforcement since use of the drug persists despite its unpredictable effects. The most common positive effects are heightened sensitivity to sounds and colours, dissociation, elevation of mood, inebriation and relaxation. Unlike LSD, animals will self-administer PCP as they will heroin, morphine, amphetamine, cocaine and alcohol.

Marijuana

Of all the drugs likely to lead to habitual use most scientists and users would argue that *marijuana* is the one which causes least harm or dependence. Nevertheless, there is still a great deal of controversy about legalization of the drug mainly because the long-term effects of heavy use are still unknown. Three major studies carried out in Jamaica, Costa Rica and Greece have carefully matched chronic users with non-users of similar backgrounds and have found few important differences between the two groups.[6] These investigations are often quoted to support the view that marijuana is totally safe. However, the total number of user–non-user pairs investigated in all three studies was too small to detect the possible occurrence of less frequent consequences. It is unlikely, for example, that the harmful effects of tobacco smoking would have been identified with such a small sample.

Marijuana consists of dried and ground leaves of the hemp plant, *Cannabis sativa*. It is usually smoked but may also be chewed, made into tea or baked into a cake. Hashish is produced by drying the resin of the cannabis plant and is therefore a much stronger preparation. Grass, pot, ganja, dagga are just a few of the dozens of other names for marijuana and related products.

It was estimated that the majority (60 per cent) of Americans between the ages of 18 and 25 had used cannabis by 1977. In spite of this large-scale exposure to the drug there are very few reports of severe dependence or compulsive use in western societies. Furthermore, animals do not self-administer cannabis and in human users withdrawal symptoms are not severely distressing. These facts must be assessed in conjunction with evidence that in Muslim and Hindu countries, where cannabis is more readily available than alcohol, the everyday heavy use of cannabis does more frequently lead to dependence and difficulty in stopping. It may be that marijuana dependence would occur more frequently if 'pot' was as easily obtained as a packet of cigarettes.

Why self-help is important

The picture of the world drug scene that emerges from international conferences and reports in scientific journals indicates that drug dependence is a growing problem. Drug use is almost universal. In 1977 one in five young adults in the United States had used amphetamines, one in five had used cocaine and 18 per cent had used a barbiturate or similar drug. At least 70 million Americans had used a tranquillizer such as Valium. Most people in the world have tried either alcohol or cigarettes and since the dependence and harm caused by these commonly available drugs is such a massive problem they have been discussed in separate chapters.

If only a tiny minority of the people who use drugs go on to develop dependence then millions of people are going to be asking: 'How can I break the habit?' Physicians won't be able to help since they are overworked and not usually trained to deal with behavioural problems. Specialized treatment centres cannot be provided on such a large scale. For example, alcoholism treatment units can deal with less than 5 per cent of the people who have drinking problems. The only sensible solutions appear to be, first, an emphasis on prevention through a knowledge and understanding of the processes leading to dependence and the types of drug which are most dangerous. Second, there must be an emphasis on self-help through an understanding of how habits develop and how they can be broken.

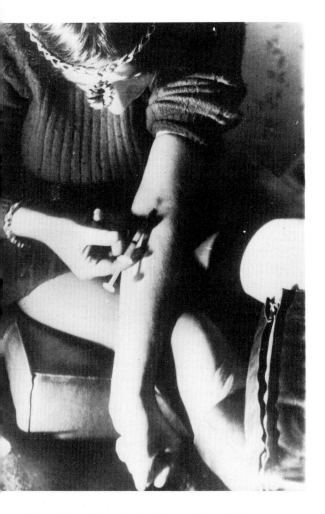

The spiral of dependency increases as the body becomes more tolerant and larger doses of opiates are needed to achieve the same effect.

Breaking a heroin habit: a selfwatching case-study

Using the approach described in this book, one of us helped a 25-year-old woman to break her heroin habit, even though she had failed many times to give up 'by willpower alone'. Very intelligent, she worked as a dress designer and a buyer for a chain of shops in London. Twice a day she would sniff a dose of heroin which she bought in Kensington Market not too far away from her place of work. Contrary to the popular stereotype, many drug users do hold down a job, even though their efficiency might be a little impaired.

As she had taken a small to moderate dose of heroin twice a day for about a year, the first step was to withdraw her from the drug and overcome withdrawal symptoms. After the situation had been explained to her mother and her family

doctor, she took two weeks off work and stayed at home with a small supply of tranquillizers prescribed by her general practitioner, to be used only during this period, and only if her withdrawal symptoms were unbearable. To stop taking drugs under these conditions is not always difficult for addicts, but this is just one small part of the battle. By far and away the biggest problem for drug addicts, smokers, drinkers and slimmers, is keeping the commitment going for more than two weeks. At this stage she had to draw up a careful plan of campaign.

For this particular woman, the easy availability of heroin was a crucial factor. She was frightened to go back to work knowing that 100 yards away, there was a pusher sitting in a café with a bagful of heroin. Fortunately, she was able to come up with a solution which was probably the key to her self-helping. She arranged to work from another shop with the same chain, but way out in the suburbs. This is sometimes scathingly called a 'geographical solution', with the implication that it is no solution at all, but there seems little doubt that for this young woman it gave her the breathing space to make other changes in her lifestyle.

She gradually started to renew her contacts with old friends who had no links with the drug-taking sub-culture. This was a slow process, but she planned some social event twice a week in order to increase the probability that her network of non-addict friends would increase, and so it did. She moved into a flat with two other girls and, for the first two months, tried to make sure that she was never alone at the weekends, since these were the times when temptation was at its highest.

The next step involved the cue-exposure procedure described in Chapter 4. She had not been back to Kensington Market and was frightened of the cravings that she might feel if she did. The cue-exposure principle was described to her as follows:

If you face up to a temptation and resist

On a trip to nowhere? Heroin (above) and opium (below) are highly addictive. Pleasantly? Only at first, though opium is less damaging.

taking drugs when you experience some craving, then gradually the craving will pass away. The next time you have to face the same situation, you will then find it easier to resist the urge to use drugs.

She then learned by heart the following quotation from *Hamlet*:

Assume a virtue, if you have it not.
. . . Refrain tonight;
And that shall lend a kind of easiness
To the next abstinence; the next more easy;

Bearing in mind that her aim was to finally break her addiction, she went with her brother to Kensington Market one Saturday morning and spent half an hour in the very café that used to be the source of her drugs. She experienced some very strange feelings, but no craving at all. Over the next three months, she carried out the same exercise by herself until Kensington Market was no longer a threat to her.

One method of coping with craving that turned out to be particularly useful in her case involved a variant of the problem-solving strategy described in Chapter 16. Whenever an incipient craving started to grow, she would counteract her feelings of helplessness by writing out a list of five things that she could do that might be pleasurable. She was taught to see herself as her own personal scientist testing these activities one at a time to see which one effectively suppressed the craving. She quickly discovered that her craving would start to disappear as soon as she wrote down her five alternatives.

It is now two years since she stopped taking heroin and all is well. She has changed her friends and her lifestyle, and greatly increased her self-confidence. In her opinion, there is no chance of a relapse.

This case is presented as an illustration of the way in which a simple self-helping strategy can break up a drug-taking habit, when the addict is ready to try it. The principles and strategies described in earlier chapters are applicable to a broad range of human behaviour, even an addiction to hard drugs. At the time of writing, however, no good controlled clinical trial has been carried out to assess the effectiveness of these procedures with a large group of drug addicts.

14
SEXUAL COMPULSION

What is normal sexual behaviour? The answer to this question has differed considerably over the years in response to changing social attitudes and mores. For example, many American states still have laws on the books against premarital sexual relationships. Fewer and fewer people consider such behaviour as deviant or immoral. Unmarried couples openly living together are commonplace in contemporary society, and it is unlikely that antiquated laws governing this behaviour will ever be enforced. Social norms simply change at a faster rate than do our political–legal bureaucracies. In some countries the present legal trend is towards the decriminalization of *all* private sexual acts between consenting adults. Such governments have decided that they cannot and should not legislate sexual mor-

als unless such behaviour infringes on someone's personal rights, such as in the case of rape or child molesting. However, there are a large number of repressive laws still in force in many different societies and cultures.

The American Psychiatric Association has recently clarified and redefined its thinking on what were formerly called sexual deviations. They now use the neutral term 'paraphilias', meaning any sexual behaviour outside that considered legally or socially acceptable. In fact, there is a wide range of conditions in which sexual arousal may occur in response to inappropriate persons, objects and activities. The newest version of the *Diagnostic and Statistical Manual of the American Psychiatric Association* reports that paraphilias are characterized by repetitive and persistent sexually arousing fantasies that are associated with either:

1. A preference for use of a nonhuman object for sexual arousal
2. Repetitive sexual activity with humans involving real or simulated suffering or humiliation
3. Repetitive sexual activity with nonconsenting partners

Homosexuality is currently not considered a sexual deviation or problem unless it results in undue anxiety, discomfort, and depression. Even so, an ethical debate has existed over the past several years about the treatment of homosexuality. For example, many clinicians argue that the goal of treatment for a depressed homosexual should be psychological adjustment to homosexuality rather than a change to heterosexuality.

Changing social attitudes

Notions of what does and does not constitute sexual deviance have changed primarily in relation to increased knowledge and understanding of sexual behaviour. Sigmund Freud was one of the first to elucidate the potential importance of sexual arousal, anxieties and frustrations. In the 1940s Alfred Kinsey of Indiana University conducted one of the first large-scale surveys on sexual behaviour. This and subsequent studies opened the way for more realistic discussions about normal and abnormal sexuality. In the 1960s and 1970s Drs Masters and Johnson conducted studies in which they actually observed, under controlled laboratory conditions, the sexual activities of volunteer couples. Since then, their Reproductive Biology Research Foundation in St Louis, Missouri, has provided new insights into the study and treatment of sexual problems.

These studies have modified attitudes about sexual deviance. Masturbation, for example, was once considered extremely abnormal behaviour. In fact, in the late 19th century the California Commission on Lunacy estimated that masturbation was the major cause of insanity in 25 per cent of patients admitted to state mental hospitals in the years 1896–7. Professionals now know that masturbation is a common occurrence that has no harmful effects. It is only considered a

Hidden thoughts . . . (above) and the purchase and exchange of pain for a vicarious pleasure (below).

The personal consequences of compulsive sexual behaviour

Compulsive sexual behaviour can be extremely devastating to a person's life. The effects, both personally and socially, are profound. In large part this is due to the moral stigma attached to 'different' sexual behaviours. For example, compare sexual compulsions with gambling or smoking excesses. Most people consider smoking and gambling to be just bad habits. At worst, compulsive gambling might be viewed as highly irresponsible behaviour. Compulsive sexual behaviour, although similar in nature to gambling and smoking in terms of its compulsive elements, is viewed quite differently. It is considered by many to constitute moral depravity and usually evokes feelings of disgust in family and friends.

The following remarks by two different patients, each suffering from compulsive sexual behaviours, illustrate the agony generated by these problems.

Case 1

Edward G. is a 25-year-old exhibitionist who was recently arrested for indecent exposure. He had been exhibiting himself to young girls for several months before he was finally caught. Upon referral for treatment by the judge, Edward described his frustration:

'I hate myself for what I've been doing. I can't stop myself. I think about it all day long. Once I tried to tell my brother. I knew I needed help and had to talk to someone. I just couldn't confide in him. What would he think of me? He would think I'm a horrible person. I couldn't tell anyone. I knew I needed help but I also knew that nobody would ever understand.'

Case 2

Beverly L. is a 29-year-old married woman who has been compulsively promiscuous for the past two years. Her husband recently caught her in bed with another man and she eventually confessed to several extra-marital affairs. She described her behaviour in this way:

'At first, a couple of years ago, I began having an affair with a man I'd met casually at a party. It started off innocently enough. Bob, my husband, and I had been arguing a lot lately. I felt hemmed in; like I was going to explode. I was angry, terribly angry, but unable to express it. I wanted to hurt him. Only the affair didn't last. I really didn't want it to. I found myself drifting from affair to affair. After a while, they weren't affairs any more – just quick sexual encounters and that's all. One week I went to bed with five different men.

'I went from one man to another. I didn't want to do it but something made me. It started to rule my life. I got less and less pleasure out of my marriage and more out of strangers. My marriage was getting worse. Bob wasn't stupid. He was always suspicious of me. I began drinking heavily and that just made matters worse. Now Bob wants a divorce and I'm on my way to having two problems – one with sex and one with alcohol.'

---

problem when it is performed compulsively, accompanied by anxiety, and takes the place of all intimate personal relationships.

Some sexual behaviours, however, are more obviously unusual and these may become compulsive and exclusive of any other sexual interest. Fetishism, compulsive promiscuity, exhibitionism, voyeurism, paedophilia, incest, and transvestism are among the types of sexual behaviour which can cause serious individual and social problems.

Fetishism

Fetishism is sexual attraction to a part of the body or to an inanimate object. Fetishes can involve such objects – animate and inanimate – as feet, hair, shoes or underwear. Usually the object alone is the target of sexual fantasy without a sexual partner involved, and in itself provides sufficient sexual stimulation. In cases where a partner is involved, a fetishist may require another person to wear the object, for example high-heeled shoes or boots, during sex. Without this condition, sexual arousal may be impossible. A man with a foot fetish may simply want to fondle and kiss a woman's feet while he masturbates.

True fetishism is relatively uncommon although some brothels in larger cities often cater to customers with fetishes. Clinically, the term fetishism is reserved for those cases in which sexual arousal can occur *only* when the fetishistic object is present and there is a compulsive drive to seek out the object.

Fetishism is rarely seen in women. It tends to occur in men who, although they are not homosexuals, are fearful of intimate sexual relationships with women. They may also show an early interest in sex but generally behave in a shy and reserved manner. Unless they get into trouble with the law (often because of stealing some object holding a fetishistic attraction for them),

The open-hearted sexuality of Tantric sculpture adorns a Hindu temple in India (right); the Chinese threesome (below right) seems unselfconscious too.

fetishists usually avoid treatment. However, feelings of depression over his sexual behaviour may prompt the fetishist to seek help. Motivation may also come from a marriage-partner or lover who finds the behaviour interferes with a good relationship.

Compulsive promiscuity

The drive to have indiscriminate heterosexual relationships can become a severe compulsion. This compulsion is characterized by the continuous urge to have sexual intercourse with many different partners. Little attention is given to the quality of the relationship or the feelings of the sexual partner.

Compulsive promiscuity by females is known as *nymphomania*. This term, however, has been largely misinterpreted and often used in a derogatory manner towards women. For example, men who have difficulty in acknowledging the normal sexuality of women might view the open expression of sexual desires from a woman as aberrant. Traditional sexual stereotypes wrongly assume that only men have active sexual desires. In addition, the view that the expression of such desires verbally and behaviourally is acceptable for men but not for women is recognized by many as outright sexual discrimination towards women. Compulsive promiscuity in women is *only* considered a problem when sexual behaviour becomes so indiscriminate and compulsive that it interferes with the individual's everyday life and keeps her from establishing close relationships with others.

Such behaviour among men has been referred to as *satyriasis* (from the Greek word for a legendary creature, half man, half goat). It is interesting to note that in terms of different sexual attitudes and stereotypes towards men and women, compulsive promiscuity among men, rather than being cause for criticism, has been viewed almost as something to be proud of. Don Juan was considered to be one of the world's greatest lovers and heroes rather than a famous example of satyriasis. The notion that a man's masculinity is tied exclusively to the frequency of his sexual conquests is, however, rapidly becoming outmoded as gender stereotypes change.

Compulsive promiscuity can dominate a person's life and cause severe problems in marital relationships. The behaviour sometimes occurs in conjunction with alcohol abuse. People with this compulsion derive little gratification from their sexual behaviour. This absence of lasting pleasure simply intensifies their promiscuity.

Little is known about this compulsion because seldom do such people seek help. When they do it is often at the insistence of a marital partner. Clinical case studies describe the presence of strong needs for love and attention together with hostility and anger in these people.

Exhibitionism

Exhibitionism, or indecent exposure, refers to the act of exposing one's genitals to a person of the opposite sex without his or her consent. Cases of exhibitionism have been described as far back as 4 BC in Greece. Dr E. C. Laseque, a French physician, first used the term 'exhibitionism' in a medical journal in 1877. Because of the public nature of their behaviour, exhibitionists constitute the largest percentage of sex offenders reported to the police. Approximately one-third of all sexual offences in Canada, England, Wales and the United States are categorized as exhibitionism. It is interesting to note that this condition is somewhat culturally determined in that it is relatively uncommon in Africa, South America and Asia.

Aroused – but to hilarity! Women are seen appreciating a male stripper in Beryl Cook's cartoon (left).

Exhibitionism usually occurs in very open, public places. Since many witnesses are present and the exhibitionist often returns several times to the same place, this compulsion frequently comes to the attention of the police. The act becomes so compulsive that the exhibitionist gives little thought to being caught.

In his book, *Indecent Exposure*, Dr J. M. MacDonald presents the results of his survey on the most likely places for an exhibitionist to expose himself.

Places where exhibitionism is most likely to occur

Place	Number	Per cent
Street	91	45.5
Alley	22	11.0
Parking lot	19	9.5
Park	6	3.0
School playground	4	2.0
House	29	14.5
Apartment	16	8.0
Launderette	9	4.5
Office or store	4	29.0

The majority of cases of indecent exposure occur in public places; most notably, streets, alleyways, car parks, offices, shops and public transport. The behaviour can become extremely compulsive and is accompanied by the desire to repeat the incident over and over again. Exhibitionists typically return to the same place on several occasions. Since indecent exposure is against the law this compulsive repetition often leads to apprehension by the police. Between 25 and 50 per cent of the time, exhibitionists expose themselves to children. The Kinsey report indicated that at least 12 per cent of a representative sample of adult women surveyed had witnessed acts of exhibitionism in early childhood.

Like many other sex offenders, exhibitionists tend to be rather inhibited people who have difficulty relating to others. There is an aggressive and defiant element to their sexual behaviour even though they are unassertive in other situations and unable to express anger easily. They are rarely dangerous and usually run away within a few seconds after the exposure. Exhibitionists say they obtain pleasure from 'shocking' their victims and the secrecy and anonymity of their behaviour tends to heighten arousal.

Voyeurism

Voyeurism refers to the act of secretly watching other people who are nude or who are engaging in sexual activity. The more commonly used term for voyeurs is 'Peeping Tom'. The origin of this term can be traced to an episode of voyeurism occurring in England over 900 years ago. Legend has it that Lady Godiva, the wife of Earl Leofric, Lord of Coventry, asked her husband to lower the heavy taxes he imposed. He agreed only if she would ride naked through the town. Lady Godiva acceded to his wishes, but asked that the townspeople should remain indoors. An unfortunate tailor named Tom 'peeped' through his window as she rode by and was struck blind.

Certainly, poor Tom's curiosity is not unusual, nor is it necessarily pathological. Going to striptease shows or looking at pornographic magazines are commonplace male activities which are not generally considered voyeurism. In fact, with the advent of male 'strip' shows and *Playgirl* magazine, a trend has developed in which women as well as men engage in these activities.

Voyeurism is different from normal sexual curiosity in three major respects. First, it often takes the place of heterosexual behaviour and is used as the exclusive means of sexual gratification. Voyeurs frequently masturbate while watching someone who is nude or undressing. Second, it is a secretive activity that violates the privacy of the victim. Third, voyeurs feel a strong compulsion to continue their behaviour in spite of the risk of being caught, arrested and, possibly, imprisoned.

Voyeurs appear to be driven to this behaviour by its excitement and danger. They are often shy, immature, and lonely people with limited sexual experience – typically, they are young (early 20s), male and unmarried. Although they are rarely dangerous, their victims may be badly frightened to discover them peering through their windows.

Paedophilia and incest

Paedophilia refers to the use of a child by an adult for sexual purposes. A related compulsion, incest, refers to sexual behaviour between people who are closely related to one another. Approximately 50 to 75 per cent of child molest-

Episodes of exhibitionism can be triggered by bouts of depression and personal problems. This was true of Lance Rentzel, a former professional football player for the Dallas Cowboys, who was arrested for indecent exposure in 1970. His episodes of public exposure were precipitated by depression over his poor performance on the football field. His arrest was met with disbelief by the public since he was a 'macho' football star and married to the beautiful actress, Joey Heatherton.

In his autobiography, entitled *When All the Laughter Died In Sorrow*, Rentzel explained how he had spent his entire life trying to prove his masculinity through football and fleeting sexual encounters with women. Close, mature relationships with women frightened him. When his team was losing or when personal relationships became too threatening he felt that he tried to prove his manhood and express his anger and frustration through exhibitionism.

ing occurs between adults and children who are either related or who know one another quite well.

Paedophiles can be either homosexual or heterosexual in their orientation. They usually fondle children or encourage them to perform oral sex but rarely initiate intercourse. Many are married but tend to be somewhat moralistic and inhibited in other sexual relationships.

Incestuous paedophilia is especially disrupting and devastating to the family in which it occurs. Such behaviour most often occurs between fathers or stepfathers and their daughters. The incest frequently goes unreported by the child who is typically confused by these sexual advances and fearful of retaliation if he or she reports the incidents. Even other family members who discover the incest, however shocked by it, fail to tell anyone. When the behaviour is finally uncovered and professional help sought, family members explain that they hesitated to seek help because of embarrassment and shame. Once the matter is made public incestuous parents are usually extremely remorseful and guilt-ridden.

Because a child is the victim of paedophilia, this compulsion is met with more public outrage than any other sexual problem. Parents of victims are understandably enraged and often

Voyeurism ancient and modern. As objects of erotic fantasy, the nudes in the old print seem natural and innocent compared with the aggressive sexuality of the 20th-century counterparts.

hysterical over the incident. Once the paedophiliac experience is over, parents can be extremely helpful in helping the child cope with the trauma. Parents must try to remain calm and avoid the natural tendency to overprotect the child. Care must be taken to treat the child as normally as possible so that he or she is not made to feel ashamed or embarrassed by the incident. In the majority of cases, paedophiliac experiences do not cause permanent psychological damage to the child.

This (male) winner of a transvestite beauty contest suggests that conventional ideas about female desirability are often no more than constructed images.

Transvestism

Transvestism refers to dressing in the clothes of the opposite sex to obtain sexual gratification. The majority of transvestites are males and are, in fact, heterosexual. Homosexual transvestites are relatively rare.

Transvestites are different from transexuals. A male transexual dresses in female clothing primarily because he thinks of himself as a female. These people often report that they feel like a woman in a man's body. The aim of a transexual would usually be to seek out a sex-change operation in order to become physically a member of the opposite sex, a role which already seems right psychologically.

Transvestites, on the other hand, do not want to change their gender. They simply obtain sex-

Leather and chains – the popular and often accurate sterotype of sexual fetishism.

ual gratification from cross-dressing. Drs P. M. Bentler and C. Prince[1] surveyed subscribers to a magazine for transvestites to determine their psychological characteristics. They found that most were males, many quite ambitious and athletic. The majority were married, participated in sexual intercourse, and expressed an above-average sexual interest in women. More than one-third reported that cross-dressing had been the major cause of divorce.

Why do sexual compulsions develop?

Although much speculation exists about sexual compulsions, few experiments on causes have been conducted. Most studies, however, indicate that several factors may be involved. Based on various theories in the field, such sexual habits may develop in the following way. First, a child may feel extremely inhibited and tense about sex, perhaps because of overprotective parents, or a puritanical upbringing. An adolescent may react to unpleasant experiences of being rejected by the opposite sex. Youthful sexual arousal, then, must be channelled in a different direction. Dr R. J. McGuire believes that, at this point, those objects or fantasies that become associated with early masturbation experiences can lead to the development of a sexual problem. In one case a fetishist accidentally discovered the sexual pleasure associated with handling a woman's panties during masturbation. Through a gradual process of associative conditioning, panties and sexual arousal became strongly linked. The subject suffered from extreme shyness and heterosexual arousal diminished because of self-doubts and severe social anxiety.

In 1966 Dr Rachman[2] of the University of London conducted a study to determine whether sexual arousal could, indeed, be conditioned to essentially non-sexual objects such as in the development of a fetish. Three rather adventurous unmarried psychologists served as the subjects. Each subject was seated in an experimental room and hooked up to a device to measure penile erections (actually, penis-volume changes). Using a classical conditioning procedure Rachman first showed photographic slides of a pair of women's black, knee-length boots. He quickly then switched to slides of nude

High technology sex for sale (above), and a bizarre use of some of the more fetishistic products (left). Do sex aids really help, or are they a symptom of failure?

women. The subjects were instructed to simply view the slides and concentrate on them. The sequence of boots → nudes was repeated over and over again. In the beginning the measurement device indicated that the subjects were becoming aroused to the photos of the nude women although they showed no sexual arousal to the boots. However, after 20 to 30 associations between the boots and nudes the subjects began to show penile volume changes not only to the women but also to the boots! Such an anticipatory physiological response could eventually become associated with more detailed fantasies and when accompanied by heterosexual inhibitions, could result in fetishistic sexual behaviour. Dr Rachman, of course, deconditioned his subjects and no deleterious after effects were experienced. The study, however, indicates how a sexual compulsion can develop relatively easily given circumstances which foster and encourage the behaviour.

Selfwatching applications
The main thrust of selfwatching treatment for sexual compulsions involves a twofold approach. First, these individuals must learn to cope more effectively with the anxiety, depression, anger, or social/marital problems that often trigger their compulsive behaviour. Second, they must learn to enhance their heterosexual skills and interests.

For men and women who experience deep anxiety about intimate relationships with the opposite sex a desensitization process can be applied in which relaxation is associated with sexual stimuli in a hierarchical fashion. First are presented those stimuli which provoke the least anxiety: these are followed by situations that induce more and more tension. Gradually, the individual learns to feel completely relaxed even when exposed to previously disturbing sexual scenes and thoughts. Desensitization can be conducted using imagined sexual stimuli, films

and videotapes, or actual sexual encounters. In their book *Sex Therapy: A Behavioral Approach* Drs W. K. Caird and J. P. Wincze[3] describe the use of video desensitization with sexual disorders. These authors have developed a set of brief videotapes depicting sexual scenes of increasingly closer intimacy. The first videotape shows a man and a woman simply carrying on a conversation, while the final one depicts nude sexual intercourse. The anxious individual is shown these tapes one at a time and instructed to practise deep muscle relaxation while viewing them. To make the scenes more realistic, people are told to imagine that they are themselves taking part in each of the scenes being portrayed.

Dr A. A. Cooper reported the case of a fetish in which he used real-life desensitization. Although the person's fetish was under control, he remained extremely tense and anxious regarding sexual intercourse with his wife. His anxiety, in fact, resulted in impotence whenever sexual contact was attempted. During the desensitization procedure the patient was instructed to lie in bed naked with his wife concentrating on relaxation. When he felt completely comfortable he was to follow a specific format of increasingly intimate sexual contact. For example, he was instructed to touch his wife's body or gently kiss her, not going any further until he felt com-

pletely comfortable and relaxed. If his anxiety became too great, the couple were advised to terminate the session and start again at another time. Such a gradual approach works well because it takes the pressure off the patient to perform. This patient gradually became more and more relaxed and confident until finally he and his wife were able to engage in satisfactory sexual intercourse.

Developing social skills

In addition to arousal and anxiety problems many people have limited interpersonal skills needed to meet and court members of the opposite sex. Such problems are not limited to sexual deviants as the mass popularity of the recent best-selling book *How To Pick Up Girls* attests. Programmes designed to teach dating skills involve practice in approaching and meeting the opposite sex and arranging a date. Therapists

Sexual adventures at home with good humour and style (left) and relaxed companionship in public (right). Becoming socially adept and integrated is something we can all learn to do.

usually have assistants provide the person with demonstrations of how to start up a conversation or how to act on a date. Patients role-play these skills with clinical assistants and receive feedback on their improvement from videotapes of their interactions. They are also taught how to provide and receive compliments, enhance their physical appearance, behave more assertively, engage in appropriate talk, and handle silences in conversations during a date. After a course of instruction, pupils are encouraged to put their newly acquired skills into practice and discuss progress and/or problems with the therapist.

Selfwatching and sexual problems
In this chapter we have described a number of techniques specifically developed to meet sexual problems, including compulsions. In addition, however, people with compulsive sexual problems may want to use several of the selfwatching techniques described in earlier chapters. The *ultimate consequences* self-management procedure discussed in Chapter 3 is often needed to keep motivation strong and to cope with urges. Urges can also be overcome using the *cue exposure* procedure (Chapter 4) in which the person gradually becomes accustomed to being in tempting situations without exhibiting his sexual compulsion. For example, an exhibitionist might drive by an alleyway repeatedly until his urges diminished.

People with sexual compulsions must develop better methods of coping with depression, anxiety and anger since such feelings often precipitate their behaviour. The relaxation and thought-control techniques discussed in Chapters 5 and 6 are essential in this regard. The overall assertiveness and social skills described in Chapter 7 are especially helpful for those who are inhibited socially and emotionally.

These approaches and strategies, we believe, will help the prisoners of sexual compulsions to work out practical methods of controlling their behaviours. The sense of victory gained from changing a habit by your own efforts is a powerful aid to maintaining behaviour change over a longer period. However, if self-help measures prove unsuccessful, the help of a qualified psychiatrist may be needed to plan and carry out effective selfwatching.

15
OBSESSIONAL COMPULSIONS

Most of the compulsions considered so far in this book have been concerned with behaviour which satisfies some basic desire or attains a pleasurable state of mind. We now turn to another form of behaviour which can be equally compulsive, although it is directed towards the avoidance of distress rather than the achievement of pleasure. At one time or another, many people will have checked their front door two or three times before they go on holiday when they really know that it is well and truly locked. This is a very short-lived and harmless example of a compulsion to check. Most people, too, have experienced repetitive nagging worries over trivial matters ('Did I address that letter correctly?'). Unfortunately, these concerns can get out of hand and become full-blown compulsions which are as troublesome as any drug or gambling problem, causing distress both to the sufferers and their families. In their work at the Institute of Psychiatry, London, Rachman and Hodgson have identified four main types of obsessional compulsion.[1] They are the following:

Obsessional checking

Repeated checking is a major problem and involves spending a great deal of time every day checking things, gas or water taps, doors, letters, etc., over and over again. This behaviour is involved in many *routine* activities, such as the morning wash, and there is also a tendency to indulge in repetitive *mental* checking (for example, did I turn off the gas tap properly?).

Obsessional cleaning

Obsessional cleaning arises from excessive concern about germs and diseases, and worries about contamination, for example, from money, public telephones, toilets, and animals. Soap and antiseptics are used excessively, and continual washing takes up a lot of time.

Obsessional slowness

A person suffering from this problem adheres to a strict routine in dressing and undressing, folding and hanging clothes. This disrupts the normal pattern of life and the sufferer is often late, for work or appointments and so on, because he or she cannot get through everything on time. The routine may involve counting as the tasks are performed. The problem does not usually include obsessional ruminations – the nagging thoughts that can come to occupy the mind to the exclusion of all else.

Obsessional doubting and conscientiousness
The person with this problem usually feels that a job has not been completed correctly, even though it was performed very carefully, and is assailed by serious doubts about simple every-day events. He or she gets behind with work because procedures are repeated over and over again and too much attention is paid to detail. Such a person has a strict conscience (probably learned from strict parents) and shows an excessive concern with honesty.

These are the main problems, but others include compulsive tidying, continued requests for reassurance and excessive repetition of simple tasks such as combing the hair. One person can, of course, suffer from more than one complaint.

The case of Howard Hughes is a celebrated example of obsessional compulsion. A brilliant engineer, aircraft designer, entrepreneur and latterly movie producer, Hughes developed a severe obsessional disorder involving a fear of contamination. Most people know that for some 20 years Hughes, one of the world's richest men, lived as a recluse in hotels in Las Vegas and Nicaragua. There, in order to avoid infection, he constructed for himself sterile, isolated environments in which his contact with potentially contaminating people and objects was kept to a minimum. For the most part he successfully avoided touching anything directly – instead, he covered himself with paper tissues and other protective materials. His barber was required to sterilize all of his instruments repeatedly by immersing them in alcohol. There was a complicated ritual for handling objects. Before handing Hughes a spoon his attendants had to wrap the handle in tissue paper and seal it with cellophane tape. A second piece of tissue was wrapped around the first protective wrapping to ensure that it would be protected from contamination. On receiving the protected spoon, Hughes

Two points on a continuum. Compulsive hand-washing (above) is more common than the total fear of contamination which led the billionaire Howard Hughes (below) to live as a recluse.

would use it only with the handle fully covered in this way. When he finished with it, the tissue was discarded into a specially provided receptacle and the spoon itself had to be carefully cleaned.

The main obsessional compulsions, namely excessive cleaning, washing and checking, are probably very common complaints but just how common is not known. Psychologists and psychiatrists have studied this kind of compulsion for many years in those people who are referred to clinics for treatment. However, these are bound to be a severely disturbed minority in whom the disturbance is so severe that daily life has been rendered impossibly difficult.

In order to provide a clear picture of the main

Obsessional compulsion assessment

This questionnaire has been devised by doctors at the Institute of Psychiatry, London. It is used to make a preliminary assessment of the degree of difficulty suffered by obsessional compulsive patients.

Please answer each question by putting a circle around the 'TRUE' or the 'FALSE' following the question. There are no right or wrong answers, and no trick questions. Work quickly and do not think too long about the exact meaning of the question.

1.	I avoid using public telephones because of possible contamination.	TRUE	FALSE
2.	I frequently get nasty thoughts and have difficulty in getting rid of them.	TRUE	FALSE
3.	I am more concerned than most people about honesty.	TRUE	FALSE
4.	I am often late because I can't seem to get through everything on time.	TRUE	FALSE
5.	I don't worry unduly about contamination if I touch an animal.	TRUE	FALSE
6.	I frequently have to check things (e.g., gas or water taps, doors, etc.) several times.	TRUE	FALSE
7.	I have a very strict conscience.	TRUE	FALSE
8.	I find that almost every day I am upset by unpleasant thoughts that come into my mind against my will.	TRUE	FALSE
9.	I do not worry unduly if I accidentally bump into somebody.	TRUE	FALSE
10.	I usually have serious doubts about the simple everyday things I do.	TRUE	FALSE
11.	Neither of my parents was very strict during my childhood.	TRUE	FALSE
12.	I tend to get behind in my work because I repeat things over and over again.	TRUE	FALSE
13.	I use only an average amount of soap.	TRUE	FALSE
14.	Some numbers are extremely unlucky.	TRUE	FALSE
15.	I do not check letters over and over again before posting them.	TRUE	FALSE
16.	I do not take a long time to dress in the morning.	TRUE	FALSE
17.	I am not excessively concerned about cleanliness.	TRUE	FALSE
18.	One of my major problems is that I pay too much attention to detail.	TRUE	FALSE
19.	I can use well-kept toilets without any hesitation.	TRUE	FALSE
20.	My major problem is repeated checking.	TRUE	FALSE
21.	I am not unduly concerned about germs and diseases.	TRUE	FALSE
22.	I do not tend to check things more than once.	TRUE	FALSE
23.	I do not stick to a very strict routine when doing ordinary things.	TRUE	FALSE
24.	My hands do not feel dirty after touching money.	TRUE	FALSE
25.	I do not usually count when doing a routine task.	TRUE	FALSE
26.	I take rather a long time to complete my washing in the morning.	TRUE	FALSE
27.	I do not use a great deal of antiseptics.	TRUE	FALSE
28.	I spend a lot of time every day checking things over and over again.	TRUE	FALSE
29.	Hanging and folding my clothes at night does not take up a lot of time.	TRUE	FALSE
30.	Even when I do something very carefully I often feel that it is not quite right.	TRUE	FALSE

types of obsessional behaviour, a number of typical cases will be described. These are people who were treated at the Maudsley Hospital and so their problems are particularly severe. Nevertheless, together they provide an overall picture of this type of problem and some idea of the intensity and degree of irrationality involved when a compulsion gets out of hand.

Obsessional-compulsive checking

An unmarried girl, aged 25, worried that her vagina would be harmed by contact with glass or contaminating substances. To avoid such harm she checked for glass on chairs and toilet seats before she sat down, and would not wear flared dresses because she thought they were more likely to pick up bits of glass. For the same reason, she kept her panties in a special part of her drawer out of harm's way and would not run for fear of knocking something over and breaking glass.

The cause of her problems was impossible to ascertain, but she did believe that a holiday at the age of 19 had exacerbated them. On this holiday she had indulged in heavy petting with a number of boys and had subsequently been disgusted by her behaviour.

The following are other examples of checking rituals. A 28-year-old patient had checking rituals precipitated by a fear of harming others. He was unable to drive his car, as this provoked intolerable anxieties and required lengthy checking rituals, and he avoided crowded streets for fear of causing harm to others. He repeatedly checked razors, pins, glass and so forth.

A 34-year-old married woman had checking rituals precipitated by contact with other people. Looking at or talking to people, or giving them food, led to checking behaviour in order to ensure that no harm came to them.

A 36-year-old man had checking rituals focused on excrement; he engaged in prolonged and meticulous inspections of any brown speck, particularly on his clothes and shoes.

A 40-year-old school teacher checked that all rugs and carpets were absolutely flat lest someone trip over them, and spent long periods looking for needles and pins on the floor and in furniture. She also repeatedly checked to ensure that all cigarettes and matches were extinguished.

Lost something valuable, or is this just another routine investigation? Some people will check anything.

A 28-year-old woman teacher spent up to three hours each night checking doors, gas taps, windows and switches before going to bed.

Obsessional-compulsive cleaning

A young woman aged 25 was almost totally pre-occupied with the harm that she might have caused to others, especially her close friends, relatives and vulnerable individuals such as the very old and the very young. Her fears were focused on the transmission of infectious diseases and poisonous substances. At the age of 20 whilst working as a hospital technician she went to a lecture during which the story of 'Typhoid Mary' was described. Typhoid Mary was the nickname of a 19th-century Irish-American woman who was chronically infected with typhoid bacteria. She worked in a restaurant and transmitted typhoid to a large number of people before being identified as the source of contamination. Shortly after this lecture the young woman had to deal with an infectious culture and her finger accidentally touched it. She scrubbed her hands diligently with disinfectant but was still very worried and in a restaurant the same evening she was unable to touch anything. This experience was crucial in determining the future development of her symptoms, although prior to this she had experienced some apprehension about causing harm to others.

During the five years prior to her admission for hospital treatment, the sources of possible contamination multiplied to include doctors' surgeries, people with illnesses, and the college where she was studying. One whole area of London was out of bounds after she met a man there who told her that he had suffered from hepatitis a few years earlier. She only spoke to the man for a few minutes but that was sufficient to ensure that she subsequently avoided an area of 10 square miles. Until she started treatment she was using a bottle of disinfectant every day.

Other examples of cleaning rituals include the following: a 22-year-old married woman had an intense fear of contamination from dogs. Over five years the problem had generalized to include many areas of England which she associated with dogs. Even reading or hearing about these places triggered prolonged washing rituals. Her fears led to repeated changes of residence.

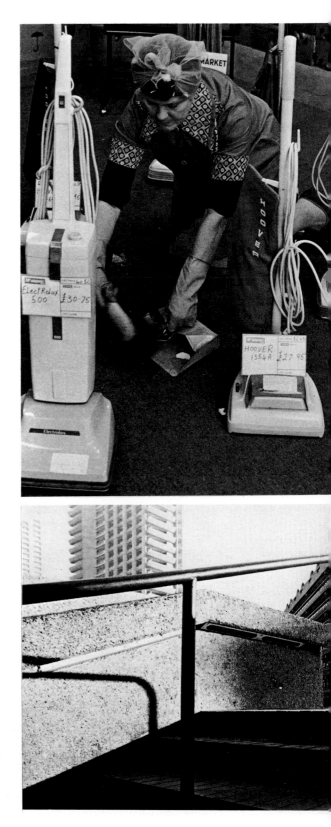

A 42-year-old woman practised hand-washing and house-cleaning rituals over a 26-year period. The rituals were prolonged and seriously interfered with her social life and her relationship with her husband. She found it impossible to truncate her rituals in order to prepare dinner for the family or get to bed at a reasonable hour. Any contact with dirt, dust, dustbins, toilets, carpets, floors and so forth triggered excessive hand-washing.

A 38-year-old mother of one child was obsessed by a fear of contamination for over 20 years. Her concern with the possibility of being infected by germs resulted in washing and cleaning rituals that invaded all aspects of her life. Her child was restrained in one room which was kept entirely germ-free. She opened and closed all doors with her feet in order to avoid contaminating her hands.

Once we have left the incubator – itself a rather frightening environment – even stranger environments await us. Learning to cope with them frees us to lead active and full lives.

Obsessional slowness

A 38-year-old man suffered from a chronic and severe obsessional disorder in which excessive slowness was the main feature. At the start of treatment the patient was taking roughly three hours each morning to prepare himself for work, although he brushed his teeth only late at night because this took, on average, 45 minutes: he bathed irregularly because he needed between three and five hours to complete the process. A second patient suffering from a similar disorder was so incapacitated as to require repeated admission to a hospital over a 20-year period. He took up to eight hours to prepare himself each day and was seldom ready for lunch before 5:00 p.m. Observation of these patients shows that they carry out routine dressing and grooming activities in a very meticulous way. They give as much attention to the act of shaving or combing their hair as a sculptor would give when administering the final touches to a masterpiece.

Obsessional doubting and conscientiousness

A married middle-aged woman, who was very religious and conscientious, suffered from persistent ruminations – persistent, threatening and inconclusive thoughts – and doubts about possible harm that she could have inflicted on her children, mostly involving sharp objects and

Excessive vanity (above) can be a means of avoiding other responsibilities. 'Be careful with knives and scissors!' A sensible precaution, but compulsive parents can instil exaggerated fears in their children, and themselves need reassurance to unlearn over-protective behaviour.

injury to her children's eyes. Here are a few examples of activities which she was frightened of performing with her children present:

1. Using knives, scissors or skewers in the kitchen
2. Cutting bread
3. Cutting the children's nails
4. Pinning a badge on to the clothing of one of her children
5. Sewing
6. Knitting
7. Writing
8. Walking round a shop, in case there should be knives or scissors on display
9. Laying the table
10. Sitting at the table at meal times

She tried to avoid these and other situations which could trigger deep anxiety, but even so

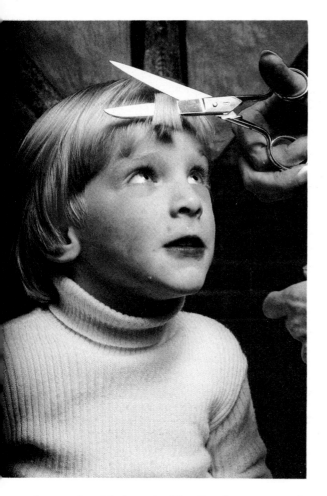

she was troubled most of the time by some rumination or other. In an attempt to terminate her persistent worrying she repeatedly asked her husband for reassurances that the children had not been harmed.

She often found that her worries were associated with a lack of confidence in the accuracy of her memory. For example, on one occasion she was transferring a brooch from one dress to another in the presence of her children. She felt relatively safe because her husband was also present but later she began to worry that her memory of the episode was faulty. Perhaps her husband had not been there after all, in which case her children might have been at risk . . . This paralysing rumination was typical.

In another example, a middle-aged man had great difficulty getting through his work as a stock controller because he was compelled to go over each task repeatedly in an attempt to allevi-

ate his doubts and be sure of avoiding mistakes. He was very conscientious and feared criticism from his boss if he made even a slight mistake.

The reinforcement of obsessional compulsive rituals

Like the 'high' produced by addictive drugs, the experience of avoiding distress is highly reinforcing. The greater the expected distress, the greater is the relief. An obsessional hand-washing compulsion might begin as a way of avoiding contamination by germs or excreta. A compulsion to straighten and tidy could begin in childhood as a way of avoiding parental punishment. In its early stages, a washing or checking ritual may appear to be merely a sensible precaution, but after many repetitions it develops into a habit which persists even when the controlling circumstances have changed. For example, tidying, which was originally carried out to avoid parental wrath, can still be compulsive and excessive even when both parents are dead. The expected unpleasant consequences change from being external (i.e. parental punishment) to internal (i.e. guilt).

A good example of this type of extension of the process was evident in one of our patients who started washing excessively in order to avoid tuberculosis after a friend died of the disease. Twenty years later when she was successfully treated (see page 4) it was apparent that a fear of tuberculosis and of spreading TB to others was not her main concern. In three weeks she was successfully treated by the cue-exposure method described in Chapter 4 which involved, in her case, deliberate prolonged exposure to hospital wards and other sources of threat. She was aware that TB could not be diagnosed until months after the contaminating event and yet she was just about cured after only three weeks of treatment. At a rational level, every person whom she touched whilst in a state of contamination during treatment could have dropped dead two months later and yet this possibility did not worry her and didn't interfere with her daily improvement during the treatment period. She was actually frightened of her own fear, not of the contamination itself. As Henry Maudsley noted in 1895, the misery is caused by 'the haunting fear of fear. It is that which is the perpetual torture, an acute agony when active, a quivering apprehension of recurrence when quiescent'.

In other cases the fear might be of guilt or of ruminations or of violent or unacceptable thoughts. The point is that a well-learned obsessional compulsive habit is reinforced by the avoidance of a distressing event, but that event is inside the mind of the victim, and often involves obsessional ruminations.[2, 3]

Factors involved in the development of obsessional compulsive rituals

First of all, some people are almost certainly more vulnerable than others but, as with alcoholism, smoking and heroin addiction, the scientific evidence of definite predisposing factors is not particularly strong. From Freud onwards, most theories of obsessional compulsive habits have implicated anxiety, and it is probable that anxious people are the most vulnerable.

Of course whether a high level of anxiety leads to alcohol use, a phobia or an obsessive compulsive problem depends on a large number of initiating factors. One person may pick up a fear from parents or relatives. For example, one of our patients modelled her childhood habits upon her father who was himself obsessional about cleanliness. She would, for instance, always imitate his habit of wearing gloves when playing with the family dog. Another patient was told as a child that there is a layer of germs on the ground, one foot deep, and consequently spent two years of his childhood making sure that, whether he was playing, fighting or resting, his face never entered this danger zone. Such an experience almost certainly influenced the course of his obsessional compulsive problem.

Persuasive communications often play an important part in the development of obsessional disorders. We have already noted that one person's problem escalated after hearing a lecture on Typhoid Mary.

Another patient used to spend five minutes obsessionally cleaning his teeth until his dentist told him that he should be a little more meticulous; thereafter, he spent at least 30 minutes morning and night cleaning and checking them. The same patient doubled the time that he spent on hair grooming activities after reading the massaging instructions on a bottle of hair oil. Once a predisposition towards obsessional behaviour has developed, persuasive communications about poison, germs, health, antiseptics and other relevant topics often result in a dramatic escalation of compulsive activities.

Another process which is right at the heart of the development of obsessional compulsive problems is usually called *sensitization*. Once a slight problem develops there can be a very rapid escalation during a period of stress or depression. A minor worry can rapidly be turned into a crippling disorder. A vicious circle is also involved here, since compulsions lead to depression and depression leads to compulsion. As Lewis points out, 'obsessional patients are in most cases depressed: their illness is a depressing one'. The advice on anxiety and depression given in Chapters 5 and 6 is very relevant if this process is to be prevented or reversed.

The *generalization* of compulsions to include many types of cues or danger signals, including thoughts, feelings or events, leads to behaviour which appears to be totally irrational. This is not surprising since generalization is based upon association and not upon reasoned argument. For example, one of our patients felt contaminated after touching a photograph of a cancer cell, although she knew logically that she wouldn't be harmed by it. Another of our patients started hand-washing frequently in an attempt to keep at bay contamination from her brother who was schizophrenic and dirty. By association the cues for hand washing gradually spread until all the domestic products used within the home by her mother were strong cues. Years later contact with them would still trigger a feeling of repulsion and excessive hand washing. For example, she had to wash if she touched Nivea Cream, Mothers Pride bread, Elastoplast, Rizla Cigarette Papers, Typhoo Tea, Lurpack Butter and 50 other products which were associated with her feelings of repulsion towards her brother.

Self-help and professional help for obsessional compulsive behaviour

As with any of the problem behaviours in this book, there is no clear dividing line between relatively useful compulsions – an urge to double

Fear and danger are relative. Many regard the fear of being alone as irrational, but would decline the offer of a job working with poisonous snakes.

check that one's parked car is locked – and the washing or checking rituals that seriously impair an individual's daily life. It is all a matter of degree. At some stage, however, it will become clear that this type of behaviour has reached a pitch where it is causing problems for the individual and for those around him or her. What hope does our selfwatching treatment hold for such victims of obsessional compulsions? Most of the research on this subject has been carried out with people with severe problems who have been referred to hospital for treatment. Evidence suggests that the cue-exposure approach described in Chapter 4 is very successful with about 60 or 70 per cent of even these difficult cases. The outlook for people who are just starting to have a problem is therefore very hopeful.

For example, one of our successes requested treatment for his washing and cleaning compulsion after he had been dismissed from his job because the excessive time involved in carrying out his cleaning compulsion reduced his working capacity. During previous hospital admissions, Alan had been exposed to drug therapy and supportive counselling and had even been given a leucotomy in an attempt to reduce the anxiety associated with his compulsive rituals.

Prior to treatment, he was spending approximately 4½ hours a day on his compulsive activities. He had to indulge in elaborate washing rituals after urinating or defecating, which he described as follows:

> In the toilet I wash my hands once under the tap with soap then wash the sink out then fill it up with hot water. I then wash my hands and arms, rinse them, then wash my face. Then I wash my hands again, dry my hands and face, undo the toilet door with a paper towel, then pull up my trouser zip, then wash my hands and arms again taking about the same time. At all cost I must not contact any item of the toilet or sink-basin or door-handle or any part of clothing after washing my hands for fear of contamination. If clothing becomes in contact with any of the above items, anything this item becomes in contact with also becomes contaminated, and so it carries on. As a rule I use my own soap. Back at the bedroom, I wash my hands again, the period before going to the toilet and after cause great worry and quite often upset me for the rest of the day.

The treatment involved repeated practice in touching the 'cues' that provoked his compulsive urges. These included grass, mud, ash, and then gradually progressed to toilets and even a tiny smear of excrement. At each stage, Alan was asked to copy his therapist. The therapist would touch the contaminating substance and then various personal belongings, his hair, face, books and anything that was frequently used. Alan was encouraged to do the same, but, of course, he was never forced.

After each cue-exposure session, Alan was asked to continue with some normal activity such as eating, conversing or playing games, in order to counteract his anxiety and the tendency to sit and brood. He was also encouraged to resist washing and cleaning during this period.

Gradually, the treatment started to have an effect and when he was discharged from hospital, there was a very marked improvement. The amount of time spent in the toilet and washing was now approximately 1½ hours instead of 4½ per day. He could now touch money, door-knobs and other items that he imagined to be contaminated without experiencing an urge to wash.[4]

Two years after treatment, Alan's mother wrote a letter of thanks which concluded:

> He was married last September and has bought a house. He and his wife have settled in well and it is a pleasure to call on them and see him gardening and doing various odd jobs around the house. This is a thing we would have thought impossible a few years ago.

Weakening the urge to check

In one experiment, people with checking problems were exposed to a provoking situation and then asked about their urge to check. For example, a woman who helplessly checked and re-checked every time she turned off the gas tap was asked to go into the kitchen and switch all the gas taps on and off. On the left of the Figure you can see the strength of her checking urge before exposure (BE), after exposure (AE) and after performing a checking ritual (AR). On the right you can see what happens to the strength of the urge when it is resisted for three hours. The change is dramatic. The urge to carry out a checking ritual and the associated discomfort decline to acceptable levels after only one hour.

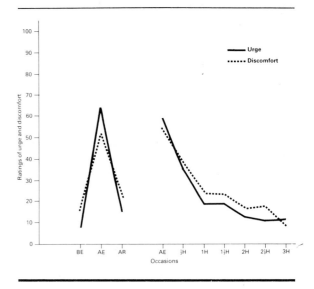

16
SELF-HELP GROUPS

In this chapter, we will put forward six reasons why a person trying to break a habit, compulsion or addiction, could benefit from joining or starting up a self-help group. Going it alone is not easy, and many people throughout the ages have discovered that getting together with fellow sufferers can help them to solve the problems in their lives and to extricate themselves from a seemingly hopeless situation. As Demone[1] notes in an introduction to a directory of self-help groups:

> It matters not what you call them – self-help, mutual aid, support systems – they are the fastest growing component of the human service industry. Nor is it surprising. Man is a social animal who throughout his history has banded together for problem solving and survival ... Thus they are as old as man in one sense or a contemporary solution to complex problems in another.

Perhaps the best known example of the power of self-help is Alcoholics Anonymous. In the summer of 1935, Bill Wilson, a New York stockbroker, and Robert Holbrook-Smith, a doctor in Akron, Ohio, worked together to overcome their

drinking problems and were able, together, to achieve and maintain the sobriety that had been so elusive while each battled alone. The subsequent evolution of Alcoholics Anonymous is a remarkable success story. From its inception in 1935, AA has grown into a world-wide organization claiming well over 1 million active members.

AA is now an institution with strong traditions and healthy links with the helping professions. It is 'a fellowship of men and women who share their experience, strength and hope with each other that they may solve their common problem and help others to recover from alcoholism'.

Many other groups now cater for the needs of people with compulsions and addictions. In recent years we have seen the development of Drink Watchers, for people with drinking problems who are aiming for sensible drinking rather than total abstinence. Weight Watchers, the largest of the weight-control organizations, was established in 1963 and in 1976 its services were used by 1,655,000 new and rejoining members. Each week, over 400,000 members attended more than 13,000 classes in all 50 states of the USA and in 25 other countries. There are now well established self-help groups for people who

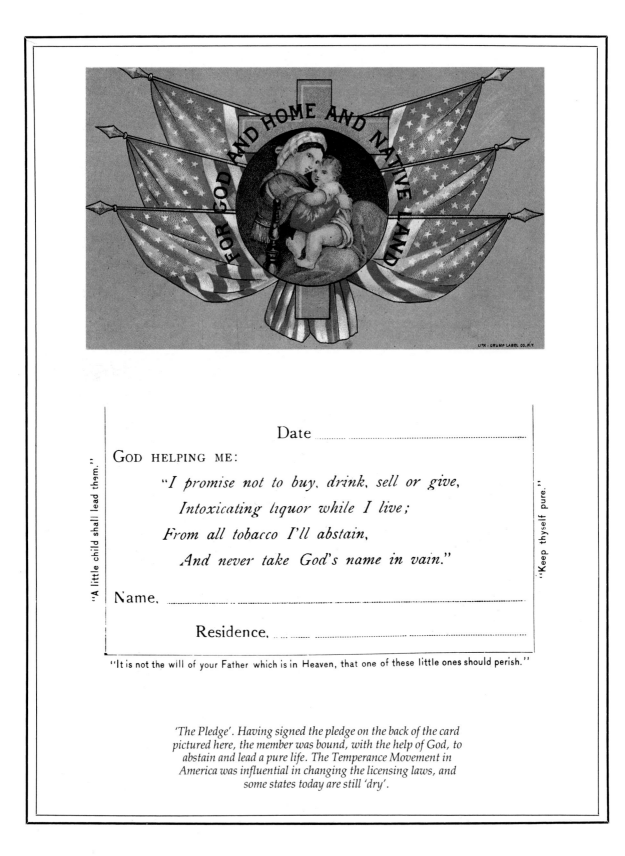

FOR GOD AND HOME AND NATIVE LAND

Date

GOD HELPING ME:

"I promise not to buy, drink, sell or give,
  Intoxicating liquor while I live;
From all tobacco I'll abstain,
  And never take God's name in vain."

Name,

Residence,

"A little child shall lead them."

"Keep thyself pure."

"It is not the will of your Father which is in Heaven, that one of these little ones should perish."

'The Pledge'. Having signed the pledge on the back of the card pictured here, the member was bound, with the help of God, to abstain and lead a pure life. The Temperance Movement in America was influential in changing the licensing laws, and some states today are still 'dry'.

I will be a teetotaler from now on!

smoke, gamble compulsively, or eat or drink to excess and a group has recently been developed in the United States to help those people who suffer from obsessive-compulsive problems.

Contact with special groups can usually be made through local social services, local radio stations and community papers. But smoker, gambler, heavy drinker or overeater will be able to locate an appropriate self-help group in his own corner of the world. If this is the case, then there is a great deal to be said for starting one. Most of the powerful forces involved in self-help groups will be present where just two or three fellow sufferers are gathered together with the aim of helping themselves and each other. As

David Robinson and Stuart Henry point out in their book *Self-help and Health*:

> . . . it does not need sociologists, psychiatrists, historians or priests to draw our attention to the simple fact that people who share a certain problem might possibly have something to offer each other. That 'something' might be emotional support, material aid, friendship, technical expertise, or a refuge from discrimination, hatred, stigma or quite simply 'the world out there'.[2]

In the following pages, we will consider some of the powerful group processes involved where people combine to solve common problems.

Brain-storming

Efficient problem solving requires that we get rid of our blinkers and look at the wide variety of possible solutions, some of which will not be immediately obvious. We have to break away from the wrong assumptions that prevent the emergence of the correct solution. Consider the following exercise as an example of the inhibitory effects of a faulty mental set:

> There are many words ending in 'ENNY' such as penny and Lenny. There are also many words ending in 'ANY' such as many, but can you think of a four letter word ending in 'ENY'?

If you get the answer within a few seconds, then either you do not suffer as much as the next man from blinkered thinking or you've come across the example before. Most of us are thrown because we are searching for a word which would rhyme with penny.*

Brain-storming is one way of breaking rigidly held assumptions. All that is needed is a blackboard or a large sheet of paper and chalks or pens. If the problem is how to help Billy Higgins to moderate his drinking at the weekend, then everybody in the group is encouraged to think of possible alternative solutions, bearing in mind the following basic rules:

1. Suspend judgements: all ideas, however wild, should be considered and their value will be assessed later.
2. Aim for quantity, not quality.
3. Let the mind wander: the most obvious ideas may not present the most appropriate solution.
4. Build upon the ideas of others. Use the ideas that have already been written up in order to associate freely. Add to and expand these ideas.

A problem-solving group brings together people with a wide range of experiences and background who will be able to generate a larger number of alternatives than any one individual alone.

Edmund Chaney, Michael O'Leary and Alan Marlatt, working at the Veterans Administration Hospital in Seattle, used this type of approach to help alcoholics cope with their craving in circum-

Role-playing increases self-confidence and social skills. An interview is simulated and recorded for later discussion with the participant.

The solution is DENY.

stances likely to increase the pressure to drink.[3] These situations were considered under four headings:

1. Frustration and anger
2. Social temptations
3. Negative emotional states
4. Temptation by other people

For each of these headings a lifelike scene was constructed in which particular feelings were likely to be experienced. Frustration and anger, for example:

> Before you entered the alcoholism treatment programme, your employer, who knew about your drinking problem, said that you could have your job back when you got out of the hospital. When you leave the programme, you find that the company has hired someone to take your place.

Social pressures to drink are among the most frequently met with temptations. For example:

> You are eating at a good restaurant with some friends on a special occasion. The waitress comes over and says, 'Drink before dinner?' Everyone else orders one. All eyes seem to be on you.

Negative emotional states – feelings such as loneliness, depression, boredom, futility, malaise, or nervousness – often occur in the absence of clear-cut environmental or interpersonal stimuli. For example:

> You get up on Saturday morning and realize that you don't have anything planned to do during the day. You sit around for a while, but you begin to feel bored and restless.

Sometimes, the person experiences a desire or compulsion to drink in the absence of any specific external or internal triggering factors. For example:

> You have been out of the hospital a couple of months now and haven't taken a single drink. However, you've been wondering how well the treatment really worked, and you consider taking a drink to test it out.

The treatment followed here, which can easily be

used by self-help groups such as Alcoholics Anonymous and Drink Watchers, simply involved the identification of high-risk situations, followed by eight brain-storming sessions to generate alternative ways of coping with them. This kind of practice, twice a week for four weeks, not only led to an increased ability to think of coping strategies, but also resulted in a decrease in the duration and severity of relapse episodes up to one year later.

So one great advantage of a self-help group is the potential for effective new approaches to problem-solving. The second involves the opportunity to learn from people who are already coping successfully.

Coping models

Members of Alcoholics Anonymous, Weight Watchers and other self-help groups are repeatedly asked to tell their stories. What were their problems and how were they able to cope? How do they now cope with high-risk situations? This kind of information provides invaluable help for the new member. It gives encouragement and hope, since he is able to identify with a model who has successfully overcome a problem similar to his own. It also provides specific strategies for coping with specific situations. Experimental psychologists have demonstrated that such a model, which is usually called a *coping model*, can have a powerful influence on behaviour.[4] Usually, one group will provide a number of coping models so that different people with diverse problems will be able to identify with and learn from at least one of them.

If we look at story-telling or self-disclosure from this point of view, then it is easy to see why some groups are more effective than others. As David Robinson[5] notes in his study of Alcoholics Anonymous, 60 per cent of members sometimes find that other people's stories tend to be rather tiresome.

> Three themes of criticism recurred. The first referred to 'drunkalogues'; when a speaker dwells on his past drinking history, talking at great length and giving repeated 'blow by blow' details of 'what, when, where and how they drank, the names of pubs and the days of the week'. Many members found these to

It can be done! Footballer Jimmy Greaves (left and above) and film and television star Dick Van Dyke provide encouraging examples of alcoholics who have kicked the habit and continued successful careers. Strategies to imitate their example as role models are often adopted.

be monotonous, laborious, boring, and having a 'sameness' which was unhelpful. A related aspect that members did not like was stories that had a 'negative attitude' towards recovery. In these members describe their drinking behaviour before joining AA, but give no emphasis to their improvement since coming to the fellowship. The third major criticism of other people's stories was the inclusion of 'irrelevant personal problems'. These 'domestic trivialities', 'war experiences', 'detailed chores' and, as one member graphically put it, 'the colour of their grandmothers', were considered to be just part of life and as such not worth talking about.

These criticisms can be avoided if a balance can be achieved between the description of the problem and a strong emphasis upon ways of coping successfully.

With a total loss of 86lbs, Mr Stan Evans (above and above right) becomes Weight Watchers Member of the Year for 1982. Keeping that smoking-hand occupied . . . these two friends (right) develop the art of controlling their yo-yo's as a form of displacement activity.

Group cohesion

Cohesion refers to the experience of being accepted by a group and being able to share thoughts and feelings without fear of criticism. It is a sense of unity and attraction that binds members together and strengthens resolve.

For example, in a study of the group treatment of agoraphobia,[6] Iver Hand, Yves Lamontagne and Isaac Marks of the London Institute of Psychiatry, looked at two types of groups: one in which cohesion was deliberately fostered and another in which members were asked not to talk to each other during assignments, but only to discuss problems individually with the therapist.

Both groups were encouraged to carry out tasks which, for them, were very frightening (e.g. walking down Oxford Street, using buses and tubes).

The therapists were very successful in their attempts to produce cohesion as shown by ratings of *help received from the group, help received from individual patients, help given to individual patients* and *liking of other patients*. On each of these items, the cohesive group gave higher ratings than the less structured group. At the end of treatment, both groups had improved equally, but *six months later the cohesive group was doing significantly better.*

Similar results were obtained by Terry Wilson and Raymond Kingsley of Rutgers in a study of obesity treatment.[7] Clients who received individual treatment and those receiving group treatment did equally well at the end of the programme, but one year later, the individually treated clients had gained more weight than those who had experienced group therapy.

We do not clearly understand this phenomenon, but cohesion does appear to be important. If each member of the group is out to help other members as well as himself, then cohesion develops, and the chances of long-term changes appear to be considerably improved.

The helper principle

Marie Killilea[8] identified seven characteristics of self-help groups which have been given particular emphasis by researchers. One of these, *the helper principle*, refers to the fact that in situations where members of a group are helping others with similar problems, it may be the helper who benefits most from the exchange.

Many people have found meaning in their lives by helping others. New recruits to self-help groups are looking for help with their own problems, but those who stay on often find that they are helped to the extent that they are able to help others. As David Robinson points out in his study of AA[5]:

> As time goes by, the focus of the member's concern gradually changes from his own problem and maintaining his own sobriety, to helping others to maintain theirs. The member's own sobriety is still the main concern, but the method of maintaining it changes from receiving support, help and encouragement and identifying with others who have succeeded, to giving support to others, being identified with and depended upon and accepting responsibility through involvement in the formal offices and activities of the fellowship.

At least two projects have successfully made use of the helper principle to bring help to the needy and, at the same time, give a *raison d'être* to the helper. The Foster Grandparents Project carried out in Summit County, Ohio, encouraged old people to spend four hours a day with an emotionally disturbed or physically handicapped child of pre-school age. The results of this project were very promising. The children became happier and more relaxed and were reported to be sleeping better, playing better and eating better. The grandparents also found the experience to be very meaningful and beneficial. As one of the foster grandfathers said, 'It gives me a reason for getting up in the morning.'

The other project was initiated by the Institute for Youth Studies at Howard University, Washington D.C. The programme aimed to help drop-outs and delinquent youths by training them to work as aides in child-care centres, as youth leaders in a community mental health centre, as counselling aides with delinquent children and as classroom aides in elementary schools. This project successfully increased the self-esteem of the helpers and, at the same time, provided a useful service to the community.

Self-help groups thrive upon the principle that both the helper and the helped benefit from the interaction and at least one self-help group has incorporated the following Hindu proverb into its guidelines – 'Help your brother's boat across and your own will reach the shore.'

Friendships and community involvement

A self-help group provides many opportunities for the development of lasting friendships. This social dimension is clearly an important ingredient of groups such as Alcoholics Anonymous. Over 80 per cent of AA members have entertained other members in their homes and 40 per cent see each other socially on other occasions. In David Robinson's study, 55 per cent of AA members recognized that such social occasions are a useful part of AA, and Robinson concludes that:

> This informal socialising between AA members could be interpreted as an incidental sideline to the real work of formal AA activities. In a sense it is, since the informal activities grew out of the formal activities which are routinely shared among as large a proportion of members as possible. But it is much more than just an accidental accretion, it is an integral part of the self-help process.

It is clear from the research on addictions and compulsions that we must consider them within a social context. Quite often, an addiction subsides when relationships change. For example, Azrin and his colleagues,[9] working at the Mental Health and Development Center in Illinois, have proved the efficacy of a form of treatment for alcoholics that they call 'community reinforcement'. They were able to strengthen social relationships and community involvement by starting up a self-help group, converting a tavern into a social club and helping their alcoholic clients to solve marital and vocational problems. Self-help groups provide an ideal base from which this kind of community integration can be achieved.

A new emphasis on community care allows previously isolated members of the community to become firm friends. Here an elderly woman takes care of a disturbed child as part of the Foster Grandparents Project in Ohio, USA.

Coping with helplessness and guilt

People who suffer from problem drinking, compulsive gambling, binge eating, drug addiction and, nowadays, smoking, usually experience helplessness and guilt because they are unable to change behaviour which causes social, financial and probably health problems. Unfortunately, these feelings, which result from past failures, set the scene for future cravings and future failures. A vicious circle is set up with failure leading to regret which, in turn, provokes compulsions and further failure. One great advantage of a good self-help group is the reduction in guilt and helplessness that naturally occurs.

Listening to other people's stories helps to put problems in a wider perspective as part of the human condition, rather than simply a sign of personal iniquity. The vicious circle is therefore broken and a cool, analytical approach to problem solving is more likely to occur.

Robinson and Henry[2] also emphasized the role of a group in helping people to cope with the stigma of being addicted.

> Coping with stigma, then, involves first of all the realisation that one is not alone; that there are others like you, and that they understand and appreciate your problems, ideas and aspirations. But coping with stigma involves self-help groups in much more than this. People, as well as problems have to be coped with. Members have often got to be encouraged to re-learn, or even learn for the first time, that they have a value, a contribution to make and a full place to occupy in the world. Outsiders have to be made to understand the members' problems, both practical and personal, to give care and support and to appreciate that having 'the problem' does not invalidate one's membership of the human race.

A good self-help group has much more to offer than is covered by the six characteristics that we have chosen to emphasize. Facilitating brain-storming and problem-solving, the opportunity to learn from multiple coping models, the power of a cohesive group to strengthen resolve, the opportunity to help others, to develop friendship and community involvement, as well as the reduction in guilt and helplessness that spontaneously occurs are nevertheless of central importance. They are all processes that groups can deliberately promote. For the person who is engaged in a lonely struggle against a compulsion or an addiction, a self-help group really can offer powerful support, and produce beneficial changes in attitude.

Receiving the encouragement needed to continue – attending meetings and having group discussions help us to resist temptation and to cope in situations of stress.

17
PERMANENT SELFWATCHING
preventing relapse

Permanent selfwatching: preventing relapse

The old joke 'Giving up smoking is easy. I've done it hundreds of times' illustrates how difficult it is to maintain a habit change permanently. Unfortunately, attempts to change addictions, habits, and compulsions can be very short-lived. While success rates for different compulsive habits vary, a similar pattern of relapse is common to most. Relapse is most likely to occur in the first three months after treatment. In fact, one study indicates that approximately 66 per cent of smokers, alcoholics and drug addicts return to their old behaviour within 90 days of their initial resolve to change. However, those who are able to curb their addiction during the first three to six months have an excellent chance of maintaining that control.

Recently, behavioural scientists have begun to examine factors that contribute to long-term success. Because prior research tended to emphasize short-term improvements due to treatment, questions crucial to long-term behaviour change have remained unanswered. What factors, for instance, determine relapse? Are some people better able to cope with brief setbacks than others? Are relapses inevitable in certain cases? How can relapses be prevented?

What causes relapse?

The notion of relapse and its causes intrigued Alan Marlatt and his colleagues[1] at the University of Washington. Their research on the subject was the first to compare the factors that cause relapse across different addictions. They were particularly interested in the idea that common psychological processes could be responsible, regardless of the sort of addiction or compulsion in question.

Marlatt and his group analysed the relapses of over 300 individuals under treatment for various addictions and compulsions. Subjects included alcoholics, smokers, drug addicts, compulsive gamblers, and overeaters. Relapse was defined as any recurrence of the addictive or compulsive behaviour after an initial period of abstinence. Subjects were asked to provide detailed written

Propping up the bar (top and above) is not the way to test your commitment to giving up drinking – or to losing weight. Avoiding social pressures to drink and eat is important. Choose a dieting schedule that suits your needs, and then stick to it. Compulsive eating followed by dieting has resulted in many women becoming anorexic.

descriptions of the circumstances that triggered their relapse.

Overall, 72 per cent of relapses were accounted for by three factors – (1) negative emotional states, (2) social pressure, and (3) interpersonal conflict. The greatest number were precipitated by negative emotional states such as anxiety, depression, anger and loneliness. These feelings were determined by internal events (for example, depression about personal inadequacies) as well as external ones (such as anger over a spouse's sarcastic remarks).

The importance of negative emotions in relapse has been corroborated in other studies. Leon and Chamberlin[2] found that unsuccessful dieters were more likely to eat when bored, depressed or lonely, whereas successful dieters ate primarily in response to hunger. Rachman and Hodgson[3] have noted that dysphoria (moods involving restlessness, impatience or a general sense of unease) contribute to an increase in cleaning and checking compulsions. It is interesting to see that in Marlatt's study, relapses in compulsive gamblers were most affected by negative emotions (47 per cent) whereas drug addicts were least affected in this way (only 19 per cent). Drug addicts were much more influenced by what are called negative *physical* states, for example, nausea, trembling, inability to concentrate.

Marlatt found that the second most frequent cause of relapse was social pressure. This included both *direct* pressure in terms of encouragement from others and *perceived* pressure, such as feeling out of place at a cocktail party when not drinking alcohol. Cigarette smokers and drug addicts were most influenced by social pressure and gamblers and overeaters were the least affected.

Interpersonal conflict, disagreements or unpleasant confrontations with relatives and friends, was the third major influence. Frequently, relapses were triggered by accusations and 'lectures' by spouses or close friends such as, 'I know you've been drinking again. You promised me you'd stop. You're going to kill yourself!', or 'You'd better not stop by the betting shop on your way to work today. You know you promised you'd never gamble again.' Accusations were especially detrimental if they were not true. For example, a dieter might respond to unfounded criticism by reasoning, 'If that's what he thinks, I'll give him something to suspect me for. I'll eat those chocolates I've been trying to avoid.'

Some factors appear to be important triggers in certain habits but not in others. Gamblers and, to a lesser extent, alcoholics seem particularly prepared to put their willpower to the test. It is common for a gambler to feel, after a period of abstinence, that he will be able to gamble in a controlled manner, stopping at will. So he purposely puts himself at risk, perhaps by walking into a betting shop just to see if he can resist temptation and walk out without laying a bet. In a sense he is testing his willpower.

Finally, one sort of trigger – social occasions – proves to be an important cause of relapse amongst overeaters but not for any other group. Celebrations, parties, and social get-togethers commonly spark off an episode of overeating. The enjoyment of good (and very often high calorie) food has historically been a part of social occasions. One is expected to overeat at birthdays, family reunions and other special events, and not indulging is often met with resentment and criticism. 'Oh, don't be such a bore. Give up your diet for one evening' are difficult, although not impossible, to ignore.

Why some people cope better than others

Although negative emotions increase the likelihood of relapse, they do not make it inevitable. In other words, some people revert to addictive behaviours when depressed or angry and others don't. The chances of a particular individual 'slipping' in a high risk situation is related both to his ability to cope and to his *perception* of that ability. Techniques of self-management, relaxation, and assertiveness can help to combat high risk factors and avoid relapse, so that people who learn and practise these methods of coping are more successful than those who don't. Several studies indicate that people who successfully control addictions in the long term use a wider variety of coping techniques than those who fail. A recent study[4] at the Addiction Research Unit of the Institute of Psychiatry in London compared the coping styles of 'relapsers' and 'survivors' who had completed treatment for alcoholism.

When temptation arose, especially under conditions of negative emotion, two major coping strategies were used. One approach was to try distraction by going for a walk or starting to do something around the house. The other was to use self-punitive thinking; thinking about the shame and guilt that might result from giving in to temptation. Simple distraction or avoiding alcohol did not prove to be very effective, whereas thought control seemed to prevent relapse more than any other technique. 'Survivors' were more likely to have used this method than 'relapsers'.

It is vital in the battle against a compulsive behaviour to be able to revise negative or self-defeating attitudes such as 'Maybe nobody can change the way they are', or, 'It's not fair that

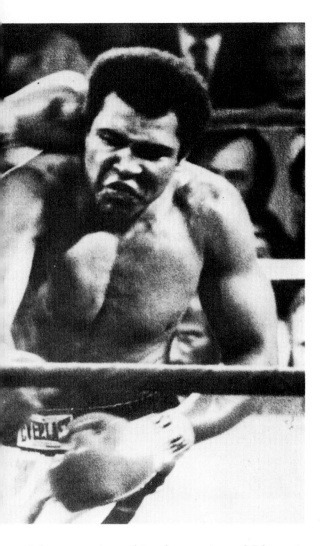

Triumph for Leon Spinks in Las Vegas, 1978. Confident but overweight and undertrained Muhammed Ali loses the World Heavyweight Championship. What finished him, age or fat?

larly used cognitive control whereas only 37 per cent of the unsuccessful patients had done so. Cognitive control had included techniques designed to offset self-defeating thoughts; the urge to nibble was delayed by reviewing the ultimate consequences of success and failure; feelings of guilt and frustration after a bout of overeating were offset against periods of successful resistance to temptation. Patients who used these techniques reported a sense of control over themselves and their surroundings. In fact, simply realizing that specific thought-control techniques were available to them was often enough to engender positive motivation.

Self-efficacy

Being aware that you can control the situations that trigger your compulsion can be as important, if not more important, than the means of control itself. The conviction that one really can achieve a desired result is what Professor Albert Bandura calls 'self-efficacy'. Bandura feels that there is an important distinction between this conviction and the belief that certain behaviour will have a positive result (in this case controlling a habit). For example, a person may believe that a set of actions will lead to a certain outcome but may seriously doubt that he or she can perform the necessary actions. The will to win in the battle against cravings or impulses is very much affected by the person's own expectations of success or failure. The stronger the expectation of successful self-control, the more energy and persistence will be exerted.

Successful habit control can be attributed to a number of sources, but success that is self-attributed is very important. A person may believe that his addiction or compulsion is controlled primarily because of medication, a therapist, good luck, or his own abilities. If he attributes his success to an external source, for example

John can eat anything he wants and I have to deprive myself.' Someone who says 'I'll never even think of alcohol again', is less likely to cope with remorse following a binge than a person who does not set such an unrealistically high standard. Amongst obese people struggling to maintain a weight loss, Peter Miller and Karen Sims[5] found that changes in negative outlook were essential for long-term success. They compared successful and unsuccessful patients after a 12-month weight-control programme. Successful patients were defined as those who had lost 35lb (15.9kg) or more, and unsuccessful patients those who had lost 20lb (9.1kg) or less. Patients were asked about the types of coping strategies they had used most during the year. Of the successful patients 75 per cent had regu-

diet pills, his expectation of self-control will be low and short-lived: once the pills are no longer available, he assumes his control is gone and so starts overeating again. If he attributes success to his own style of behaviour, the expectation of his own effectiveness will be reinforced and tend to last longer regardless of external circumstances.

If belief in one's power to cope is so important, how do people develop this positive attitude? Primarily, success breeds success. For example, a reformed smoker facing a room full of cigarette smoke at a party may feel anxious and unsure of himself. If he successfully overcomes his craving and avoids smoking, belief in his self-control is enhanced, and the next party becomes much easier to deal with. But if such experiences are so important, what about the person who simply avoids temptation? The compulsive gambler who simply steers clear of betting shops may be able to control his habit *most* of the time. But by always avoiding risks he is ill-prepared to deal with them effectively. If he inadvertently finds himself amongst gamblers he may panic and succumb to compulsion simply because he has not had a chance to test his self-control.

Strengthening one's self-control by deliberate exposure to temptation is similar to the 'cue exposure' technique described in Chapter 4. The following case illustrates this technique well. Alison is a 17-year-old high-school girl who has had a considerable weight problem for most of her life. About a year ago she embarked on a weight control programme which emphasized diet, exercise and changes in behaviour. She was determined to lose 40lb (18kg) before she went to college. After three months she had lost 25lb (12kg) and was doing well. The biggest potential problem was her extreme craving for 'fast foods' from the local McDonald's restaurant. Merely driving past 'fast food' restaurants caused considerable apprehension and summoned up thoughts of Big Macs, French fries and chocolate milkshakes. Confronted with these food cues Alison felt completely helpless and out of control. To make matters worse, McDonald's was the local rendezvous for Alison's school friends. This posed an added problem. She didn't want to avoid her friends – but she didn't want to fall victim to temptation either.

To solve this conflict a plan was devised to build up Alison's belief in her self-control. The scheme involved gradually and systematically exposing her to the goodies at McDonald's. Initially, she was instructed to visit McDonald's under relatively 'safe' conditions, such as immediately after a meal or in the company of a supportive friend who was aware of her dieting goals. She was then instructed to sit in the restaurant, pay close attention to the sights and smells of food around her, and allow her craving to develop. To overcome the craving she was then to practise specific selfwatching techniques – deep relaxation on some occasions and on others concentration on the 'ultimate consequences' of overeating (described in Chapter 3). At times she was advised to order a diet drink and remain in McDonald's for at least twenty minutes practising self-control. These procedures were repeated several times. As training progressed Alison's sense of self-control increased. Throughout the training period her belief in her ability to cope was rated on a scale similar to the one shown below.

She was asked to rate the probability that she would be able to cope with temptation immediately prior to each visit to McDonald's. At first her rating was only 10 per cent. As training proceeded, the rating increased rapidly until after

0%   100%

Completely   Completely
convinced that   convinced that
I will *not* be   I *will* be able
able to cope   to cope

|___|___|___|___|___|___|___|___|___|___|___|___|

three visits it was 60 per cent and after six it rose to 90 per cent.

Alison's ultimate test came one day when she was walking home with several friends and they decided to stop at McDonald's for an after-school snack. Even under these unforeseen circumstances Alison triumphed. She felt completely certain of her self-control and sat for 30 minutes watching her friends devour all the fast food they could eat. She simply ordered a diet drink and told her friends she was not hungry. Needless to say, she was exuberant after this success.

Keeping the habit at bay

The first line of defence against relapse, then, is to identify situations of risk and develop self-watching skills to defuse them. There are four important ways of ensuring that the habit remains broken – monitoring the risks, planning ahead, developing positive addictions, and controlling 'slips'.

Monitoring risks

At the start of an anti-habit campaign one is usually buoyed up by plenty of motivation and enthusiasm. After several weeks or months that motivation often dwindles. Highs and lows are quite natural and to be expected. However, when the first battles have been won and initial enthusiasm is at a low ebb, complacency can set in. Compare this with the first Mohammed Ali–Leon Spinks confrontation. Ali was so cock-sure of his ability to win that he did not take the time to prepare fully. He was overweight and undertrained. No one, in fact, expected Spinks to win. Sure enough, Ali was beaten and badly beaten – not by Spinks but by complacency. He was simply off his guard and unprepared. So it is vital to keep a constant eye on current and poten-

The end in sight! Giving-up a bad habit, like running a marathon is hard going but ultimately worth the effort (top). Making a change in lifestyle (below) helps develop assurance, and old habits die away more easily as the old life fades away.

tial risks and remember that new, unexpected risks can crop up at any time. Dr Ovide Pomerleau of the University of Connecticut Medical Center found that continued self-monitoring (as described in Chapter 2) was *the* most important predictor of success in an anti-smoking clinic.

Though daily written monitoring of both risks and behaviour changes is essential for many people, others find that *periodic* monitoring serves the same purpose and is less intrusive on their time. Miriam, for example, is a 50-year-old, overweight housewife who has lost a total of 25lb (11kg). She is 5ft 4in (1.64m) tall and now weighs 175lb (79kg) but she still has a long way to go. Her ideal weight is 121lb (54kg) so she will have to diet and exercise for at least another five or six months. Miriam has discovered that about once every three or four weeks her willpower begins to fade. Luckily, she can sense this change early enough to prevent a relapse. She immediately begins a daily eating diary, writing down everything she eats along with the times and circumstances. She also records urges to eat and particularly the situations, thoughts and feelings which precipitate them. To monitor her physical activity she begins wearing a pedometer, a small device, worn at the waist, which measures the distance she walks. She keeps an exercise and

activity diary and pays particular attention to factors associated with inactivity. Then she hangs up large graphs of her daily calorie intake and pedometer distances in a conspicuous place in the kitchen. Almost immediately she recovers her momentum. Self-assessment has provided feedback, reinforced her self-control, and enabled her to pinpoint risks and plan accordingly.

Planning ahead

It is extremely helpful, at least once a week, to set aside a 'planning time' when you think through business for the following week, consider what family and friends will be doing, and mull over how to spend your spare time. Each day needs to be scrutinized for potential pitfalls and a plan of action worked out for each. Imagine temptations as vividly as you can and go through the self-watching techniques you would use to deal with them. This sort of rehearsal makes the real temptation easier to resist, as Simon, a man prone to long drinking binges, found.

Simon is a 52-year-old married man whose drinking problem was treated by Peter Miller. He was employed as a freelance business consultant and travelled frequently. At the time of treatment his drinking was limited to binges lasting

Keep a score of how many hits and misses you make but don't be wooden in your approach – sneaking one chocolate is not the end of the world as long as you stop yourself from going on and re-affirm your commitment to diet.

three to five days during business trips. No drinking ever occurred at home. Here is Simon's own description of a typical sequence of events that led to one drinking bout.

> I had been at the Hilton Hotel in New York City conducting a business seminar for high-level executives. I felt under tremendous pressure to make a good impression. The seminar ended at 4 o'clock in the afternoon. Although my presentation went well I felt extremely fatigued when it was over. I was physically drained.
>
> Three executives from a large oil company wanted me to have a drink with them to discuss the possibility that I might work for their firm. I hesitated at first but they were very insistent. I remember thinking to myself, 'It's very important that they like me. I must make a good impression.' My plan was to order a Perrier water once we got into the bar. When we sat down all three were quite insistent that I join them in a drink – an alcoholic one, that is. They said I needed to unwind. I remember thinking, 'Oh, well, one drink won't hurt me. I'll just have one and stop there. Besides, I deserve to relax. I owe it to myself!' After one drink my thinking began to change. As I started to feel the effects of the drink, I thought that a couple more wouldn't hurt me. Finally, my companions left but I remained in the bar for the rest of the evening. I continued drinking for the next 2 days.

At the beginning of treatment these drinking episodes were occurring approximately once every month. With selfwatching treatment Simon gradually improved. Initially, he went for four consecutive months without a bout of drinking and was feeling quite proud of himself. Unfortunately, this proved to be his undoing. During a business trip to Chicago he consciously avoided self-management strategies in order to test his willpower. One drink with business associates led to another and after eight martinis he (fortunately) fell asleep. He woke up the next morning full of remorse, convinced that he must be more vigilant. Prior to each business trip thereafter Simon carefully planned ahead. He would prepare a detailed written schedule of his activities during the trip. This was mapped out on an hour by hour basis to keep 'unstructured' times to a minimum. He was careful to plan activities for times when drinking was likely, such as at the end of the business day. Here is a sample of one of his schedules.

7 am	Wake up
7 am–7.20 am	Calisthenics
7.20 am–8 am	Shower and dress
8 am–9 am	Breakfast
9 am–12 pm	Business meetings
12 pm–1.30 pm	Lunch with business associates
1.30 pm–2 pm	Practise stress-management technique in hotel room
2 pm–5 pm	Business meetings
5 pm–5.45 pm	Jog, walk or swim
5.45 pm–6.30 pm	Shower and change
6.30 pm–7 pm	Practise relaxation routine
7 pm–8 pm	Dinner
8.30 pm–10 pm	Alcoholics Anonymous meeting
10.30 pm–11.30 pm	Read, prepare for tomorrow's meeting, call home promptly at 11.30 pm. Go to bed

He also planned to avoid talking business over cocktails by arranging breakfast or luncheon meetings instead. By openly discussing his newly acquired jogging and physical fitness interests he anticipated that he would find companions in these activities who were likely to be light drinkers or abstainers, and so a good influence.

To prepare himself for really risky situations Simon would conjure up in his mind a likely predicament, imagine exactly what might happen and how he would successfully avoid temptation. This is his verbal version of one of the scenes he invented.

I can see myself in the offices of G. Corporation. I have just signed a very profitable 2-year consultation contract. Mr. R, the president of the company, invites me to his home for cocktails and dinner. When I arrive I meet a few other guests that are present. I feel a bit anxious since I want to make a favourable impression. Mr. R says 'Simon, I've got a fine batch of martinis made up. As I recall when we last met in Los Angeles a few months ago you've got quite a taste for gin and vermouth.' Even though I'm tense and unsure of myself I quickly respond with, 'I'm trying to keep a clear head for some meetings I have tomorrow. I'll just have a soda water.' Mr R, who I remember as a rather heavy drinker, says, 'Oh, come on, Simon, we're celebrating. Don't spoil the party.' In a serious and assertive tone I remark, 'No, I'm positive. Just a plain soda.' He finally gives up and accedes to my wishes.

At dinner Mr. R brings out 2 bottles of rare wine that he has been saving for a special occasion. As he begins pouring for the guests I think, 'Now I'm really in trouble. Maybe I should just have one glass of wine so I won't hurt his feelings. Besides, this is a special occasion. Wine isn't really that strong anyway.' As soon as I recognize my negative thinking I quickly counteract these thoughts with more appropriate ones such as, 'He's not going to get hurt over my not drinking his wine. That's silly. Even if he does make a big deal out of it, that's his problem, not mine. Anyway, a special occasion is not an excuse for drinking. I've given up all forms of alcohol forever. I've felt so good over the past few months by not drinking. My life is great just now. I'm *not* going to spoil it.' After that I begin to relax myself. I take a deep breath, let it out and let all of my muscles get loose and relaxed. As Mr. R approaches me, I say, 'No wine for me, thanks. I appreciate the thought, though.' To my surprise he simply goes on to the next person.

After the dinner is over and I leave Mr. R's house, I feel exhilarated. I have a real sense of accomplishment and control. I feel a physical and psychological strength growing inside me.

Simon repeatedly rehearsed several such scenes in his mind. Each time he felt more and more in

control. These rehearsals, together with his carefully planned schedules, were a great help in keeping the drinking demon at bay. Simon now enjoys the benefits of long-term success. But in spite of this he continues to plan ahead before each business trip.

Developing positive addictions

An addiction may provide a source of satisfaction and pleasure even though, in the long run, it damages mental or physical health. Without an addiction, be it food, cigarettes or alcohol, we can experience a considerable void in our lives. Smokers often go through a period of mourning after they give up smoking almost as if a good friend had died. One ex-smoker remarked 'I could always count on that cigarette to be there to satisfy me, excite me, comfort me or calm me down.' Such a lost source of satisfaction needs to be replaced by a healthier alternative as quickly as possible, otherwise the risk of relapse remains high.

Dr William Glasser advocates the development of 'positive addictions' – habits that provide satisfaction but are healthy. The only criteria for developing such addictions are that they should bring you pleasure, pure and simple. A positive addiction could grow from an interest or hobby that you once had but gave up, one you've always wanted to try but have never got around to, one your friends or family are involved in, or one you indulge in only occasionally. However, it is common for sheer procrastination to prevent people developing positive addictions. A 60-year-old over-stressed workaholic once remarked to me, 'One of these days I'm going to take flying lessons. That's always been a great desire of mine and as soon as I get time I'm going to do it.' When I queried him about the history of this plan it transpired that he had been saying that to himself for over 20 years!

Learn to anticipate the difficulties you will have to confront, but an occasional slip is not too painful. Pick yourself up, dust yourself off and start all over again!

Possible positive addictions could include relaxation and meditation, running, walking, tennis, golf, woodworking, painting, sculpture, skiing, writing, poetry ... the list is infinite. Once such activities are started on a regular basis they can become so addictive, that if you miss your morning walk or afternoon meditation session your day simply isn't the same. Runners frequently become so habituated that if unable to run because of circumstance or injury they suffer withdrawal symptoms such as restlessness, agitation, irritability – ironically the same 'void' experienced by the ex-smoker or ex-gambler.

Controlling 'slips'
Many people trying to control habits are likely to give way to temptation on occasions. These slips are perfectly natural and happen despite the best-laid stratagems for maintaining self-control. Whether or not the slip is followed by total backsliding is determined largely by the way in which you view it. If you see it as a failure, personal weakness or proof that willpower is lacking, then a relapse into old habits will be very likely. If, on the other hand, your slip is viewed as a one-off error that you can learn from in the future, then relapse is unlikely. Unfortunately, people often perceive addictive behaviour in terms of black and white – they view themselves or others as either smokers or non-smokers, dieters or non-dieters. Even one puff of a cigarette may make them think, 'Well, I've really done it now. I'm a smoker again! I'll never have enough willpower to give up. I'll go and buy a packet and try to give up again next week.' A smoker in this situation must realize that one puff does not magically change him or her into a different person. One slip does not eradicate the days, weeks or months of abstinence that preceded it.

It is better to think of your efforts to control a habit as a continuum, ranging from 0 per cent – no control – to 100 per cent control. The diagram shows two views of the inevitable slips and problems which will occur along the way. Suppose someone is aiming to control weight by eating three low-calorie meals a day, keeping a written record of food consumed and taking a three-mile daily walk. Ideally the person aims to progress smoothly along the control continuum B, increasing control until the programme can be

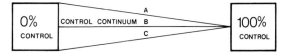

maintained without any sense of undue effort. In real life, however, some days will show better progress than others. Many people will see their control campaign as an uphill path C. When they slip, they imagine themselves as having fallen back, and think of the way forward as a renewed uphill struggle. It is far better to see progress as path A – a downhill run towards total control. Any relapse then becomes not so much a ques-

---

Reminders to help prevent relapse

Continued vigilance and review of progress are necessary to prevent relapse. The following is a checklist designed to determine if a person is remembering the selfwatching alternatives:

1. I am continuing to monitor my high risk situations.
   _____ Yes _____ No
2. I change my daily routine to decrease temptations from old conditioned associations.
   _____ Yes _____ No
3. I plan enjoyable alternative activities for times of day when I am most tempted.
   _____ Yes _____ No
4. I try to reward myself for positive habit changes.
   _____ Yes _____ No
5. I have tried using a behavioural contract to motivate myself.
   _____ Yes _____ No
6. I practise the selfwatching relaxation technique on a regular basis and use it when I am tense.
   _____ Yes _____ No
7. I practise analysing and changing my negative thinking that leads to depression, anger, or anxiety.
   _____ Yes _____ No
8. I refuse offers to return to my old habit assertively.
   _____ Yes _____ No
9. I have instructed my family and friends on how they can help me.
   _____ Yes _____ No
10. I practice techniques of controlling my cravings such as *cue exposure* and the *ultimate consequences* procedure.
    _____ Yes _____ No

tion of lost ground but more a case for ignoring guilt, relaxing and gradually resuming control.

Dr Alan Marlatt postulates that a slip is particularly likely to cause relapse if a person feels a strong disparity between his actions, and what he thinks about himself. For instance, a smoker who has just smoked a cigarette after a long period of abstinence may believe, 'I am an ex-smoker and I completely abstain from all cigarettes', yet there he is holding the burning stub. This disparity makes him feel guilty and anxious, so to reduce these feelings he may change his self-image to be more in line with his behaviour. 'I must be really addicted to cigarettes. I guess my body still needs nicotine.' In effect he has

opted to view the incident not as a temporary slip, but as proof that the old bad habits should be the norm for him. Dr Terence Wilson of Rutgers University advocates using an 'emergency drill' to counteract this train of thought. Immediately after a slip, his patients are instructed to take 10 minutes to remind themselves of the following things:

1. Deviations from your programme are not unusual. You simply made a mistake. You are *not* a failure
2. A slip simply indicates that you have to be more careful
3. Acknowledge your mistakes and learn from the experience. What techniques could you use to control temptation under similar circumstances?
4. Do *not* feel guilty, frustrated or discouraged
5. Get back to your programme *now*. Not tomorrow, not next week, but *now*!

Before and After! An achievement to be proud of, and evidence that with the help of selfwatching techniques it is possible to change our behaviour.

NOTES AND REFERENCES

Chapter 2
[1] Miller, P. M. *Personal Habit Control*. New York, Simon and Schuster (1978).
[2] Glad, W. & Adesso, V. J. 'The relative importance of socially induced tension and behavioral contagion for smoking behavior', *Journal of Abnormal Psychology*, 85, 119–121 (1976).
[3] Knapp, T. & Shodahl, S. 'Ben Franklin as a behavior modifier: A note', *Behavior Therapy*, 5, 656–660 (1974).
[4] Franklin, B. *Autobiography*, New York, International Collector's Library (1923).
[5] Watson, D. L. & Tharp, R. G. *Self-Directed Behavior*, Monterey, California, Brooks/Cole (1981).

Chapter 3
[1] Rosenbaum, M. 'A schedule for assessing self-control behaviors: Preliminary findings', *Behavior Therapy*, 11, 109–121 (1980).
[2] Mahoney, M. J. 'Self-reward and self-monitoring techniques for weight control', *Behavior Therapy*, 5, 48–57 (1974).
[3] Horan, J. J. 'Coverant conditioning through a self-management application of the Premack Principle: its effects on weight reduction', *Journal of Behavior Therapy and Experimental Psychiatry*, 2, 243–249 (1971).

Chapter 4
[1] Rachman, S. & Hodgson, R. J. *Obsessions and Compulsions*. Englewood-Cliffs: Prentice-Hall (1980).
[2] Rachman, S., Hodgson, R. J. & Marks, I. M. 'The treatment of chronic obsessive-compulsive neurosis by modelling and flooding in vivo', *Behavior Research and Therapy* (1973).
[3] Hodgson, R. J. & Rachman, S. 'The modification of compulsive behaviour, in *Case Studies in Behavior Therapy*, ed. H. J. Eysenck. London: Routledge and Kegan Paul (1976).
[4] Marks, I. M., Hodgson, R. J. & Rachman, S. 'Treatment of chronic obsessive-compulsive neurosis by in vivo exposure', *British Journal of Psychiatry* (1975).

Chapter 5
[1] Holmes, T. H. & Dale, R. H. 'The Social Readjustment Dating Scale', *Journal of Psychosomatic Research*, 11, 213–218 (1967).
[2] Marks, I. M. 'Perspectives on Flooding', seminar in *Psychiatry*, 4, 129–138 (1972).
[3] Christensen, A., Arkowitz, H. & Anderson, J. Practice Dating as Treatment for College Dating Inhibitions. *Behaviour Research and Therapy*, 13, 321–332 (1975).
[4] Jacobson, E. *Anxiety and Tension Control*. Philadelphia: Lippincott (1964).
[5] Orme-Johnson, D. W. & Farrow, J. T. (eds.). *Scientific Research on the Transcendental Meditation Program: Collected Papers* (Vol. 1). Pheinweiller, German Federal Republic: Meru Press (1976).
[6] Corey, P. In Orme-Johnson, D. W. & Farrow, J. T. (eds.), op. cit., p. 95 (1976).
[7] Benson, H. *The Relaxation Response*. New York: Marrow (1975).
[8] Novaco, R. W. *Anger Control: The Development and Evaluation of an Experimental Treatment*. Lexington, Mass.: D. C. Heath, Lexington Books (1975).

Chapter 6
[1] Reid, E. C. 'Autopsychology of the Manic-depressive', *Journal of Nervous and Mental Disease*, 37, 606–620 (1910).
[2] Beck, A. T., Rush, J. A., Shaw, B. F. & Emery, G. *Cognitive Therapy of Depression*. New York: Wiley (1979).

[3] Seligman, M. E. P. *Helplessness*. San Francisco: W. H. Freeman (1975).
[4] Adler, A. *What Life Should Mean to You*, A. Porter (ed.). New York: Capricorn (1958).
[5] Ellis, A. & Harper, R. A. *A New Guide to Rational Living*. Englewood-Cliffs, N.J.: Prentice-Hall (1975).
[6] Bandura, A. & Simon, K. M. 'The Role of Proximal Intentions in Self-regulation of Refractory Behaviour', *Cognitive Therapy and Research*, 1, 177–193 (1977).
[7] Rush, A. J., Beck, A. J., Kovacs, M. & Hollon, S. 'Comparative Efficacy of Cognitive Therapy and Imipramine in the Treatment of Depressed Out-Patients', *Cognitive Therapy and Research*, 1, 17–37 (1977).
[8] Blackburn, I. M. & Bishop, S. 'Is There An Alternative to Drugs in the Treatment of Depressed Ambulatory Patients?' *Behavioural Psychotherapy*, 9, 96–104 (1981).
[9] Beck, A. & Greenberg, R. L. *Coping with Depression*. New York: Institute for Natural Living (1974).

Chapter 7
[1] Eisler, R. M., Hersen, M. & Miller, P. M. 'Shaping components of assertive behavior with instructors and feedback', *American Journal of Psychiatry*, 30, 643–649 (1974).
[2] Foy, D. W., Miller, P. M., Eisler, R. M. & O'Toole, D. H. 'Social skills training to teach alcoholics to refuse drinks effectively', *Journal of Alcohol Studies*, 37, 1340–1345 (1976).
[3] Miller, P. M. 'Behavior therapy in the treatment of alcoholism', in G. A. Marlatt & P. E. Nathan (eds.), *Behavioral approaches to the assessment and treatment of Alcoholism*. New Brunswick, N.J.: Center of Alcohol Studies (Rutgers University) (1977).
[4] Brownell, K. D., Heckerman, C. L., Westlake, R. J., Hayes, S. C. & Ponti, P. M. 'The effect of couples training and partner cooperativeness in the behavioral treatment of obesity', *Behavior Research and Therapy*, 16, 323–333 (1978).
[5] Miller, P. M. *Personal Habit Control*. New York: Simon & Schuster (1978).

Chapter 8
[1] Ikard, F. F., Green, O. E. & Horm, I. 'A scale to differentiate between types of smoking as related to the management of affect', *The International Journal of the Addictions*, 4, 649–659 (1969).
[2] Fagerstrom, K. 'Measuring degree of physical dependence to tobacco smoking with reference to individualization of treatment', *Addictive Behaviors*, 3, 235–241 (1978).
[3] Schachter, S., Silverstein, B., Kozlowski, L. T., Perlick, D., Herman, C. P. & Liebling, B. 'Studies of the interaction of psychological and pharmacological determinants of smoking', *Journal of Experimental Psychology: General*, 103, 3–40 (1977).
[4] Marlatt, G. A. 'Perception of "control" and its relation to behavior change', *Behavioral Psychotherapy*, 9, 190–193 (1981).
[5] Eiser, J. R., Sutton, S. R. & Wober, M. 'Smoking, seat belts, and beliefs about health, *Addictive Behaviors*, 4, 331–338 (1979).
[6] Flaxman, J. 'Quitting smoking now or later: Gradual, abrupt, immediate, and delayed quitting', *Behavior Therapy*, 9, 260–270 (1978).
[7] Puska, P., Bjorkquist, S. & Koskela, K. 'Nicotine-containing chewing gum in smoking cessation: A double blind trial with half year follow-up', *Addictive Behaviors*, 4, 141–146 (1979).

Chapter 9
[1] Bray, G. A. *The Obese Patient*. Philadelphia: W. B. Saunders (1976).

[2] Garo, J. *Energy Balance and Obesity in Man.* New York: American Elsevier Publishing Co. (1978).

[3] Herman, C. P. & Polivy, J. 'Anxiety, restraint and eating behavior', *Journal of Abnormal Psychology*, 84, 666–672 (1975).

[4] Schachter, S. & Rodin, J. *Obese Humans and Rats.* Washington: Erlaum-Halstead (1974).

[5] Stunkard, A. J. & Fox, S. 'The relationship of gastric motility and hunger: a summary of the evidence', *Psychosomatic Medicine*, 33, 123–124 (1971).

[6] Rodin, J. 'The Externality Theory Today', in A. Stunkard (ed.), *Obesity*. Philadelphia: Saunders (1980).

[7] Monedo, L. F. & Mayer, J. 'Hunger-sensation in men, women, boys and girls', *American Journal of Clinical Nutrition*, 20, 253–261 (1967).

Chapter 10

[1] Nora, J. J. *The Whole Heart Book.* New York: Holt, Rinehart and Winston (1980).

[2] Suinn, R. M. & Bloom, L. J. 'Anxiety management training for Pattern A behavior,' *Journal of Behavioral Medicine*, 1, 25–35 (1978).

[3] Novaco, R. W. 'The cognitive regulation of anger and stress', in P. C. Kendall & S. D. Hollon (eds.), *Cognitive Behavioral Interventions: Theory, Research, and Practice.* New York: Academic Press, 241–286 (1979).

Chapter 11

[1] Custer, R. L. *Gambling in America: Final Report of the Commission on the Review of the National Policy on Gambling.* Washington, D.C.: U.S. Government Printing Office (1977).

[2] Lewis, D. J. & Duncan, C. P. 'Effect of different percentages of money reward on extinction of a lever pulling response', *Journal of Experimental Psychology*, 52, 23–27 (1956).

[3] Dickerson, M. G. 'FI schedules and persistence at gambling in the U.K. betting office', *Journal of Applied Behaviour Analysis*, 12, 315–323 (1979).

Chapter 12

[1] Schmidt, W. 'Cirrhosis and Alcohol Consumption: An Epidemiological Perspective', in G. Edwards & M. Grant (eds.), *Alcoholism: New Knowledge and New Responses.* London: Groome Helm (1977).

[2] Plant, M. A. 'Occupational Factors in Alcoholism', in M. Grant & W. H. Kenyon (eds.), *Alcoholism in Industry*, Alcohol Education Centre and MLCCA. London (1975).

[3] Edwards, G., Chandler, J., Hensmon, C. & Peto, J. 'Drinking in a London suburb. II. Correlates of trouble with drinking among men', *Quarterly Journal of Studies on Alcohol*, Supplement 6, 94–119 (1972).

[4] Litman, G. K., Eiser, J. R., Rawson, N. S. B. & Oppenheim, A. N. 'Towards a typology of relapse', *Drug and Alcohol Dependence*, 2, 157–162 (1977).

[5] Higgins, R. L. & Marlatt, G. A. 'Fear of Interpersonal Evaluation as a determinant of Alcohol Consumption in Male Social Drinkers', *Journal of Abnormal Psychology*, 84, 644–651 (1975).

[6] Miller, P. M., Hensen, M., Eisler, R. M. & Hilsman, G. 'Effects of Social Stress on Operant Drinking of Alcoholics and Social Drinkers', *Behaviour Research and Therapy*, 12, 67–72 (1974).

[7] Boyatzis, R. E. 'The Effect of Alcohol Consumption on the Aggressive Behaviour of Men', *Quarterly Journal of Studies on Alcohol*, 35, 959–972 (1974).

[8] Wilson, G. T. 'Alcohol and Human Sexual Behaviour', *Behaviour Research and Therapy*, 15, 239–252 (1977).

Chapter 13

[1] World Health Organisation Expert Committee on Drug Dependence. Twentieth Report. Technical Report Series 551, WHO Geneva (1974).

[2] Woods, J. H. 'Behavioral Pharmacology of Drug Self-Administration', in *Psychopharmacology: A Generation of Progress*, M. A. Lipton, A. DiMascio & K. Killam. New York: Raven Press (1978).

[3] Jaffe, J. H. 'Drug Addiction and Drugs Abuse', in *The Pharmacological Basis of Therapeutics*, 5th ed., L. S. Goodman & A. Gilman (eds.). New York: Macmillan (1975).

[4] Ellinwood, E. J., Jr. 'Amphetamine and cocaine', in *Psychopharmacology in the Practice of Medicine*, M. E. Jarvik (ed.). New York: Appleton-Century-Crofts (1977).

[5] Wesson, D. R. & Smith, D. E. *Barbiturates: Their Use, Misuse and Abuse.* New York: Human Sciences Press (1977).

[6] Jaffe, J., Petersen, R. and Hodgson, R. J. *Addictions: Issues and Answers.* London: Harper & Row (1980).

[7] *Marijuana and Health*, Seventh Annual Report to the U.S. Congress from the Secretary of Health, Education and Welfare. Washington, D.C.

Chapter 14

[1] Bentler, P. M. & Prince, C. 'Personality characteristics of male transvestites: III', *Journal of Abnormal Psychology*, 74, 140–143 (1969).

[2] Rachman, S. 'Sexual fetishism: An experimental analogue', *Psychological Record*, 16, 293–296 (1966).

[3] Card, W. K. & Wincze, J. P. *Sex Therapy: A Behavioral Approach.* Hagerstown, Md.: Harper & Row (1977).

Chapter 15

See references for Chapter 4.

Chapter 16

[1] Demone, H. W. *Director of Mutural Help Organisations in Massachussetts* (4th edn.). Massachussetts: Blue Cross on a Blue Shield (1974).

[2] Robinson, D. & Henry, S. *Self-Help and Health: Mutual Aid for Modern Problems.* London (1977).

[3] Chaney, E. F., O'Leary, M. R. & Marlatt, C. T. A. 'Skill Training with Alcoholics', *Journal of Consultancy and Clinical Psychology*, Vol. 46, pp. 1092–1104 (1978).

[4] Meichenbaum, D. 'Examination of model characteristics in reducing avoidance behavior', *Journal of Personality and Social Psychology*, 17, 298–307 (1971).

[5] Robinson, D. *Talking Out of Alcoholism.* London: Croom Helm (1979).

[6] Hand, I., Lamontagne, Y. & Marks, I. 'Group exposure (flooding) in vivo for agoraphobics', *British Journal of Psychiatry*, 124, 588–602 (1974).

[7] Kingsley, R. & Wilson, G. T. 'Behavior therapy for obesity: A comparative investigation of long-term efficacy', *Journal of Consulting and Clinical Psychology*, 45, 288–298 (1977).

[8] Killilea, M. 'Mutual help organisations: Interpretations in the literature: III', G. Caplan & M. Killilea (eds.), *Support Systems and Mutual Help.* New York : Grune & Stratton (1976).

[9] Azrin, N. H. 'Improvements in the community reinforcement approach to alcoholism', *Behaviour Research and Therapy*, 14, 339–48 (1976).

Chapter 17

[1] Cummings, C., Gordon, J. R. & Marlatt, G. A. 'Relapse: Prevention and Prediction', in W. R. Miller (ed.), *The Addictive Behaviors.* New York: Pergamon (1980).

[2] Leon, G. R. & Chamberlain, K. 'Emotional arousal, eating patterns, and body image as differential factors associated with varying success in maintaining a weight loss', *Journal of Consulting and Clinical Psychology*, 40, 474–480 (1973).

[3] Rachman, S. J. & Hodgson, R. J. *Obsessions and Compulsions.* Englewood-Cliffs, N.J.: Prentice-Hall (1980).

[4] Litman, G. K., Eiser, J. R., Rawson, N. S. B. & Oppenheim, A. N. 'Differences in relapse participants and coping behavior between alcohol relapses and survivors', *Behavior Research and Therapy*, 17, 89–94 (1979).

[5] Miller, P. M. & Sims, K. 'Evaluation and component analysis of a comprehensive weight control program', *International Journal of Obesity*, 5, 57–62 (1981).

INDEX